Transitions to Early Care and Education

EDUCATING THE YOUNG CHILD

VOLUME 4

This academic and scholarly book series will focus on the education and development of young children from infancy through eight years of age. The series will provide a synthesis of current theory and research on trends, issues, controversies, and challenges in the early childhood field and examine implications for practice. One hallmark of the series will be comprehensive reviews of research on a variety of topics with particular relevance for early childhood educators worldwide. The mission of the series is to enrich and enlarge early childhood educators' knowledge, enhance their professional development, and reassert the importance of early childhood education to the international community. The audience for the series includes college students, teachers of young children, college and university faculty, and professionals from fields other than education who are unified by their commitment to the care and education of young children. In many ways, the proposed series is an outgrowth of the success of *Early Childhood Education Journal* which has grown from a quarterly magazine to a respected and international professional journal that is published six times a year.

DeAnna M. Laverick • Mary Renck Jalongo
Editors

Transitions to Early Care and Education

International Perspectives on Making Schools
Ready for Young Children

 Springer

Editors
DeAnna M. Laverick, D. Ed.
Department of Professional Studies
in Education
Indiana University of Pennsylvania
570 South Eleventh Street
Indiana, PA 15705
USA
laverick@iup.edu

Mary Renck Jalongo, Ph. D.
Department of Professional Studies
in Education
Indiana University of Pennsylvania
654 College Lodge Road
Indiana, PA 15701-4015
USA
mjalongo@iup.edu

ISBN 978-94-007-0572-2   e-ISBN 978-94-007-0573-9
DOI 10.1007/978-94-007-0573-9
Springer Dordrecht Heidelberg London New York

Library of Congress Control Number: 2011921327

Cover design: eStudio Calamar S.L.

Printed on acid-free paper

Springer is part of Springer Science+Business Media (www.springer.com)

Preface

The assertion that early experience affects later experience represents a triumvirate of theory, research, and conventional wisdom. A basic tenet in the study of human development theory is that the early childhood years leave an indelible imprint across the lifespan. Likewise, research in neuroscience suggests that the brain seeks patterns in complexity, drawing upon previous experience to interpret subsequent experiences (Jensen 2005; Rushton and Larkin 2001). Even from the perspective of the general public, the conviction that initial experience shapes later experience is widely accepted and reflected in everyday expressions such as "starting out right," "getting a head start," or the old adage that "first impressions are lasting ones." For all of these reasons, most parents/families, early childhood educators, and professionals from other fields are in agreement that children's first experiences with child care, preschool, kindergarten, and other academic programs are important (Einarsdottir et al. 2008).

Some of the more common transitions that characterize the early years are from home care to group care, from home or preschool to kindergarten, and from kindergarten to more formal educational experiences. In addition to these fairly predictable transitions, individual children often are expected to make an extra effort of adaptation to many other circumstances, such as adjusting to a different cultural context, coping with changes in family configuration, or learning in a second language—to name just a few. Thus, transitions can be one of the most challenging issues for children, families, and educators because they frequently involve not just one change, but complex interactions among various changes. The child who cries on the first day of kindergarten also might be one who witnessed violence in his family, fears his mother will abandon him as his father did, lives at a shelter, grieves for the dog he was forced to surrender, and worries about expectations for him at school. In fact, researchers estimate that 48% of children experience moderate to serious problems with adjustment to kindergarten (Pianta et al. 2007). Other studies, including the recommendations of the National Governor's Task Force on School Readiness (2005), research on parents'/families' involvement in children's transitions (McIntyre et al. 2007), teachers' evaluations of young children's adjustment issues (Rimm-Kaufmann et al. 2000), and cross-cultural comparisons of transition practices all concur that transitions are not necessarily managed well when they very much need to be.

In this volume of the *Educating the Young Child* Series, we have gathered together the insights of a group of distinguished teachers/scholars on transition practices throughout the world. The book's primary purpose is to support early childhood educators as they strive to make transitions as seamless as possible. The ways in which such stressors are handled are etched into the child's memory and often have lifelong significance for ways of coping. Consider, for example, the situation of three-year-old Laura. She could not contain her disappointment when her sister, cousins, and friends boarded the big yellow school bus in late August and left her behind. Laura yearned to join their ranks and flatly refused to accept the explanation of "you're too little to go." Those "big kids" had backpacks and lunchboxes, library books and homework; they carried home tales about school that surprised and fascinated her. When Laura's aunt came to visit, she was well aware of the child's eagerness to attend school so she presented the three-year-old with a toy school bus loaded with chubby passengers and a plastic lunchbox that included containers for food and drink. These items led to hours of play about being at school, riding the bus, eating in the cafeteria, and the good/bad behavior of children. Laura would line up her stuffed toys to represent a group of students, scribble on the board, give them assignments, reprimand their misbehavior, and pretend to read them a book. Whenever possible, she would draw her extended family into the play, and new dramatic possibilities would be added to the school theme, such as being sent to the principal's office, having a mean teacher, or getting sick and needing to come home. This "going to school" theme dominated Laura's play for two years, an indicator of the personal relevance that transitions have for the very young.

Three points serve as preparation for readers as they explore these distinguished authors' perspectives on transitions during the early years of life. First, to consider the child's point of view; second, that adults often have misconceptions about the kind and amount of support young children need; and finally, that the human costs of poorly managed transitions are considerable.

Perhaps the first lesson adults need to learn is that the child's perspective is qualitatively different from that of grown-ups. The experience of five-year-old Justin underscores this point. He attended a church-affiliated preschool two days a week at ages 3 and 4, and was ready to begin kindergarten at the local public school. Justin's grandparents, who were his primary caregivers, attended an orientation program sponsored by the school district. Justin also had the opportunity to spend the afternoon at his new school prior to beginning. The evening before his first official day of kindergarten, his grandmother laid out the clothing Justin would wear. Together they equipped his backpack with school supplies and packed a special lunch. The next morning, Justin and his grandfather walked to the school a few blocks away and that afternoon, his grandfather accompanied him on the walk back home. Justin's grandparents were relieved to hear that things had gone very well. That evening, as they began preparations for the second day of kindergarten, the preschooler appeared to be puzzled and then said, "You mean I have to do this *every day*?!" As Justin's perspective illustrates, young children often have very different questions and concerns than the ones adults anticipate. If ever we hope to effectively smooth transitions from one early childhood experience to another, we first need to identify with the child and really listen to what that child has to say.

Of course, adults can have misconceptions about the best way to support a young child's transitions; this is another important point addressed in this volume. Often, these misconceptions are based on what they recall from their own lives as children or spring from a desire to hasten the developmental process. When an international group of parents and their teachers convened for a workshop on helping their child adjust to a new country, language, culture, and school, a father from Germany asked it is best to ignore a crying child. The presenter said that being cold and rejecting, while *seeming* to be a way to put crying to a stop, would actually tend to have the opposite effect if a young child is genuinely distressed. She then stated, "I assume that you now have a warm, caring relationship with your son; otherwise, you would not have attended this session and bothered to ask." The father nodded affirmatively. "Then consider this," the presenter went on, "your son sees his big, strong father acting strangely. He understandably becomes worried, fearful, and clingy—and that is the very thing you had hoped to prevent. What he really needs is to 'borrow' some of your calm and emulate your confidence so that he can learn how to cope with stressful situations." The father appeared to be satisfied with this answer and afterwards, when the teachers were meeting with the presenter over lunch, they expressed their gratitude for explaining the issue in a way that the parents could understand. This is another goal that *Transitions to Early Care and Education: International Perspectives on Making Schools Ready for Young Children* strives to accomplish. The authors demonstrate how early childhood educators can bring all of their compassion, experience, and wisdom to bear on the issue of transitions as they work with families.

When a transition is managed poorly, it ripples out to affect every person in the process. If, for example, a child does not want to go to school and dreads it so much that he or she becomes physically ill before the bus arrives each day, then the family is in crisis, opportunities for that child's learning are diminished, peer relationships are disrupted, and reciprocal trust and respect between the family and school personnel is compromised. Consider the case of six-year-old Chris. His mother decided to keep him out of kindergarten for a year on the advice of family, friends, and neighbors. Chris was, in her words, "a little backward" and spoke with a lisp. When the child attended kindergarten, other children teased him about "talking like a baby" and his teacher would insist that he repeat after her, drawing out the "r" sound in words. One morning Chris arrived at his classroom door where the two kindergarten teachers stood and one of the teachers said derisively, "Here comes Cwis." Then both of them laughed.

When Chris came home that day, he went directly to his room and could not be coaxed into talking. Hours later, he said tearfully, "My teachers made fun of me today at school." The inexcusable behavior of Chris' first teachers formed a lifelong rift between his family and the educational system; they never again viewed the school or district positively because of this one, thoughtless and heartless act. From that point forward, Chris believed that he wasn't good at anything. His teachers were worse than incompetent, they are a disgrace to the profession.

As educators enter the early childhood field, they must, above all, embrace their solemn responsibility to put children first. We need to identify with the very young, advocate for their needs, protect them from harm, support their development, and optimize their learning. As children wend their way through various educational programs, settings, and policies, our role is to offer gentle guidance and support. We have an obligation to make new educational experiences, affirming and welcoming ones; we need to make schools ready for young children.

Mary Renck Jalongo

Contents

About the Contributors

Tomoko N. Arimura is a doctoral candidate in the School and Clinical Child Psychology Program at OISE/University of Toronto. She is a member of the Toronto First Duty (TFD) research team, and has investigated effects of service integration on everyday family life.

Nancy Balaban has been on the Bank Street College Graduate School of Education faculty for many years as course instructor and advisor in the Infant and Family Development and Early Intervention Program. She is author of *Everyday Goodbyes: Starting School and Early Care: A Guide to the Separation Process* (2006) and co-author of *Observing and Recording the Behavior of Young Children* (2009, 5th edn.), both published by Teachers College Press, as well as many articles and book chapters.

Carl Corter, Ph. D. is the Atkinson Charitable Foundation Chair in Early Child Development and Education and a professor in human development and applied psychology at OISE/University of Toronto. His research on parenting and early childhood programs is designed to inform policy and practice in schools and other community services.

Nancy Freeman is an associate professor of early childhood education and director of the Yvonne and Schuyler Moore Child Development Research Center at the University of South Carolina. She has published widely on professional ethics in early childhood, and issues related to quality programming, with a particular focus on preschoolers.

Allison Sidle Fuligni is assistant professor of child and family studies at California State University, Los Angeles, and associate research scientist in the Graduate School of Education and Information Studies at the University of California, Los Angeles (UCLA). Her research focuses on longitudinal and evaluation studies of early development, school readiness, and the educational and family contexts supporting early development, with a particular focus on urban children living in poverty and dual-language learners.

Susan Grieshaber is professor of early years education at the School of Early Childhood, Queensland University of Technology, Brisbane, Australia. Her research interests include early childhood curriculum, pedagogy, assessment, and policy, with a focus on equity and diversity. She has published widely, and co-edits the international refereed journal *Contemporary Issues in Early Childhood.*

Susan Hill works in teacher education and conducts research in the area of language and literacy development in the years before school and the early years of schooling.

Annemarie H. Hindman is an assistant professor in the College of Education at Temple University. Her research focuses upon early language and literacy learning, particularly among children in poverty, with a particular interest in how families and educators can, independently and in collaboration, support these early skills.

Palmina Ioannone, Ph. D. is the director of research and evaluation at Invest in Kids. She has spent more than 15 years working with young children, families, and early childhood professionals in various settings including schools, childcare centers, and family support programs.

Zeenat Janmohamed is the coordinator of the Atkinson Centre for Society and Child Development at the Ontario Institute for Studies in Education (OISE), University of Toronto, and a faculty member in the School of Early Childhood Education at George Brown College. She is a member of the Toronto First Duty research team and a specialist in early childhood professional education.

Dr. Magdalena Janus is an associate professor at the Department of Psychiatry and Behavioural Neuroscience at McMaster University where she holds the Ontario Chair in Early Child Development. Since joining the Offord Centre for Child Studies at McMaster University in 1997, Magdalena, together with the late Dr. Dan Offord, developed the Early Development Instrument (EDI), a measure of children's readiness to learn at school entry, which has been used widely in Canada and adapted in a number of international sites, e.g., Australia, Jamaica, Jordan, Kosovo, and Mexico. She regularly serves as a consultant with various national and international organizations, including the World Bank and UNICEF, on the measurement and indicators of early child development. Magdalena's research interests also include the transition to school, with a particular emphasis on children with special needs, and communities' engagement in children's early development and health.

James E. Johnson is professor of early childhood education at the College of Education, The Pennsylvania State University, USA.

Lynn A. Karoly is a senior economist with the RAND Corporation whose research has focused on child and family well-being, human capital investments, labor market behavior, and social welfare policy. In the area of child policy, she has examined the benefits and costs of early childhood programs and completed an in-depth study of preschool use and quality in California and the publicly funded preschool system in the state.

Margaret A. King is professor emerita in the School of Human and Consumer Sciences at Ohio University, Athens. She is a former teacher, director, and teacher educator. Her research interests are the schooling of young males and emotional maltreatment in the classroom.

Sandraluz Lara-Cinisomo is an assistant professor of child and family studies at the University of North Carolina, Charlotte. Her research focuses on early childhood academic and behavioral outcomes, teacher belief systems, school readiness, youth well-being among children from military families, and maternal mental health among civilian and military populations.

Laura Lee McIntyre, Ph. D. is an associate professor and director of the School Psychology Program in the Department of Special Education and Clinical Sciences at the University of Oregon. Her interests are in (1) parent training, education, and support, (2) kindergarten transition, and (3) child risk factors and family well-being.

Joann Migyanka taught children on the autism spectrum for 8 years in the public school system. She was awarded the Autism Professional of the Year from the Autism Society of America (ASA) in July 2000. She has presented at national and international conferences on topics related to autism spectrum disorders.

Saba Mir is a doctoral student in the Developmental Psychology and Education Program at the Ontario Institute for Studies in Education (OISE), University of Toronto. She is the manager of the Toronto First Duty (TFD) research team.

Dr. Frederick J. Morrison is a professor in the Department of Psychology at the University of Michigan. His program of research examines early language and literacy development, with a particular interest in identifying the cognitive and social foundations of this skill set and isolating the learning opportunities at home and school that support children's early competence in these domains.

Dr. Regena F. Nelson is a professor in early childhood education with over 20 years of research, teaching, and consulting experience in the field. She has conducted numerous research studies on school readiness, authentic assessment, early childhood program evaluation, culturally appropriate practices, and mentoring.

Sejal Patel, Ph. D. is a strategic training fellow of the Canadian Institutes of Health Research (CIHR) and Peterborough K. M. Hunter Foundation Fellow at the Centre for Research on Inner City Health at St. Michael's Hospital. As a member of the Toronto First Duty (TFD) research team, she investigated parent engagement, outreach, and the effects of integrated early childhood program participation on children's developmental outcomes.

Janette Pelletier, Ph. D. is an associate professor in human development and applied psychology at the Ontario Institute for Studies in Education (OISE), University of Toronto. Her research examines children's perspectives and learning, family literacy programs, and early childhood service integration in several projects, including Toronto First Duty. She is a specialist in early childhood professional education.

Anne Petriwskyj is a lecturer in inclusive early childhood education and care at the School of Early Childhood, Queensland University of Technology, Brisbane, Australia. She has extensive experience in the area of inclusivity and is currently challenging some deeply held beliefs about inclusive education. Her research focuses on transition to school and inclusive pedagogies in early childhood.

Beth Powers-Costello is an assistant professor of early childhood education at the University of South Carolina. She leads annual study abroad trips to Reggio Emilia through a partnership with Clemson University. She has published on early childhood education, curriculum, and teaching for justice.

Jaipaul L. Roopnarine is Jack Reilly Professor of Child and Family Studies and director of the Jack Reilly Institute of Early Childhood and Provider Education, Syracuse University, Department of Child and Family Studies, Syracuse, NY, USA.

Dr. Lori E. Skibbe is an assistant professor in the Department of Child and Family Ecology at Michigan State University. Her research examines children's literacy development in the context of schools and families, the optimal interventions for providing a strong foundation in this area, and the long-term consequences of depressed language and emergent literacy skills.

Leah K. Wildenger is a doctoral candidate in school psychology in the Department of Psychology at Syracuse University. She has interests in young children with developmental delays and disabilities, early intervention, and kindergarten transition.

Suzanne M. Winter is an associate professor of early childhood education and the principal investigator of early childhood research projects examining the health and school readiness of children with particular focus of on preschool obesity prevention strategies. She has sole-authored two books on theory and practice in inclusive early childhood classrooms and has published numerous research reports and articles in scholarly journals. Dr. Winter is currently serving a three-year term as the vice president for infancy and early childhood on the Executive Board of the Association for Childhood Education International.

Dr. Yaoying Xu is an associate professor in the Department of Special Education and Disability Policy at Virginia Commonwealth University. Dr. Xu's research focus is on early assessment and intervention for children and students from culturally and linguistically diverse backgrounds.

About the Editors

DeAnna M. Laverick, D. Ed. is an assistant professor at Indiana University of Pennsylvania and a former kindergarten teacher. She most recently authored a book chapter titled "The Development of Expertise in Teachers of Early Literacy," which was published in A. M. Columbus (Ed.), *Advances in Psychology Research* (vol. 69). Her other publications include "Starting School: Welcoming Young Children and Families into Early School Experiences" and "Motivation, Metacognition, Mentors, and Money: Ingredients that Support Teaching Expertise," both of which were published in *Early Childhood Education Journal*. Dr. Laverick was interviewed by *Early Childhood Today* on "Using Stories for Character Development" and also wrote "Home Visits and More: How to Ease the Transition to Kindergarten," which was published in *Classroom Leadership*. Dr. Laverick has made international conference presentations on topics that relate to transitions to new school experiences, literacy strategies, teacher expertise, and educational technology.

Mary Renck Jalongo, Ph. D. is a professor at Indiana University of Pennsylvania where she earned the university-wide Outstanding Professor Award and coordinates the Doctoral Program in Curriculum and Instruction. She is a co-editor of Springer's *Educating the Young Child* book series and has written, co-authored, or edited more than 25 books, including *Early Childhood Language Arts* (6th edn.), *Creative Thinking and Arts-Based Learning* (5th edn.), *Exploring Your Role in Early Childhood Education* (4th edn.), and *Major Trends and Issues in Early Childhood Education: Challenges, Controversies, and Insights* (2nd edn.). In addition, she has written two books (*Learning to Listen, Listening to Learn; Young Children and Picture Books*) for the National Association for the Education of Young Children (NAEYC), edited two for the Association for Childhood Education International (ACEI), and earned various national awards for writing. Since 1995, Mary Renck Jalongo has served as editor-in-chief of the *Early Childhood Education Journal*.

Chapter 1
Introduction

DeAnna M. Laverick

There are many transitions to new experiences that occur throughout one's lifetime. From infancy to the onset of formal school, transitions in the early childhood years involve a variety of stakeholders in the process and evoke a myriad of feelings for all involved. By putting the needs of children and their families first, early childhood educators support the transition process. The diverse experiences, traits, and needs exhibited by young children and their families worldwide provide early childhood educators with what may be a potentially challenging role. Yet it is by putting the children's and their families' needs first that successful transitions transpire.

Purpose of the Book

Transitions to Early Care and Education: International Perspectives on Making Schools Ready for Young Children focuses on the transitions that young children make to early care and education settings, along with the issues that surround this very important time in their lives. The purpose of this book is to communicate an enlarged view of the transition process in early childhood education. Rather than approaching the topic from a deficit-based readiness for school view, a broader examination of transitions guides the reader to appreciate and honor the promise and potential of all children worldwide. This book responds to the call for helping early childhood educators become ready to recognize the strengths and meet the diverse needs of all children.

A plethora of research-based practices and strategies for promoting successful transitions for children in a variety of social and cultural contexts are described in this book. It serves as a resource for teacher education programs and in-service early childhood professionals. The book links early childhood educational theories

D. M. Laverick (✉)
Department of Professional Studies in Education, Indiana University of Pennsylvania,
570 South Eleventh Street, Indiana, PA 15705, USA
e-mail: laverick@iup.edu

D. M. Laverick, M. R. Jalongo (eds.), *Transitions to Early Care and Education,*
Educating the Young Child 4, DOI 10.1007/978-94-007-0573-9_1,
© Springer Science+Business Media B.V. 2011

with practical applications. Additionally, it provides international perspectives on the ways that schools can institute practices and policies that promote successful transitions for all young children. The recommendations and strategies discussed will assist the reader in responding to the diverse abilities and needs of children worldwide in order to promote successful transitions in the early childhood years.

Overview of the Book

The book is comprised of three parts, beginning with Part One: Programs and Practices. Key themes that emerge in this section include programs and practices that teachers employ to meet the diverse needs of children and their families through the transition process. Practices that support the needs of children with exceptionalities are a focus in this section. This focus aligns with research conducted by the National Early Childhood Transition Center, which associated positive transitions with "the consistent use of developmentally appropriate practices across programs, especially for children with disabilities" (Rouse et al. 2007, p. 15).

In the first chapter of Part One, Nancy Balaban describes transition to group care for infants, toddlers, and families. This chapter concludes with information on transition for children receiving early intervention. Chapter 3, written by Laura Lee McIntyre and Leah K. Wildenger, then reviews empirical research on kindergarten transition practices for students with disabilities. Chapter 4, written by Joann Migyanka, provides strategies for supporting transition to formal school for students on the autism spectrum. In Chap. 5, Susan Hill examines connections and disconnections between oral language and literacy. The last chapter of this section, Chap. 6, is an article written by Hindman et al. (2010) that was originally published in *Early Childhood Education Journal*. This article describes teachers' outreach practices for families of children in preschool, kindergarten, and first grade and the impact that these practices make on early academic outcomes.

Part Two, Policies and Issues, begins with Chap. 7. This chapter, written by Anne Petriwskyj and Susan Grieshaber, reframes the debate about school transitions from the perspectives of critical theory and critical pedagogy. The focus then turns to the role of the teacher, with regard to teachers' histories and beliefs about transitions in Chap. 8, written by Margaret King. Then, in Chap. 9, Sandraluz Lara-Cinisomo, Allison Sidle Fuligni, and Lynn A. Karoly share findings from a study on teachers' beliefs about preschoolers' transitions to kindergarten. The discussion continues to focus on preschoolers from urban areas in Chap. 10, as Regena Nelson reports research findings from a study of preschool teachers' ability to work effectively with children from minority and low-income backgrounds. Chapter 11, written by Suzanne M. Winter, is the last chapter in this section and describes the linkages among culture, health, and school readiness.

Part Three, International Perspectives, begins with Chap. 12, written by Nancy K. Freeman and Beth Powers-Costello. This chapter provides a rationale for making schools ready for children by sharing practices in the United States and Northern

Italy. Transitions within the early childhood educational system in China are then described in Chap. 13 by Yaoying Xu. In Chap. 14, the socio-cultural context of early childhood education in English-speaking Caribbean countries is described by Jaipaul L. Roopnarine and James E. Johnson. The discussion then turns to perspectives from Canada. First, in Chap. 15, Magdalena Janus discusses influences on school readiness in Canada and Mexico. The book concludes with Chap. 16 as Tomoko N. Arimura, Carl Corter, Janette Pelletier, Zeenat Janmohamed, Sejal Patel, Palmina Ioannone, and Saba Mir share an integrated service model in which schools become hubs for support of children and their families.

Given the barriers that inhibit successful transitions, particularly for children with disabilities from linguistically and culturally diverse backgrounds (Rouse et al. 2008), the implementation of research-based developmentally effective transition practices is crucial. The authors' collective expertise provides readers with information to guide the transition process throughout the early years. Their work serves as a touchstone for early childhood educators worldwide as they strive to make programs at various levels and in different contexts ready for the children they serve.

References

Hindman, A. H., Skibbe, L. E., & Morrison, F. J. (2010). Teacher outreach to families across the transition to school: An examination of teachers' practices and their unique contributions to children's early academic outcomes. *Early Childhood Education Journal, 38*(4). doi:10.1007/s10643-010-0410-4.

Rouse, B., Myers, C., & Stricklin, S. (2007). Strategies for supporting transitions of young children with special needs and their families. *Journal of Early Intervention, 30*(1), 1–18.

Rouse, B., Schroeder, C., Stricklin, S. B., Hains, A., & Cox, M. (2008). *Transition issues and barriers for children with significant disabilities and from culturally and linguistically diverse backgrounds.* Lexington: University of Kentucky, Human Development Institute, National Early Childhood Transition Center. http://hdi.uky.edu/SF/Home.asp.

Part I
Programs and Practices

Chapter 2
Transition to Group Care for Infants, Toddlers, and Families

Nancy Balaban

The focus of this chapter is to shed light on the significance of infants, toddlers, and their families making the *transition* from care-at-home to out-of-home care. Parents or primary caregivers as well as their children profit from focused support during this process because the event arouses deep feelings and uncertainties. How the transition itself is accomplished sets the stage for the child's *entire* experience in the early care or Early Intervention (EI) group setting.

Infant and toddler care is a major and rapidly growing form of child care in this country today. With 56% of women with children under age three employed outside the home, child care for infants and toddlers is in high demand. Although nearly 6 million infants and toddlers spend all or part of their day being cared for by someone other than their parents, more than 40% of those infants and toddlers are in child care classrooms of poor quality (Cohen and Ewen 2008). This deeply disheartening fact challenges the accepted requirements for healthy early child development in quality care settings.

> Good-quality childcare has been associated with a range of outcomes, including better cognitive, linguistic, and social development. Moreover, good-quality care can promote the school readiness and success of children from at-risk families. (Zigler et al. 2009, p. 90)

According to Zero to Three (2009), the pre-eminent national organization devoted to the optimal development of children from birth to age three and their families, the central components of *quality care* for infants and toddlers are:

- Small groups
- High staff-to-child ratio
- Primary caregiving (see p. 11)
- Adherence to health and safety policies
- A highly trained, well-compensated staff
- Well-planned physical environments
- Cultural and linguistic competence and continuity

N. Balaban (✉)
Bank Street Graduate School of Education, 610 West 112th Street, New York, NY 10025, USA
e-mail: nbalaban@bankstreet.edu

D. M. Laverick, M. R. Jalongo (eds.), *Transitions to Early Care and Education,*
Educating the Young Child 4, DOI 10.1007/978-94-007-0573-9_2,
© Springer Science+Business Media B.V. 2011

The Nature of Transitions

Transitions form a life-long matrix of human life through which all children and adults move gradually from known into unknown realms of experience. Birth, the original transition propels infants from their warm, dark, nine month inner home into the outer world of light and variability. Many transitions follow this first foray: an infant or toddler goes to child care, an adolescent starts high school, an adult takes a new job, one graduates from college, another gets married, some get divorced, a worker retires, and at the ultimate transition, a person dies.

These transitions are mileposts on the path from babyhood through adulthood. Each involves a *separation* from a familiar environment and an entry into an unfamiliar one. A range of emotions from anticipation to apprehension often accompanies each transition. Inevitably, these transitions offer challenges and hopefully, new opportunities for accomplishment and competence.

A potential for growth and change exists in every separation experience even though a temporary sense of loss predominates. Few people set out on a new venture without thoughts of what they have left behind. Sometimes ceremony lessens the impact of a loss by acknowledging a particular separation as a legitimate transition to a new phase of development. In some primitive cultures, rituals such as shaving a child's head may symbolize cutting him off from his past connections and indicate his entry into another stage of life. Spanking at a birthday party may be an old-fashioned counterpart of this custom. In an elaborate ceremony in some Hispanic communities, a 15-year-old girl, wearing a floor length dress, makes her debut before church and society in a rite of passage from childhood to adulthood known as quinceañera. Other present-day events such as baptisms, bar and bat mitzvahs, graduations, and weddings mark the transition from one stage of life to another. Entering early care and education is a transition to a new stage for children as well as parents, but there is no unique ritual that is culturally shared (Balaban 2006, pp. 16–17).

Entering Early Care

The entry process itself can be considered a microcosm, containing significant characteristics of a high-quality program. The *essence* of high-quality care, on which all the above features depend, is the *relationship* the caregiver creates with the child (Shonkoff and Phillips 2000).

> **The quality of the relationships between child care providers and the children for whom they are responsible carry the weight of the influence of child care on children's development [emphasis added].** The relationship between the child care provider and parent is also critical. However, in order for these relationships to flourish, program policies as well as caregiving environments need to facilitate their growth. It is the skilled and stable relationship-oriented provider working in the high quality conditions described above that promotes positive development. Mentoring and coaching supports, a stable workforce with

low turnover, and adequate compensation have also been linked to high quality of care. (Cohen and Ewen 2008, pp. 1–2)

This relationship is set in motion the moment infants, toddlers, and their families arrive at the child care setting on their first day, facilitated by the program's *gradual entry* policy that eases them into the new setting, encouraging the growth of trust. The infant/toddler care teacher starts to forge a connection with the *whole* family, recalling the words of psychiatrist D. W. Winnicott, "There is no such thing as a baby…if you set out to describe a baby, you will find you are describing a baby and someone. A baby cannot exist alone, but is essentially part of a relationship" (Winnicott 1978, p. 88).

If the center's policy also involves a prior home visit, the care teacher can make another alliance by reminding the toddler that they have met before. "I remember that I saw your teddy bear when I came to your house." As a welcome gesture, the teacher may offer a toy that will engage the family members with their child. If the care teacher is not familiar with the child's home language, she or he might ask for few key words to use when speaking with the child. The care teacher's goal is to help the child and family feel comfortable, safe, and welcome in the room.

The Developmental Meaning of Transition for Infants and Toddlers

Although most school age children rely on their solid sense of self as a bulwark to ease their passage from one life condition to another, the same is not true for infants and toddlers. Infants and toddlers are still in the *process* of forming their preliminary sense of self (Lally 1995) and must rely on caring, familiar adults for psychic stability. Thrusting babies into a strange child care setting without thoughtful preparation and support invites difficulties.

Infants and toddlers learn the lesson of who they are by the way they are cared for. "Through multiple experiences, the child builds an internal working model or representation that says: 'This is how my caregiver cares for me. This is how I am.'" (Howes 1998, p. 8). Because infants and toddlers rely on the care of others in the process of defining themselves, entry to child care demands sensitive, responsive, well-trained infant/toddler care teachers who possess an understanding of early development. The entry process itself requires a well-designed plan that includes several features:

- A director's meeting with family members prior to the child's starting in the program. This gives parents an opportunity to ask questions, to learn the program requirements, and to meet other adults whose children will be attending.
- A gradual entry that welcomes and supports a family member to stay with the child in the classroom until both feel safe. This may take place over a few days with each day's stay shorter than the day before. If a parent cannot manage this,

another family member or close friend can substitute. This process is an investment in a baby who feels safe and trusting in the new environment.

- A discussion between the care teacher and the family about the baby's home routines.
- An acknowledgement that separation reactions, crying and clinging, are appropriate and expected. Care teachers always respond to the infants' and toddlers' demonstrations of these emotions and soothe them.
- A primary caregiver system. (see p. 11)
- Photographs of the family, covered with clear, adhesive plastic and posted low on a wall where the baby can see and touch it.
- A welcome for *transitional objects*—favorite stuffed animals, or a piece of blanket that bring the infant/toddler's home into the center and provide a large measure of security.
- A book of photos of the child taken at the center to keep at home.

Recognizing and legitimizing the wide range of emotions that accompany this transition is not only basic but *essential*. Parents of very young infants have been known to burst into tears after leaving the room. Others may phone to make sure all is well with their toddler. After saying "goodbye" many children cry—sometimes every day, sometimes for weeks. It is important to legitimize these feelings rather than try to distract them. Children need to know "You feel sad when your mom leaves. I will try to help you feel better. Your mom (dad, grandma, aunt) *always* comes back."

Sensitive early care teachers can engage in play that enables infants and toddlers to work through their separation reactions. There are many variations on the "hide and seek" game that essentially recapitulates, symbolically, parents' leaving and returning. In the sand table, one teacher hides individual photos of all the children enabling each to "find" him/herself again. Here is a description of a 31-month-old boy at play as he copes with the daily *hello* and *goodbye*. In play he is in charge, unlike the real situation in which his family is in charge of leaving and returning.

> Mano holds a small shovel and two plastic figures in the sand table saying, "Bye-bye people. I'm going to make you go bye-bye." He buries the figures under a mound of sand. Once they are out of sight, he digs into the sand, grabs them and raises the two figures high in the air. "I found you!" he exults. (Rajan 2009)

Feelings about the morning separation may surface at the end of the day when the child is tired and eager to go home. Lisa (19 months) is standing by her cubby watching the care teacher help another toddler with his sweater.

> Lisa takes out her coat and sticks one arm through the sleeve, trying to put on her jacket. Dragging her jacket on the floor, she walks to her teacher saying, "Ugh-ugh." "It's not time to go home yet, Lisa," the teacher says as she hangs Lisa's jacket back in the cubby. Lisa walks over to a child who is bundled up in his coat and tries to unzip it. She tugs at the other child's sleeve yelling, "Home! Home!" The teacher sits on the floor close to Lisa, saying "Your mom will be here soon to take you home" and guides her to a table where other toddlers are doing puzzles. Uninterested, Lisa walks back to her cubby, reaches for her jacket and yells, "Home!" (Eastzer 2009)

Caregiver–Child Attachment: The Bottom Line

Infant/toddler care teachers build intimate and important relationships with infants and toddlers over time out of their day-to-day interactions, as they soothe distress, repair conflicts, observe and support play, change diapers, assist napping, and share the children's successes as well as their disappointments.

When these interactions are sensitive, responsive, and caring, infants and toddlers become *attached* to their care teachers in ways that are reminiscent of their attachment to their parents. Both these important relationships are powerful because they produce emotions, thoughts, and special meanings. A number of studies show that young children prosper when they have strong, positive relationships with their teachers. They do better with peers, are happier, and are more successful later in school. Having a close, supportive relationship with a caregiver/teacher in early childhood has been seen as a "resiliency factor" for high-risk children (Elicker and Fortner-Wood 1995 p. 72). Tierney and Nelson (2009) state that "psychosocial experiences are necessary for the development of a healthy brain" (p. 13). During the early years of life, brain development is rapid and highly reliant on positive and supportive relationships. "Sensitive and responsive caregiving becomes a powerful regulator of emotional behavior" and "of the stress response to the threat of separation" as well (Gunnar and Cheatham 2003, p. 195, 204). The attachment engendered by attentive caregiving creates a *secure base* from which the baby and toddler can explore, learn, and form wider relationships with peers and other adults. Secure attachment is the foundation of an independent, resourceful, self confident, and learning child.

Infant/toddler care is personal. A *primary caregiving system* (Bernhardt 2000) in which each caregiver has primary, but not exclusive, focused care of two or three children, assures very young children that attention will be paid. The primary caregiver is the one who greets the child and family each day, diapers or toilets, feeds and puts to nap—is an anchor in a sea of activity. The child knows to whom to go for special comfort. The family knows whom to contact for daily information. This is *secure base* behavior. It has many advantages:

> [I]nfants explore more, have more productive play, and interact more and more resourcefully with adults in group settings when their attachments to teachers are secure. (Raikes 1996, p. 61)

Some infant/toddler programs use a "school model" rather than an "attachment model," grouping children

> according to age—babies in one room, one-year-olds in another, and two-year-olds in yet another-[which] may require children to move from one group to another before they or their families are ready. When infants begin to walk, for example, they move to the toddler group. However, transitions are stressful for both children and teachers because they disrupt attachments. Babies' departure for a toddler group affects their caregivers, who miss them and the experience of following their development. These transitions also affect parents, who must disconnect from familiar caregivers. To counteract these disruptions, some centers enact a continuity of care model in which the teachers stay with the same children for their entire three years in a center. (Casper and Theilheimer 2009, p. 327)

The Impact of Culture

It is not unusual for early care teachers to assume that they share the same values as the children and families in their care. Yet families differ widely in their beliefs about the role of children in the family and society. "A number of contemporary researchers have observed that adults set goals for their children with one of two cultural ideas in mind: individualism or collectivism" (Pena and Mendez-Perez 2006, p. 35). Groups favoring an individualistic orientation view children as independent and self-directed, while those incorporating a collectivistic approach regard children as part of and responsible to the family group. While these two ideas produce different parental behaviors and expectations, they are not mutually exclusive. "Every culture depends on children's ability to do both, but in some cultures, one or the other can take greater priority. Even within a family, various ideas about what is best for a child may be in competition" (Casper and Theilheimer 2009, p. 324). Nevertheless, teachers need to be aware not only of these differences, but of their own child rearing beliefs as well. Becoming alert to other's ideas of what behavior is important for young children is necessary in our increasingly diverse society. Cultures vary greatly in their childrearing practices such as multigenerational households that share child care, children co-sleeping with parents, use of pacifiers, and age of self-feeding and of toilet learning. These practices are highly potent issues in the first three years of life.

> Since most early childhood programs in this country value independence and individualism, it is a formidable task for teachers to distinguish a "collective" cultural style from dependence. In order to embrace both major cultural patterns, perhaps teachers should think about separation and attachment not only as a child's movement *away* from a parent but also as movement *toward* a connection with others. (Balaban 2006, p. 20)

Transition for Children Receiving Early Intervention (EI) Services

EI programs provide critical services for infants and toddlers from birth to age two regardless of income or citizenship. "EI can enhance the healthy development of children by providing vital health, developmental, and therapeutic services to promote early learning and strengthen crucial relationships with caregivers" (Dicker 2009, p. 1). Currently all states participate in EI provided by Part C of Public Law 105-17 (Individuals with Disabilities Education Act of 1997).

Although some information is available about the transition from home-based care to a group-based EI program or an inclusion program serving both typically developing and children with special needs (Bennett et al. 1991; O'Brien 1997), major attention is focused on the Part B transition process, at age three, to preschool special education and/or from preschool programs to kindergarten or primary school (Hains et al. 1991).

Since the law requires that EI services take place in "natural environments—settings that are natural or normal for the child's age peers who have no disabilities," (www.Wrightslaw.com), it is evident that a *quality* program designed for typically developing infants and toddlers is obligatory for EI group programs. The fact that so little is written about the transition from home to group setting for infants and toddlers with disabilities is surprising since the central thrust of the law recognizes the predominant role of the family in making decisions about the education and care of their child. Such a decision is difficult for a family to make without sufficient information.

Suggestions below for enabling the transition of infants and toddlers, in EI, from home to center are based on plans described by Bennett et al. (1991). Other suggestions, drawn from Rous et al. (2007) that are focused on three-year-olds entering special education preschool or kindergarten, can also be applied to the EI home-to-group-care transition. We must always remember that the baby is an infant or toddler *first*, and has special needs *second*.

Arrangements designed to stabilize the transition include those described above as well as:

- Clarifying objectives and discussing roles and responsibilities
- Developing a transition plan from the home-based EI sending staff to the center's receiving staff
- Developing a checklist of the infant/toddler's abilities and needs
- Securing support of the child's place in the program from the receiving administrator and staff
- Preparing and supporting families via specific meetings with the receiving administrator and staff focused on the transition
- Visiting and evaluating the receiving program prior to a family's enrolling their child, accompanied, if possible, by the home-based service provider
- Visiting, on a frequent, regular basis by the parent and toddler before the actual attendance. Attending thereafter for short periods of time, gradually working up to full-time
- Building interagency relationships

A short history of Sarah and Tom and their twelve-month-old daughter Kate, who had many medical complications as a result of premature birth, making a transition from home-based EI to an integrated child care setting is described in Bennett et al. (1991).

After 12 weeks in the NICU (Neonatal Intensive Care Unit) Kate was sent home on an apnea monitor. Her parents

> were concerned about how she would fare in a child care setting when Sarah returned to work during Kate's second year of life. Would the classroom staff be able to give her the kind of attention she needed? Would Kate be safe in a group of freely mobile children? Would she be left out of activities because she couldn't follow the other children? How would Kate respond when Sarah left her?
> Sarah and Tom shared these concerns with the home visitor [Debbie] who had seen Kate during her first year. [They] planned to designate one classroom teacher as Kate's "special person," who initially would respond to Kate and set up situations that would allow her to interact with a limited number of children at a time. (1991, p. 19)

The center staff, naturally, had concerns about Kate's apnea monitor that they discussed with Sarah and Tom. In order to ease the family's settling-in, the staff arranged Kate's first day at the center many days before Sarah had to return to work.

> Sarah and Tom brought Kate to the center and stayed for several hours, helping to involve Kate in activities and introduce her to other children. For the next few days, Sarah stayed with Kate at the center, becoming...more familiar with the program as the staff and children got to know her. After Kate had attended the center for several days part-time, Sarah was ready to leave Kate for the full day.... Gradually, over several days, Sarah decreased the time she spent in leave-taking, and parting became easier for Kate.
> The classroom teacher was careful to make frequent contact with Sarah and Tom, both formal and informal, to give them information about Kate's daily activities and to discuss [their] questions and concerns. (1991, p. 20)

Family Concerns Unique to Early Intervention

Families have many concerns related to and during the transition to an infant/toddler center-based program that must be recognized by the receiving program.

> Stress for families of young children with special needs increases when the diagnosis is made, during entry into early intervention services, and during the child's transition to a new program. Parental adjustment and adaptation to the child's disability typically is most difficult at the beginning of each of these events. A planned approach by the early intervention team can help families prepare for and better cope with early transitions. (Hains et al. 1991, p. 39)

Such concerns include "saying goodbye to their current intervention team and form[ing] new relationships with new service staff" (Hains et al. 1991, p. 39). Although a therapist who served in the home might arrange to continue working with the child in the new setting, it is more usual to find itinerant occupational therapist, physical therapist, and speech therapists providing services at an inclusion site. An EI group will very likely have their own on-site staff of therapists. Because of their widely differing schedules, communication among the therapists, teachers, and family is a demanding, often overwhelming task.

Many infant/toddler care teachers have limited experience with children with disabilities and look to the EI team for consultation and support. When that consultation and support is difficult to arrange, the child's progress may be at risk. When making the transition from home-based EI services to group care, the emphasis on family involvement and family services remains as a crucial element in the process, as required by law.

Some family concerns are related to the bus transportation provided to EI programs. Concerns relate to the child's safety and security as well as limiting contact between the family and the infant/toddler care teacher. Although arrangements can be made for parents to ride the bus, it is not always convenient, especially if they need to be at work at a certain time. Unwittingly, the bus can be a barrier between the family's familiarity with the program and their daily ability to support an ongoing separation process with their child. *The onus is on the teacher to find ways to communicate.* Teachers may need to make special arrangements to bridge this gap. For example, one program creates a communication book that travels daily from center to home and back, in which the teacher writes comments to the family and the family responds with their comments to the teacher. The book may also include comments from any therapist who is providing services at the center. Below is an entry to a communication book:

> *Teacher:* G. was very sad when his dad left but he was able to be comforted by teacher W. He played with play dough and made a birthday cake. He worked on reducing his tongue thrust.
> *Parent:* G's turtleneck shirt is missing. He didn't sleep well last night. Make sure he eats lunch. He's been lining up toys. What does that mean?

If a family member and a teacher feel the need to talk together they may set up a face-to-face conference time, arrange a telephone call, exchange e-mails, or make a plan for the parent to bring the child in one day. The parent may share some of her thoughts with the teacher who needs to listen carefully. Is there a "hidden message" behind the disclosure that "he didn't sleep well" or "Make sure he eats lunch."? A response of "How are *you?* You must be tired or worried." will be closer to the parent's real concern and desire for understanding. Parents of these babies with special needs require huge amounts of support, encouragement, and patient understanding from teachers.

Parents of children with disabilities may have a host of worries. "Will she fall down? Will he get hurt? Will she be protected? He has a language delay—will teachers understand him? Will other children like her? He's not walking yet; will they think he's a baby? How will she do in this setting? She's used to adults in our family helping her—will the teachers have enough time to attend to her? What will other parents think of him?" Parents, confronted with a group of children who are developing typically, may experience what one teacher called "re-wounding"—a reminder that their child is different and needs special attention. It may, therefore, be harder for the parent to leave the child at the initial transition period than it is for the child to leave the parent. This places an additional responsibility on the teacher to help both parent and child feel comfortable and reassured. Here we see the vital role of the primary caregiver as described previously.

A *central issue* for many parents in the transition to group care is that they are no longer in charge of managing the EI home services. While this may be a relief for some parents, it is a conflict and loss for many others. Without the case management load, the parent now "has to learn to be *only* a parent" (Murray Kelley, 1 April, 2010, personal communication). Teachers need to be sensitive to this issue should it arise in their relationships with the parents.

Attachment: Children with Disabilities

Supporting and encouraging the attachment that exists between children with disabilities and their parents falls under the teacher's and the program's purview. Compared to the attachment of children without disabilities, the attachment of children with disabilities may appear "less complex, less provocative, and less differentiated" (Blacher 1984, p. 181). Conversely, it may appear quite complicated, because in some parent-child pairs the "existence of a developmental disability has been found to impair the normal development of attachment" (Foley 1986, p. 58). Foley reported on a small study showing that children with disabilities may not be able to engage in behaviors that promote interaction and reciprocity—the building blocks of attachment. Children may exhibit reduced cueing, delayed locomotion, unpredictable temperament, irritability, and/or a high incidence of illness that interfere with the usual give and take of attachment formation. For example, a child who is born blind is unable to make the eye contact that the mother anticipates when nursing or holding the baby face-to-face (Fraiberg and Fraiberg 1977). These impediments to attachment may require more of the care teacher's capability than she is able to do without support of expert consultation. In some states EI may provide funds for a staff to hold clinical meetings focused on specific children and their families. Crucial to the integrity of *every* program is the need for reflective supervision and mentorship.

All Infant/Toddler Care Teachers Need Support

There are challenges to creating relationships with infants and toddlers whether they are developing typically or have special needs. Teachers may rely on their own experiences of being parented or on social myths about relating to children. If the well-regarded technique of following a baby or toddler's lead is an unfamiliar way of working, care teachers may tend to "entertain" in their effort to play, or hold a baby too long in their attempt to be close.

Many demanding situations arise every day. What does the early care teacher do with his/her frustration when a baby doesn't stop crying, or a toddler has frequent, inconsolable tantrums, or a two-year-old refuses to comply? Infants and toddlers may not *love the teacher back* when she stops an unsafe interaction like a toddler climbing on the table, throwing sand, or hitting or biting another child. Infant/toddler care is physical and emotional hard work (Eliot 2007). It calls for regular, supportive, reflective "supervision and mentorship [that] offer ongoing opportunities to recognize, understand, and cope successfully with the challenges of becoming an infant/family practitioner" (Fenichel 1992, p. 103).

Teamwork that forges the endeavors of care teachers and assistants is fundamental to a relationship-based quality program. When the room team meets regularly, works together with a spirit of cooperation and trust, it provides a model for children of how adults get along. The well functioning team creates a safe and affectionate environment. There must be space, and time, however, for disagreements and for confronting, and resolving, issues that have the potential for disruption.

Optimistic Outlook

Parents who are searching for infant/toddler care, are often at a loss as to what constitutes good care and what features to look for. They may not know key questions to ask a center director or a family child care provider. They may not understand the significance of transition planning. They may be unsure where to get information, other than from friends or neighbors. What they can afford is a serious consideration because care for children from birth to age three is "labor intensive" and therefore expensive. In addition, there are more infants and toddlers needing care than available slots. This report from the mother of a 26-month-old toddler is not atypical.

> I started looking for child care when I was 6 months pregnant. I've yet to come across a class or workshop for new parents-to-be that discusses what child care is really about and what the options are for families who have to go back to work. In fact, no one discusses how difficult it is for new parents to put a three-month-old baby into an environment for up to ten hours a day. It is usually such a traumatic break for the primary caregiver and though an infant can't tell you with words, it can also be a very difficult adjustment for the baby. (McSharry 2009)

Although this mother contacted a local child care bureau, she found it difficult to get information on what is "really going on in daycare centers and family care." She had to change child care arrangements several times because of bad experiences. Finally, she settled for what she could afford—"but it falls short of what my child needs" (McSharry 2009).

This scene has been replicated in various forms across our country for many years. Although our early childhood programs have remained inadequate, often compromising children's development, there *is* optimism.

> Today, the quest for quality has been invigorated by a dramatic shift in national policy. The research is driving unprecedented federal support for early childhood quality initiatives, which promises to move the field forward in ways that were previously unimaginable. (Policy Brief 2009, p. 2)

This Policy Brief describes the Quality Rating and Improvement Systems (QRIS) as

> a strategy for assessing, improving, and disseminating information about the level of quality across the full continuum of ECE programs, including school-based pre-kindergarten, Head Start, and center- and home-based child care…creating an industry-wide standard for quality assurance and a framework for improving consumer knowledge and influencing choice.
>
> The standards used to assign ratings are based on research about the characteristics of programs that indicate quality and are linked to positive outcomes for children…. Standards may be aligned with a state's early learning guidelines, and are based on widely accepted existing quality standards for programs and practitioners, such as those developed by the National Association for the Education of Young Children (NAEYC), Head Start, and the National Association for Family Child Care (NAFCC). In many states, programs that have been accredited by NAEYC, or NAFCC, in the case of family child care, automatically receive the highest rating. (Policy Brief 2009, p. 3)

According to Zero to Three Policy Center, the Obama administration and Congress, using vehicles such as the economic stimulus package, health care reform, and student loan reform, have worked together to increase federal support for Early Head Start, child care, and EI, as well as challenge states to improve the quality of early learning settings for very young children. Signed into law on Feb. 17, 2009 the American Recovery and Reinvestment Act includes significant funds targeted for infants and toddlers much of which is dedicated to improving the quality of infant and toddler care as well as funding for Part C EI services for infants and toddlers.

Among the programs established, a Congressional Baby Caucus was formed in May 2009 to educate members of Congress about the role federal policymaking plays in the healthy development of very young children and to advance federal policy change on behalf of infants, toddlers, and their families (Zero to Three, 2009). "Elements of such early care and education systems are interrelated and rely on effective collaboration and the interaction of participants to be effective" (Goldstein 2006, p. 30).

> Across the country, states and communities are developing comprehensive systems to help all children from birth to five years old have good health, strong families, and positive early learning experiences. In aligning policies and programs across the ages of children served, states can establish an array of services supporting the healthy development of babies, toddlers and their families. A variety of strategies represent the initiatives that states and federal government are using. (Goldstein 2006. p. 30)

These indications of a focus on children's very early development are encouraging and a cause for an optimistic outlook.

References

Balaban, N. (2006). *Everyday goodbyes: Starting school and early care: A guide to the separation process.* New York: Teachers College Press.

Bennett, T., Raab, M., & Nelson, D. (1991). The transition process for toddlers with special needs and their families. *Zero to Three, XI*(3), 17–21.

Bernhardt, J. L. (2000). A primary caregiving system for infants and toddlers: Best for everyone involved. *Young Children, 55*(2), 74–80.

Blacher, J. (1984). Attachment and severely handicapped children: Implications for intervention. *Developmental and Behavioral Pediatrics, 5*(4), 178–183.

Casper, V., & Theilheimer, R. (Eds.). (2009). *Early childhood education: Learning together* (p. 328). New York: McGraw-Hill.

Cohen, J., & Ewen, D. (2008). *Infants and toddlers in child care.* Zero to Three Policy Center & CLASP, Center for Law and Social Policy. Policy brief. http://www.clasp.org/federal_policy/pages?id=0006. Accessed 10 Nov. 2008.

Dicker, S. (2009). The promise of early intervention. EITI newsletter. New York: Early intervention training institute. Rose F. Kennedy Center, University Center for Excellence Developmental Disabilities. Albert Einstein College of Medicine.

Eastzer, N. (2009). *Student journal.* New York, NY: Bank Street College.

Elicker, J., & Fortner-Wood, C. (1995). Adult-child relationships in early childhood programs. *Young Children, 51*(1), 69–78.

Eliot, E. (2007). *We're not robots: The voices of daycare providers.* Albany, NY: State University of New York Press.

Fenichel, E. (Ed.). (1992). *Learning through supervision and mentorship*. Arlington, VA: Zero to Three.

Foley, G. (1986). Emotional development of children with handicaps. In N. Curry (Ed.), *The feeling child: Affective development reconsidered* (pp. 57–73). New York, NY: Haworth Press.

Fraiberg, S., & Fraiberg, L. (1977). *Insights from the blind*. New York: Basic Books.

Goldstein, A. (2006) State early care and education systems can support the healthy development of babies and toddlers. *Young Children, 61*(4), 30–32.

Gunnar, M. R., & Cheatham, C. L. (2003). Brain and behavior interface: Stress and the developing brain. *Infant Mental Health Journal, 24*(3), 195–211.

Hains, A. H., Rosenkoetter, S. E., Fowler, S. A. (1991). Transition planning with families in early intervention programs. *Infants and Young Children, 3*(4), 38–47.

Howes, C. (1998). Continuity of care: The importance of infant, toddler, caregiver relationships. *Zero to Three, 18*(6), 7–11.

Lally, J. R. (1995) The impact of child care policies and practices on infant/toddler identity formation. *Young Children, 51*(1), 58–67.

McSharry, T. (2009). Student journal. New York, NY: Bank Street College.

O'Brien, M. (1997) *Inclusive child care for infants and toddlers: Meeting individual and special needs*. Baltimore, MD: Paul H. Brookes.

Pena, E. D., & Mendez-Perez, A. (2006). Individualistic and collectivistic approaches to language learning. *Zero to Three, 27*(1), 34–41.

Policy Brief. (2009, Summer). *Improving the quality of early childhood education through system-building II*(1). New York, NY: New York City Early Childhood Professional Development Institute. The City University of New York.

Raikes, H. (1996). A secure base for babies: Applying attachment concepts to the infant care setting. *Young Children, 51*(5), 59–67.

Rous, B., Myers, C. T., & Stricklin, S. B. (2007). Strategies for supporting transitions of young children with special needs. *Journal of Early Intervention, 30*(1), 1–18.

Rajan, M. (2009). *Student journal*. New York, NY: Bank Street College.

Shonkoff, J., & Phillips, D. (2000). *From neurons to neighborhoods: The science of early childhood development*. Washington, DC: National Academy Press.

Tierney, A. L., & Nelson III, C. A. (2009). Brain development and the role of experience in the early years. *Zero to Three, 30*(2), 9–13.

Winnicott, D. W. (1978). *The child, the family and the outside world*. Harmondsworth, Middlesex: Penguin Books. www.wrightslaw.com/info/ei.index.htm#natenv

Zero to Three. (2009). *Caring for infants and toddlers in groups: Developmentally appropriate practice* (2nd ed.). Washington, DC: Zero to Three. (Zero to Three National Center for Infants, Toddlers, and Families: Celebrating improvements in infant-toddler policy: Top 10 Policy achievements of 2009. Retrieved from www.zerotothree.org/policy (June 2009) Navigating the opportunities for families with young children in the American Recovery and Reinvestment Act: An interactive tool).

Zigler, E., Marsland, K., & Lord, H. (2009) *The tragedy of child care in America*. New Haven & London: Yale University Press.

Chapter 3
Examining the State of the Science

Empirical Support for Kindergarten Transition Practices for Students with Disabilities

Laura Lee McIntyre and Leah K. Wildenger

One of the first rights of passage children experience in their formative years is the transition from early care and education to elementary school. This move brings increased responsibility, expectations, and opportunities for success and failure for children and their families. Successful adaptation to school is influenced by many factors, including academic, social, emotional, behavioral, and cognitive competencies of the child (McIntyre et al. 2006; Perry and Weinstein 1998), as well as family and community factors (McIntyre et al. 2007; Rimm-Kaufman and Pianta 2000). Some researchers have even conceptualized the kindergarten transition as a "sensitive period" (Rimm-Kaufman and Pianta 2000) necessary to establish positive, academic, and social trajectories in a child's educational experience (Eckert et al. 2008; Rimm-Kaufman et al. 2000). Given the developmental flux often experienced by many children at this age, coupled with changing systems of support, it is important for professionals to partner with families to make formal school entry for children as smooth as possible. Successful kindergarten transition, although important for all children, may be especially important for children with disabilities given their risk for school difficulties (Fowler et al. 1991; McIntyre et al. 2006; Quintero and McIntyre 2010). As a group, children with developmental delays or disabilities may require additional supports to facilitate successful elementary school entry.

The Ecological and Dynamic Model of Transition, proposed by Rimm-Kaufman and Pianta (2000), provides a fundamental theoretical framework describing the transition to school and articulates the necessary supports for students, families, and school personnel. A key assumption of this model is that child-centered models of transition emphasizing only children's internal characteristics or "readiness," while important, are inadequate to fully explain transition outcomes. Indeed, it has been argued that within-child factors such as cognitive ability explain less than one-quarter of the variance in children's academic outcomes (Rimm-Kaufman and Pianta 2000). Instead, the Ecological and Dynamic Model of Transition focuses on changing contexts and relationships amid the transition to school. This model describes

L. L. McIntyre (✉)
Department of Special Education & Clinical Sciences,
University of Oregon, Eugene, OR 97403-5208, USA
e-mail: llmcinty@uoregon.edu

D. M. Laverick, M. R. Jalongo (eds.), *Transitions to Early Care and Education,*
Educating the Young Child 4, DOI 10.1007/978-94-007-0573-9_3,
© Springer Science+Business Media B.V. 2011

how connections among child, family, school, peer, and community factors create a dynamic network of relationships that impact children's transition to school both directly and indirectly (Rimm-Kaufman and Pianta 2000). Another key component of The Ecological and Dynamic Model of Transition is the transactional nature of the interactions between child and ecological contexts. These theorists contend that dynamic patterns and relationships can operate to either enhance or impede a child's transition to kindergarten. Thus, this model is particularly helpful for identifying both risk and protective factors that affect transition outcomes.

Rimm-Kaufman and Pianta (2000) recommend that kindergarten transition research adhere to their proposed theoretical framework. Although no studies have explicitly examined kindergarten outcomes through the lens of this model, limited preliminary evidence in support of this model has emerged from a small number of outcome studies of kindergarten transition.

Chapter Goals

The primary goal of this chapter is to review the empirical literature on kindergarten transition for students with disabilities. Studies published between 1986 and 2008 are included. The state of the science will be examined and future research directions and recommendations for practice will be articulated.

Although there is a wealth of theoretical literature addressing best practices to support children with disabilities during the transition to kindergarten, there is a relative lack of high-quality, data-based studies. Specifically, 15 empirical studies to date have examined the kindergarten transition for children with disabilities (see Table 3.1). These studies can be divided into the following categories: (1) caregiver perspectives on transition, (2) teacher perspectives on transition, (3) future environments, (4) intervention studies, and (5) comprehensive kindergarten transition preparation interventions.

Caregiver Perspectives on Transition

It is well-recognized that kindergarten transition presents a major challenge to caregivers of children with special needs (e.g., Johnson et al. 1986). Thus, several studies have explicitly investigated caregiver perspectives on transition (i.e., Conn-Powers et al. 1990; Fowler et al. 1988; Hamblin-Wilson and Thurman 1990; Janus et al. 2008; Johnson et al. 1986). As a group, these studies provide a preliminary empirical basis for best practice recommendations to support kindergarten transition for children with disabilities and their families. In general, the literature addressing parent perspectives emphasizes the importance of family–school collaboration, the involvement of *both* sending and receiving programs in high-quality planning, and the use of proactive, individualized practices. In particular, the involvement of families as equal partners in transition planning, in light of the special needs of this population,

Table 3.1 Empirical studies of transition for children with disabilities ($N = 15$)

Study	Category	Results
Beckoff and Bender (1989)	Teacher perspectives	Pre-K teachers considered child social and academic skills more critical for school entry than K teachers
Carta et al. (1990)	Future environments	Major differences between Pre-K and K environments in instructional arrangement and activities
Conn-Powers et al. (1990)	Parent perspectives	Parents and professionals expressed satisfaction with collaborative school transition planning model
Fowler et al. (1988)	Parent perspectives	Parents identified aspects of transition planning they viewed as most important
Hains (1992)	Intervention	Intervention reduced dependence on teacher and increased independent work success
Hamblin-Wilson and Thurman (1990)	Parent perspectives	Parents participated in transition activities and were satisfied with services. Parents received more support from Early Intervention than kindergarten
Hutinger and Johanson (2000)	Intervention	Positive child, family, and staff outcomes with technology system designed to increase participation in transition activities
Janus et al. (2008)	Parent perspectives	Kindergarten parents reported less impact of disability than Pre-K parents and reported lower quality of care
Johnson et al. (1986)	Parent perspectives	Parents reported involvement and satisfaction in transition process
LeAger and Shapiro (1995)	Future environment intervention	Students receiving template matching had school environments more closely aligned to kindergarten
McIntyre et al. (2006)	Teacher perspectives	Students with intellectual disability had poorer adaptation to kindergarten than students without disabilities
Redden et al. (2001)	Comprehensive transition preparation	Children in intervention were less likely to be labeled MR or ED in 3rd grade, but more likely to be labeled with Speech-Language Impairment
Rimm-Kaufman and Pianta (1999)	Teacher perspectives	Teacher-family contact more frequent in preschool than kindergarten
Rule et al. (1990)	Future environment intervention	Students taught survival skills for kindergarten environment. Students maintained and generalized skills
Vaughn et al. (1999)	Teacher perspectives	General Education teachers rated transition practices as desirable but not feasible; reported lack of preparation for students with disabilities

emerges as a priority (Conn-Powers et al. 1990; Fowler et al. 1988; Hamblin-Wilson and Thurman 1990; Johnson et al. 1986). It is also clear from this set of studies that parents regard early intervention and preschool staff as more involved and helpful during transition compared with kindergarten staff (Hamblin-Wilson and Thurman 1990; Johnson et al. 1986). Research conducted in Canada by Janus et al. (2008) corroborates this sentiment (see also Chap. 15). This study assessed the transition experiences of 40 caregivers of children with special needs at school entry and found that parent perceptions of quality of care were significantly higher when children were in preschool compared with kindergarten. Finally, these studies overwhelmingly suggest that caregivers of children with special needs tend to be highly involved in many aspects of transition planning and program selection (Conn-Powers et al. 1990; Fowler et al. 1988; Hamblin-Wilson and Thurman 1990; Johnson et al. 1986).

Teacher Perspectives on Transition

A second group of studies have focused on teacher perceptions of the kindergarten transition for children with disabilities (i.e., Beckoff and Bender 1989; McIntyre et al. 2006; Rimm-Kaufman and Pianta 1999; Vaughn et al. 1999). Taken together, the empirical investigations of teacher perspectives on the kindergarten transition for children with special needs suggest that although teachers perceive children with special needs to have more difficult transitions (McIntyre et al. 2006), kindergarten teacher implementation of transition practices to support these students may not reflect best practices (Vaughn et al. 1999). Evidence suggests that family–school communication decreases drastically in kindergarten (Rimm-Kaufman and Pianta 1999), kindergarten teachers regard transition practices as more desirable than feasible to implement (Vaughn et al. 1999), and that sharp differences exist between preschool and kindergarten teachers' behavioral and academic expectations and use of classroom management strategies (Beckoff and Bender 1989). The disconnect between preschool and kindergarten may place children with disabilities in a precarious position upon transition. Studies assessing caregiver and teacher perceptions of transition illuminate some of the key issues and problems surrounding transition for children with disabilities. That is, both parent and professional stakeholders identify children with disabilities as at particular risk for transition difficulty, yet usual care practices may not be sufficiently intensive or individualized to provide adequate support during the early education to elementary school transition.

Future Environment/Comparison of Preschool and Kindergarten Settings

A third group of studies has directly examined inclusive kindergarten environments to identify child skills and behaviors that are critical for successful functioning (i.e., Carta et al. 1990; LeAger and Shapiro 1995; Rule et al. 1990). These "future environment studies" have relied on direct behavioral observations in the identification of kindergarten survival skills to inform academic, social, and behavioral goals and objectives for preschool children with disabilities (Fowler et al. 1991). The descriptive information that emerges from this group of comparative environment studies has important implications for the preparation of children with disabilities for successful kindergarten transitions. The data gleaned from direct observational studies help to elucidate the difficulties inherent in the transition from special education preschool settings to regular kindergarten classrooms. As demonstrated by three different studies (Carta et al. 1990; LeAger and Shapiro 1995; Rule et al. 1990), preschool and kindergarten environments are markedly different and thus require different child skills. Observational studies consistently indicate that kindergarten students often participate in activities that require skills for working independently, with minimal teacher direction, and participating in sizeable groups. In stark contrast, children in early childhood special education settings spend much of their time in smaller grouping arrangements and receive substantially more teacher prompting, feedback, and support. Because successful functioning in kindergarten requires higher levels of independence and self-regulation, the transition may pose challenges for children with disabilities (McIntyre et al. 2006).

Following directly from these observed differences, the theoretical literature consistently suggests that preparation of children with disabilities for success in kindergarten necessitates the teaching of generic, functional skills to increase independence and appropriate engagement alongside typically developing peers as opposed to teaching specific preacademic or readiness skills (Atwater et al.1994; Wolery 1999). Indeed, kindergarten survival skills, such as the ability to work independently and follow directions, are generally socio-behavioral in nature (LeAger and Shapiro 1995; Rule et al. 1990). As a result, many have suggested that socioemotional and behavioral functioning is just as important, if not *more* critical than academic skills in early educational settings (Atwater et al. 1994; Fowler et al. 1991; McIntyre et al. 2006). The future environment studies for children with disabilities clearly lend empirical support for this sentiment.

Intervention Studies

In several studies, information gathered from future environment observational and survey work has informed interventions to facilitate the kindergarten transition for children with disabilities (Hains 1992; Hutinger and Johanson 2000; LeAger and Shapiro 1995; Rule et al. 1990). The majority of studies in this fourth category focus on teaching children survival skills in order to prepare them to function successfully in the demanding kindergarten classroom. Thus, the general goal of the intervention work is to foster better matching or alignment of preschool and kindergarten environments. Taken together, these intervention studies consistently demonstrate that when preschool and kindergarten environments are aligned, children with disabilities can be successfully taught survival skills to strengthen independence and group participation and facilitate transition to kindergarten (Atwater et al. 1994).

These studies are very valuable in their examination of actual interventions and measurement of child outcomes in kindergarten. They have also utilized relatively rigorous experimental designs and direct behavioral assessment methods, which are well suited to measure child outcomes. It should be noted that the developmental appropriateness of teaching kindergarten survival skills to preschoolers has been questioned by some (e.g., Atwater et al. 1994; LeAger and Shapiro 1995). Despite their methodological strengths, transition intervention studies have tended to use small and idiosyncratic samples of children with disabilities.

Comprehensive Kindergarten Transition Preparation Interventions

A study by Redden et al. (2001) is the only investigation to examine the impact of a comprehensive kindergarten transition preparation intervention on child outcomes in kindergarten. This study, in the fifth category, departs from the special education kindergarten transition intervention literature in several respects. Most notably, the intervention did not grow out of the future environment work and thus, did not focus explicitly on teaching preschool students survival skills or aligning preschool and kindergarten environments. This study also utilized a group design with a significantly larger sample compared to the other intervention studies. Redden et al. (2001) examined elementary special education identification rates in a national sample of Head Start children ($N=7,079$). Approximately half had been provided with systematic transition programming from kindergarten through third grade, while a comparison sample of children had not received such programming. Children were randomly assigned to intervention or control conditions. The multicomponent transition program was intended to enhance and extend Head Start experiences. Therefore, the intervention comprised school transition and curricular modifications, parent involvement activities, health screening and referrals, and family social services, similar to Head Start services. In order to assess the impact of the intervention, child psychoeducational assessments, teacher ratings, and special education services were investigated. Results indicated that the total percentage of Head Start children eligible for special education in the transition intervention group was significantly higher than the comparison group. In addition, fewer children who had received transition programming were identified as having mental retardation (MR) and emotional disturbance (ED) in third grade, while more were identified as having speech-language impairment. Few statistically significant differences were discerned on psychoeducational outcome measures for children in the four major special education categories between intervention and nonintervention groups. The authors suggest that a prevention effect may have occurred such that the intervention was particularly effective for children at risk for MR and ED due to the benefits of family support and preventive referrals and screenings. Redden et al. (2001) also speculate that minor speech-language difficulties may either have been detected earlier for children in the intervention group or that they may have been mistakenly identified in the less socially stigmatizing "triage" category of speech-language impairment.

The study by Redden et al. (2001) provides tentative support for the value of a comprehensive kindergarten transition intervention targeting children at risk for disabilities. However, it is important to note that the study primarily used diagnostic labels and disability categories to represent intervention outcomes. The authors failed to identify evidence suggestive of a positive impact on other academic and sociobehavioral outcomes. Additionally, this study focused on a very specific intervention confined to and particularly appropriate for a Head Start population.

Recommendations for Research

Given that the Redden et al. (2001) study is the sole investigation addressing the impact of comprehensive transition preparation activities on children's kindergarten outcome, this constitutes a major gap in the early childhood special education literature. Instead, most studies focus on parent and teacher perceptions of, concerns about, and satisfaction with transition preparation. There is a pressing need for additional studies to examine the impact of transition preparation conceptualized more broadly, and from the perspectives of multiple stakeholders, on more general child outcomes, including sociobehavioral and academic readiness dimensions. It is also important for studies of transition preparation to utilize samples of children previously identified as eligible for special education services rather than at risk for poor developmental outcomes. Because children eligible for special education may have existing significant risk factors, intervention studies geared at identifying the most effective intervention supports are sorely needed. Such intervention supports may be at the level of the child (e.g., survival skills training, social skills intervention), parent (e.g., parent training, education, and support), preschool (e.g., aligning early education and elementary curricula), kindergarten (e.g., increasing communication and problem-solving across systems), or may involve all important stakeholders in important transition planning. Research supporting multicomponent interventions aligned with the Ecological and Dynamic Model of Transition (Rimm-Kaufman and Pianta 2000) will be an important advance in the research literature.

Given that the overwhelming majority of the transition to kindergarten empirical literature is descriptive in nature, we recommend that at least five areas of intervention research be addressed. First, we recommend that the feasibility of implementing high quality, individualized, and specific transition preparation practices be examined. There is a need to examine specific transition practices that involve various stakeholders. For example, transition practices implemented by family members, preschool personnel, elementary school staff, and parent–school liaisons can be examined to determine the most feasible and efficacious means of providing children with disabilities and their families support during kindergarten transition.

Second, it is imperative that more research be conducted that examines child outcomes as a function of transition preparation and practices. The kindergarten transition intervention literature for students with disabilities is sparse, with only one large-scale comprehensive study conducted investigating transition programming on child outcomes (Redden et al. 2001). In the general education literature only two studies have investigated child outcomes linked to transition preparation and activities for students attending schools in the United States (LoCasale-Crouch et al. 2008; Schulting et al. 2005). Schulting et al. (2005) examined the effects of kindergarten teachers' use of transition practices on child academic outcomes, while LoCasale-Crouch et al. examined the effects of preschool teachers' use of transition preparation on child sociobehavioral outcomes. Results of both studies suggested that kindergarten transition practices were related to better child outcomes. In both studies, researchers found the greatest effect for children from lower socioeconomic status backgrounds. Furthermore, Schulting et al. found that parent-initiated school involvement was positively correlated with more transition practices and suggested that parent involvement had a mediating effect on students' academic outcomes. Schulting et al. argued that transition practices stimulated parent involvement which, in turn, resulted in higher child academic achievement. The findings of LoCasale-Crouch et al. (2008) and Schulting et al. (2005) may have relevance to students with disabilities; however, much more research is necessary to determine which practices are predictive of positive outcomes for students with disabilities.

Third, we recommend that studies include both direct observation and indirect (rating scales, interviews, checklists) data collection procedures that involve multiple informants across settings. Fourth, we recommend including longitudinal procedures investigating the effects of randomized intervention trials to investigate child outcomes over time. Such analysis will provide information on sustainability and generalization of intervention effects. Finally, we recommend that cost-effectiveness studies be included in intervention studies to determine cost savings of preventive or early intervention efforts designed to reduce early school academic and sociobehavioral difficulties for students with disabilities.

Recommendations for Practice

At least three recommendations for practice emerge from this literature review, including teacher training, family involvement, and the need for early childhood partnerships. Each area is described briefly below.

Research suggests that early childhood special education staff are valuable resources to families as children with disabilities transition to kindergarten (Hamblin-Wilson and Thurman 1990); however, the involvement of receiving elementary schools may be minimal (Janus et al. 2008). This may be due, in part, to fewer resources and the perception that transition practices are unrealistic to implement (Vaughn et al. 1999). Results of a large-scale study of kindergarten teachers suggest that very few kindergarten teachers receive specialized kindergarten transition programming at either the preservice or the inservice level (Early et al. 1999). Thus, training to increase preschool and kindergarten teachers' knowledge of transition programming is critical. In a study of general education kindergarten teachers, Early et al. (2001) found that teachers who received training in transition practices were more likely to utilize such practices. Thus, we recommend that preservice and inservice teacher training include transition preparation practices. Practices such as school and home visits, communication with parents and preschool staff, transition planning meetings, and developing specific child interventions may be especially useful.

Second, we recommend early and continued family involvement in both early childhood education and elementary school settings. The results of Schulting et al. (2005) suggest that parental involvement may be important for both transition practices and children's school achievement. Findings from the small number of studies investigating parent perceptions of their involvement in kindergarten transition preparation activities suggest overall satisfaction with their efforts (e.g., Conn-Powers et al. 1990; Hamblin-Wilson and Thurman 1990). Schools can reach out to families by developing two-way communication between home and school; can reach out to families prior to the first day of school; and can utilize a range of activities to encourage parent and family participation in transition programming (Pianta and Kraft-Sayre 2003).

A final recommendation involves developing early childhood partnerships to enhance children's and families' transition experiences. Kraft-Sayre and Pianta (2000) describe "school and program transition teams" which are multidisciplinary units headed by a transition coordinator. The transition coordinator could serve to contact and link community and school personnel (e.g., parents, community agency representatives, elementary school principals) with staff at the individual school building level (e.g., kindergarten teacher). Involving families, community leaders, and early childhood and elementary educators ensures the input of all important stakeholders. These parent-professional partnerships may be especially important for students who are at risk for school difficulties. Children with disabilities may be experiencing a number of cognitive, social, behavioral, and developmental risk factors making their transition to school especially complex (McIntyre et al. 2006). Such transition teams may lay the foundation for continued support and partnership through kindergarten and beyond.

References

Atwater, J., Orth-Lopes, L., Elliott, M., Carta, J., & Schwartz, I. (1994). Completing the circle: Planning and implementing transitions to other programs. In M. Wolery & J. Wilbers (Eds.), *Including children with special needs in early childhood programs* (pp. 167–188). Washington, DC: National Association for the Education of Young Children.

Beckoff, A., & Bender, W. (1989). Programming for mainstream kindergarten success in preschool: Teachers' perceptions of necessary prerequisite skills. *Journal of Early Intervention, 13*(3), 269–280.

Carta, J., Atwater, J., Schwartz, I., & Miller, P. (1990). Applications of ecobehavioral analysis to the study of transitions across early education settings. *Education and Treatment of Children, 13*(4), 298–315.

Conn-Powers, M., Ross-Allen, J., & Holburn, S. (1990). Transition of young children into the elementary education mainstream. *Topics in Early Childhood Special Education, 9*(4), 91–105.

Early, D. M., Pianta, R. C., & Cox, M. J. (1999). Kindergarten teachers and classrooms: A transition context. *Early Education and Development, 10,* 25–46.

Early, D. M., Pianta, R. C., Taylor, L. C., & Cox, M. J. (2001). Transition practices: Findings from a national survey of kindergarten teachers. *Early Childhood Education Journal, 28,* 199–206.

Eckert, T. L., McIntyre, L. L., DiGennaro, F. D., Arbolino, L., Begeny, J., & Perry, L. J. (2008). Researching the transition to kindergarten for typically developing children: A literature review of current processes, practices, and programs. In D. H. Molina (Ed.), *School psychology: 21st century issues and challenges* (pp. 235–252). Hauppauge, NY: Nova Science Publishers.

Fowler, S., Chandler, L., Johnson, T., & Stella, E. (1988). Individualizing family involvement in school transitions: Gathering information and choosing the next program. *Journal of the Division for Early Childhood, 12*(3), 208–216.

Fowler, S., Schwartz, I., & Atwater, J. (1991). Perspectives on the transition from preschool to kindergarten for children with disabilities and their families. *Exceptional Children, 58*(2), 136–145.

Hains, A. (1992). Strategies for preparing preschool children with special needs for the kindergarten mainstream. *Journal of Early Intervention, 16*(4), 320–333.

Hamblin-Wilson, C., & Thurman, K. (1990). The transition from early intervention to kindergarten: Parental satisfaction and involvement. *Journal of Early Intervention, 14*(1), 55–61.

Hutinger, P., & Johanson, J. (2000). Implementing and maintaining an effective early childhood comprehensive technology system. *Topics in Early Childhood Special Education, 20*(3), 159–173.

Janus, M., Kopechanski, L., Cameron, R., & Hughes, D. (2008). In transition: Experiences of parents of children with special needs at school entry. *Early Childhood Education Journal, 35,* 479–485.

Johnson, T., Chandler, L., Kerns, G., & Fowler, S. (1986). What are parents saying about family involvement in school transitions? A retrospective transition interview. *Journal of the Division for Early Childhood, 11*(1), 10–17.

Kraft-Sayre, M. E., & Pianta, R. C. (2000). *Enhancing the transition to kindergarten: Linking children, families, and schools.* Charlottesville, VA: University of Virginia, National Center for Early Development & Learning.

LeAger, C., & Shapiro, E. (1995). Template matching as a strategy for assessment of and intervention for preschool students with disabilities. *Topics in Early Childhood Special Education, 15*(2), 187–219.

LoCasale-Crouch, J., Mashburn, A., Downer, J., & Pianta, R. (2008). Pre-kindergarten teachers' use of transition practices and children's adjustment in kindergarten. *Early Childhood Research Quarterly, 23,* 124–139.

McIntyre, L. L., Blacher, J., & Baker, B. L. (2006). The transition to school: Adaptation in young children with and without intellectual disability. *Journal of Intellectual Disability Research, 50*(5), 349–361.

McIntyre, L. L., Eckert, T. L., Fiese, B. H., DiGennaro, F. D., & Wildenger, L. K. (2007). The transition to kindergarten: Family experiences and involvement. *Early Childhood Education Journal, 35,* 83–88.

Perry, K. E., & Weinstein, R. S. (1998). The social context of early schooling and children's school adjustment. *Educational Psychologist, 33*(4), 177–194.

Pianta, R., & Kraft-Sayre, M. (2003). *Successful kindergarten transition.* Baltimore: Paul H. Brookes.

Quintero, N., & McIntyre, L. L. (2010). Kindergarten transition for students with developmental disabilities and autism: Family concerns and involvement. Manuscript submitted for publication.

Redden, S., Forness, S., Ramey, S., Ramey, C., Brezausek, C., & Kavale, K. (2001). Children at risk: Effects of a four-year Head Start transition program on special education identification. *Journal of Child and Family Studies, 10*(2), 255–270.

Rimm-Kaufman, S., & Pianta, R. (1999). Patterns of family–school contact in preschool and kindergarten. *The School Psychology Review, 28*(3), 426–438.

Rimm-Kaufman, S., & Pianta, R. (2000). An ecological perspective on the transition to kindergarten: A theoretical framework to guide empirical research. *Journal of Applied Developmental Psychology, 21*(5), 491–511.

Rimm-Kaufman, S., Pianta, R., & Cox, M. (2000). Teachers' judgments of problems in the transition to kindergarten. *Early Childhood Research Quarterly, 15*(2), 147–166.

Rule, S., Fiechtl, B., & Innocenti, M. (1990). Preparation for transition to mainstreamed post-pre-school environments: Development of a survival skills curriculum. *Topics in Early Childhood Special Education, 9*(4), 78–90.

Schulting, A., Malone, P., & Dodge, K. (2005). The effect of school-based kindergarten transition policies and practices on child academic outcomes. *Developmental Psychology, 41*(6), 860–871.

Vaughn, S., Reiss, M., Rothlein, L., & Hughes, M. (1999). Kindergarten teachers' perceptions of instructing students with disabilities. *Remedial and Special Education, 20*(3), 184–191.

Wolery, M. (1999). Children with disabilities in early elementary school. In R. C. Pianta & M. J. Cox (Eds.), *The transition to kindergarten* (pp. 217–251). Baltimore, MD: Paul H. Brookes.

Chapter 4
Supporting and Sustaining the Transition to Formal Schooling for Children on the Autism Spectrum

Joann M. Migyanka

Defining Autism

> In May, the spring before Charles (not his real name) was to be part of my kindergarten classroom, I attended the IEP (Individualized Education Program) meeting. I quickly became aware of the fact that I knew little about autism. I must admit that what I was hearing about possible behaviors and difficulties that may arise made me feel very uneasy. As I expressed my concerns, I was told that Charles would have a full-time aide and I was given an array of handouts to read. Surely, this literature would enlighten me with the information on typical behaviors of children with autism and strategies to use with a child.
> There, I was ready…I thought…until the first day of school. It would soon become very clear to me that those handouts were not quite enough. Reading general statements regarding the needs of children with autism did not necessarily cover the realm of all children and general strategies were not enough to aid all children. (Tracy Carpenter 1998, personal communication)

Tracy's frustration is common among teachers trying to understand the broad range of abilities and disabilities of children on the autism spectrum. When defining autism it is important to understand the general characteristics of this spectrum disorder; however, it is also essential for teachers to understand that inter- and intra-individual differences exist for children with autism.

Autism spectrum disorders are a group of developmental disabilities, typically diagnosed during the first three years of life, which can cause significant social, communication, and behavioral challenges (Centers for Disease Control and Prevention 2009). Autism affects the normal development of the brain in the areas of social interaction, communication skills, and cognitive function. Individuals with autism typically have difficulties in verbal and non-verbal communication, social interactions, and leisure or play activities (National Autism Association n.d.). Children with autism also have trouble with the integration of the body's sensory system. The cause of autism remains unknown. Research suggests that there may be a

J. M. Migyanka (✉)
Department of Special Education & Clinical Services, Indiana University of Pennsylvania,
Davis Hall Room 213, Indiana, PA 15705, USA
e-mail: migyanka@iup.edu

D. M. Laverick, M. R. Jalongo (eds.), *Transitions to Early Care and Education,*
Educating the Young Child 4, DOI 10.1007/978-94-007-0573-9_4,
© Springer Science+Business Media B.V. 2011

link to genetics, environmental insults, or a combination of both (Muhle et al. 2004; London and Etzel 2000).

Autism spectrum disorders fall under the umbrella of Pervasive Developmental Disorders (PDDs). Children can carry one of the diagnostic labels associated with the spectrum, which include autism, Asperger syndrome, Rett syndrome, childhood disintegrative disorder, fragile X syndrome, and pervasive developmental disorder—not otherwise specified (PDD-NOS). "Spectrum" indicates that every person with autism is unique. Although having similar characteristics, each child has a different profile of strengths and challenges. "No two individuals manifest the same characteristics in the same degree of severity" (Grandin 2008, p. xix). However, diagnostic labels are beneficial for providing individuals with disabilities, families, and professionals a common language, framework, and mechanism for connecting with resources, information, funding, and support services (Kluth 2003).

Although labels may be useful, the boundaries among the differential diagnoses of the spectrum disorders are not static (Grandin 2008). Therefore, the diagnostic label should never be used to define the child or to dictate the educational placement of the child. Labels are often limiting and may result in lowering reasonable expectations of the child's capacity to learn and color attitudes and perceptions. Positive attitudes, perceptions, and expectations are critical for the successful transition and inclusion of children with autism into formal schooling.

The Role of the Teacher

The attitudes and perceptions of teachers are consistently identified as important factors in the inclusion of children with disabilities (Avramidis et al. 2000; Brady and Woolfson 2008; Ernst and Rogers 2009; Hammond and Ingalls 2003; McGregor and Campbell 2001; Sze 2009). Too often teachers and administrators focus on the disabilities of the child and respond reactively when a particular deficit interferes with the social or academic functioning of the child. A paradigm shift from deficit-reactive to ability-proactive can lead to academic and social success.

Kluth (2003) sees the role of the teacher as an educational leader and stresses how central attitudes, beliefs, and the actions of teachers are to the success of students in an inclusive environment. The teacher's perspective on his or her role in supporting the child with autism has a profound effect on the success of that child. Kluth (2003) suggests that educators make an attitudinal shift from seeing *differences* that pose difficulties as something that needs fixed or changed to fit the classroom environment to seeing *differences* as something to be desired and valued. Differences can serve as valuable assets on which to capitalize when planning for instruction and socialization. Fully recognizing the strengths, interests, and challenges of the individual requires the teacher to develop a supportive and authentic relationship with the child. Students know when and if the teacher believes they can learn and achieve (Kluth 2003). Even with the most positive, proactive attitudes and expectations, teachers can experience disappointment and frustration without thoughtful and appropriate planning for transition and sustained support.

Preparing for the Transition into Formal Schooling

Transitions for children with special needs occur when the individual moves from preschool to formal schooling, from grade to grade, from primary/elementary school to middle school to high school, and when the child ages out of formal schooling. "Children with autism are particularly vulnerable in the transition process," (Forest et al. 2004, p. 103). The communication, social, and adaptive behavior deficits associated with autism can lead to a difficult transition into a new setting. Children with autism have difficulty generalizing skills acquired in one setting to another and often require specific and individualized strategies in the educational environment (Forest et al. 2004). Careful planning to minimize the effects of transition for these children is essential. The goal of transition planning is to make a potentially stressful and difficult situation as seamless and successful as possible.

The Transition Plan

The transition plan should focus on continuity of services and implementation of the necessary supports to ensure a successful transition for the child. Successful planning requires a concerted effort among parents, agencies, and professionals working with the child and family, as well as personnel from the receiving school. This effort must begin well in advance, at least six months prior to the child starting into formal schooling, and should include site visits. The child and his family should be given the opportunity to visit the classroom and meet the teacher at least once but preferably on multiple occasions. During site visits, the child and family should be introduced to essential personnel with whom the child may have contact (i.e., school nurse, secretaries, principal, etc.) and do a walk-through of the school's important areas where the child will be expected to go. In addition to site visits, it is important to share detailed information about the child's history, strengths, challenges, specific needs, readiness skills, and assessment information (Forest et al. 2004). Critical components of the transition plan include a timeline, description of the transition activities, definition of the roles and responsibilities of each team member, professional development for school personnel, and a specific plan to review, revise, and ensure accountability for success throughout the entire school year.

Professional Development

In the opening scenario, Tracy indicated that in the five months prior to the start of kindergarten she participated in an Individualized Education Program (IEP) meeting for the child with autism transitioning into her classroom. Tracy spent the next five months preparing for this student by reading the supplied literature, learning about communication and behavior difficulties often exhibited by children with autism, planning for the classroom paraprofessional, and designing the structure and routine for the classroom that was suggested. Despite these efforts, the school year proved difficult for her and the children in the class. Tracy found that the paraprofessional did not have any training with children with autism or with children having any type of disability. The autistic support consultant and occupational therapist visited once a week for thirty minutes.

> Although helpful, these visits were not enough. I found what was needed was the intervention of one strategy after another.... Charles (not his real name) needed continuous intervention...something was wrong.... I knew it, the parents knew it, outside services knew it, administration knew it, others in my classroom knew it, and ultimately, Charles knew it. (Tracy Carpenter 1998, Kindergarten Teacher, personal communication)

Ongoing Support

Tracy's experience reinforces the need for ongoing, targeted support and intervention. Simply knowing the plethora of strategies is not enough. Teachers need to understand *how* to implement the strategies and, just as important, *when* to choose and apply a specific strategy. Even if the teacher has taught another child with autism, the unique and splintered skills of children with autism require that teachers and school personnel receive professional development that is sustained, specific, and applicable to a particular individual and for targeted situations. Support personnel must be highly knowledgeable and well trained in educating students with an autism spectrum disorder. In addition, involving families in providing professional development and support is important. Families can provide the teacher with more rich and detailed information about their child than can be obtained through reading any report or professional consultation (Kluth 2003).

Families as Partners

The pervasive nature of autism has a powerful effect on the dynamics of family life. Family life is often stressful as parents and siblings cope with the relentless behavior and sleepless nights of some children with autism. The child's difficulty functioning in many social situations often leaves the family socially isolated and searching for support and answers. In many cases, the intensity of having a child with autism spurs parents to research the disorder, gain expertise in medical and educational treatments, and become fierce advocates for their child. On the other hand, some parents may become so overwhelmed that they distance themselves.

Reciprocal Expertise

Professionals frequently view themselves and other professionals as the experts and parents as consumers of that expertise. However, parents often understand the intent of the unique or unusual behavior exhibited by their child that school professionals fail to recognize or understand. Families can provide valuable information in understanding the strengths, challenges, and strategies needed in planning for instruction and intervention for their child. Developing a collaborative partnership with the family requires establishing a reciprocal relationship and gaining a true appreciation for the diversity of families (Kluth 2003).

Family Diversity

Connecting with students begins with learning about the shared life with family members (Kluth 2003). It is important to understand the structure of the family including siblings and extended family who may play an important supportive role. Gargiulo (2009) contends that families operate as an interactive and interdependent unit. What happens to one member affects the others. Professionals should work to establish support structures and resources for families. Awareness and sensitivity to the needs of the family as a whole is a prerequisite to establishing a successful cooperative relationship (Gargiulo 2009).

Communication is Critical

Central to the education for a child with autism is constant, open, and productive communication with families. Kluth (2003) states several reasons for this critical need for communication. First, some students with autism cannot communicate reliably; thus, the home–school communication is dependent on the teacher–family interaction. Secondly, the unique needs of the child with autism may require frequent sharing of information about the child's physical well-being. Finally, families can provide useful information about the child's specific characteristics and disability.

Opportunities for sharing information and giving or receiving support must be created and clearly articulated. Some ways to structure and facilitate communication is through a weekly or daily notebook entry, daily e-mail, an established time to conference, and/or weekly or daily telephone calls (Kluth 2003). However, the method of communication should be mutually agreed upon and meet the needs of all members of the partnership.

Breakdown in communication is often the result of parents feeling left out of the loop (Kluth 2003). Academic and social successes or difficulties should be communicated in a timely manner. All reports of successes or difficulties should have

the support of specific examples to avoid miscommunication or making errone-
ous judgments. In addition, when problems arise, families should be involved in
solution building to ensure consistency between home and school (Kluth 2003).
Establishing a collaborative and caring working relationship with families increases
the likelihood that the child will succeed. Extending the spirit of collaboration and
caring into the classroom environment is essential.

Creating a Safe and Nurturing Learning Environment

Unfamiliar or novel situations and environments are often a source of anxiety for
children with autism. Noise, light, movement, verbal commands, and tactile stimulation can prove overwhelming. Scheuermann and Webber (2002) describe the primary classroom as often highly stimulating in décor, materials, and dialogue. This
type of environment does not always facilitate learning for the child with autism.
Children with autism rely on spatial orientation and rote memory to make sense of
their world; therefore, routine and sameness create a safe and comforting environment (Scheuermann and Webber 2002). Reliance on routine and sameness requires
that the classroom environment and teaching strategies be calming, highly structured, and visually supportive.

The Sensory System

According to Heflin and Alaimo (2007), information received from different sensory systems is processed, organized, and combined to produce an adaptive motor response. In some cases, sensory information may lead to an adaptive response that is
protective in nature if the central nervous system perceives the stimuli to be threat-
ening. For example, lighting, sound, smell, and temperature that are unobtrusive
for most individuals can be distracting and overwhelming for the child with autism.
Grandin (2008) contends that children who are overwhelmed by their senses have
little time to relax enough to attend to learning opportunities. An impaired sensory
system also accounts for many of the perceptual difficulties the child experiences.
Grandin (2008) found that the faulty processing of incoming information falls into
three basic categories: (1) sensory oversensitivity; (2) perceptual problems; and (3)
difficulties with organizing information. All three of these can have a profound effect on the child's ability to function within the classroom environment.

Sensory Oversensitivity

The response to sensory input varies from child to child and ranges from mild anxiety to severe tantrums. Individual children may experience sensitivity to fluorescent

lighting, while others may find loud noises painful. Smells that are barely noticeable to many can be overpowering to the child with autism. The sight, taste, or texture of certain foods can induce a sense of repulsion. Light touch or tactile stimulation may result in the child pulling away (Heflin and Alaimo 2007). The child's inability to attend and concentrate during classroom activities and learning opportunities may be the result of an impaired sensory system. Therefore, careful examination of the learning environment should be considered to determine if sensory oversensitivity is the cause of maladaptive behavior.

Perceptual Difficulties

Scheuermann and Webber (2002) contend that the perceptual and cognitive brain function of children with autism often results in specific differences in their thinking ability and the way they receive external input. Many children with an autism spectrum disorder have auditory processing difficulties. Because much of traditional instruction, directions, and activities rely on verbal input and dialogue, the child with autism may be at a distinct disadvantage. These children may hear and be distracted by conflicting background noise or experience the fading in and out of voices leading to missed information (Grandin 2008). This child will learn best by presenting information in a visually and highly structured manner.

In addition to difficulties with auditory perception, some children may experience visual perception difficulties or a combination of both auditory and visual perceptual deficits. A visual perceptual disparity may result in the brain receiving an accurate picture but an inability to make sense of the picture because of cognitive or perceptual interference. Therefore, the child may not learn what type of visual information to attend to and may lose the ability to attend selectively to relevant visual details necessary for learning (Kurtz 2006). Children with autism who have visual perceptual problems often see things in parts. It is like looking through a kaleidoscope; images may appear flat and broken into pieces. Others may lack peripheral vision and perceive an almost tunnel-like vision (Grandin 2008). Children with visual perception deficits often fail to see things as a whole but rather focus or become fixated on a minor detail. Think about the common practice of using a picture book to do a "picture walk" strategy to enhance reading comprehension. Where most children will attend to the picture as a whole to make sense of the story, the child with autism may attend to a minor detail in the picture and misperceive the main idea. For children who have global perceptual deficits, it is important to use concurrent, multiple modalities for instruction such as manipulatives, pictures, symbols, and books on tape.

Organizing Information

A very early learning skill for young children is the ability to categorize information. The ability to form categories is the foundation for later concept formation

(Grandin 2008). Forming categories often requires the ability to multi-task or recognize the variable aspects of the item. The brains of children with autism may have not developed certain circuits or connections; therefore, impairment in the ability to quickly form and expand categories may occur (Grandin 2008). This is evident in the literal interpretation of language and the difficulty with idioms, sarcasm, inferences, and perspective taking. Because concept formation may be difficult, it is very important to help children with autism organize information and expand categories. An example of this might be the concept of "cup." If *cup* is taught as a cup with a handle used for drinking, the child may not make the connection that the object holding pencils on the teacher's desk is also a cup. This inability to expand categories may interfere with the child's comprehension of written or spoken words and the acquisition of complex or abstract thinking skills. Information or concepts should be presented using as many exemplars as possible to aid in the ability to generalize information learned and build upon that foundation to increase the breadth and depth of concept understanding as well as higher level thinking skills.

Organizing the Learning Space

Many modern classrooms have moved from passive learning environments, where students sit in seats aligned in rows and columns, to configurations that are more conducive to active, engaged, and cooperative learning. While this may have advantages for all children, even those with autism, teachers may need to be more flexible in creating the learning spaces (Kluth 2003). Children with autism often need a personalized, structured work area removed from noise and chaos and an area to calm themselves when feeling overwhelmed by sensory input. Kluth (2003) recommends setting aside a space for a desk or small table for quiet study or work on a project to meet their needs. Careful thought to matching the activity and learning space will help the child with autism experience greater success. Creating a well-organized, calming learning environment allows children with autism the ability to maximize their attention and concentration for learning. A caring and nurturing learning environment is conducive to increasing cognitive and social–emotional development and fostering a sense of belonging for all children. However, children with autism may need additional intervention in building friendships, relationships, and promoting social acceptance.

Friendships, Relationships, and a Sense of Belonging

Fostering socialization skills is considered an important part of best practices for children with severe disabilities (Scheuermann and Webber 2002). This is especially true for children with autism. The social skill deficits associated with autism make it very difficult for some children with autism to make and keep friends. The restricted and narrow repertoire of interests and the inability to understand the perspective of others significantly impairs sustained socialization. When interacting with others, the child with autism will consistently want the interaction to center around his or her narrow topic of interest and often fails to recognize that others do not share the same level of interest. Even if the interaction veers from that topic, the child with autism will often attempt to steer the interaction back to his or her interest. This can lead to others losing the motivation to interact with the child and moving on to other friends.

Another impediment to successful social interaction is the deficits in reading social cues. For example, non-disabled peers can typically survey a room and quickly determine what he or she should do based on what they observe. Children with autism are often unaware of the social context of what is occurring in the room. This can result in misperception and inappropriate behavior, again stressing the need for intervention in the acquisition of appropriate social skills. Intervention is best implemented and more effective when conducted in socially rich and naturally occurring environments (Scheuermann and Webber 2002). Scheuermann and Webber (2002) recommend the focus of intervention should include: teaching activities preferred by non-disabled peers; teaching pivotal behaviors that serve a similar purpose in a variety of areas of functioning; reducing inappropriate behavior; and emphasizing generalization. Intervention approaches may require direct instruction of social skills. Social skills curricula, instructional scripts, social stories, role-play, and video modeling can aid in social skill development (Kluth 2003; Scheuermann and Webber 2002). Finally, building the communication skills of the child with autism may add to the child's social competence.

Building Communication Competencies

The ability to express wants and needs and to understand others is powerful, liberating, and essential for independence. The capacity to communicate in a meaningful way contributes to cognitive growth. All children on the autism spectrum have trouble with expressive and receptive language to varying degrees. The inability to process auditory stimuli also plays a part in receptive language problems (Scheuermann and Webber 2002). Some children with auditory processing deficits have problems attending to and deriving meaning from the spoken word, especially when there is impairment in the ability to attend to contextual clues. Children with autism may overemphasize the syntactic structure of language rather than the semantic content. The child gains more meaning from the order of the words than from the meaning of the word itself (Scheuermann and Webber 2002). For example, the child may understand that "time to go" means to stop what they are doing and go, but fail to recognize "it's time" as meaning the same thing. In addition, children with autism may respond to and understand directive statements far better than asking a question.

The expressive language skills of children with autism are variable. Some children are verbal, hyper-verbal, or echolalic while others are non-verbal. Higher functioning individuals may develop a large vocabulary because they can memorize what words mean but fail to use the words properly or to organize their speech (Scheuermann and Webber 2002). The use of referents in speech (verb tenses and articles) is often impaired because they change depending on the point of view (Scheuermann and Webber 2002). Another common characteristic of children with autism is the misuse of the personal pronouns "I" and "you." "I" is often replaced with "you" as it is heard from another. For example, "you want to go home" means "I want to go home." Echolalia is the inappropriate repetition of words, phrases or sentences of others, videos, or books. It is important to determine if the echolalic speech carries the intent to communicate. Temple Grandin (2008) believes that echolalia is related to the child's inability to expand categories. The limited repertoire and understanding of the words and labels makes it difficult for him or her to retrieve and use words to convey meaning more appropriately.

It is important for teachers to recognize the diversity in communication skills and work to help children acquire new skills. Kluth (2003) contends that educators must constantly seek ways to connect and communicate with their students. This includes a deliberate effort to provide rich and varied opportunities for the child to communicate throughout the day in varied contexts and, if necessary, with the use of pictures, symbols, sign language, or communication devices. Communication is the lynchpin for all academic and behavioral learning. Helping students to improve their communication skills may alleviate many of the inappropriate behaviors often linked to language, communication, and social deficits.

Defining How We Think About Behavior

Behavior is contextual and serves a function. It does not occur in isolation but rather manifests from interrelated influences. Children with autism characteristically display challenging behaviors commonly referred to as behavioral excesses (Scheuermann and Webber 2002). The range of behaviors includes noncompliance by ignoring directions to very disruptive behaviors such as screaming, crying, biting, pinching, and hair pulling. Aggressive behaviors may be self-directed or other directed. It is important to take a proactive approach to reducing challenging behavior. The first step is to determine the function of the behavior by conducting a Functional Behavior Analysis (FBA). Questions such as "Why is the child exhibiting such a behavior?" and "What purpose is the behavior serving for that child in this particular context?" should be considered. By addressing function, new and more appropriate skills and replacement behaviors can be taught to serve the same purpose and satisfy the child's need. When the child is in crisis, it is important for the teacher to remain calm, speak quietly and gently, avoid restraint of the child, and allow the child time to calm. Yelling, raised voices, or physical restraint of the child usually leads to increased anxiety, escalated behaviors, and the need for a longer recovery time. Teachers can use rewards and reinforcement but should avoid the use of punishment. Adaptability and flexibility is essential in meeting the child's need and reducing challenging behaviors.

Summary

Children with autism are unique, diverse, and fascinating. They can enrich the dynamics of the classroom while making significant developmental gains. Teachers play an important role in the success of the child's physical, cognitive, and social development. A positive, proactive attitude and the belief that the child with autism can learn and meet expectations are essential but not enough. Children with autism, their families, and school personnel need preparation and support for successful transition into formal schooling. For young children with autism, the transition to formal schooling can be a source of anxiety. Focused transition planning and personnel professional development is central to address the challenges that children with autism, their families, and schools may encounter. Particular attention to planning for and sustaining a safe and nurturing learning environment is essential. Families play an important role in developing the plan and sustaining the necessary support. Families share vital information in understanding the child's strengths, interests, and challenges; therefore, a collaborative relationship is crucial. Curricular considerations should include enhancing the child's ability to communicate, build relationships, and reduce inappropriate behavior, all of which directly influence the child's cognitive growth. With careful planning, concerted effort, and a proactive, positive attitude, the transition to formal schooling can ensure continuity of services and increase the likelihood of success for the child with autism.

References

Avramidis, E., Bayliss, P., & Burden, R. (2000). A survey into mainstream teachers' attitudes towards the inclusion of children with special educational needs in the ordinary school in one local education authority. *Educational Psychology, 20*(2), 191–211.

Brady, K., & Woolfson, L. (2008). What teacher factors influence their attributions for children's difficulties in learning. *British Journal of Educational Psychology, 78,* 527–544.

Centers for Disease Control and Prevention (2009). Autism Spectrum Disorders (ASD). http://www.cdc.gov/ncbddd/autism/facts.html. Accessed Feb 2010.

Ernst, C., & Rogers, M. R. (2009). Development of the inclusion attitude scale for high school teachers. *Journal of Applied School Psychology, 25,* 305–322.

Forest, E. J., Horner, R. H., Lewis-Palmer, T., & Todd, A. W. (2004). Transitions for young children with autism from preschool to kindergarten. *Journal of Positive Behavior Interventions, 6*(2), 103–112.

Gargiulo, R. M. (2009). *Special education in contemporary society: An introduction to exceptionality*. Thousand Oaks: Sage.

Grandin, T. (2008). *The way I see it*. Arlington, TX: Future Horizons.

Hammond, H., & Ingalls, L. (2003). Teachers' attitudes toward inclusion: Survey results from elementary school teachers in three rural school districts. *Rural Special Education Quarterly, 22*(2), 24–30.

Heflin, L. J., & Alaimo, D. F. (2007). *Students with autism spectrum disorders.* Upper Saddle River, NJ: Prentice Hall.

Kluth, P. (2003). *You're going to love this kid!.* Baltimore, MD: Paul H. Brookes.

Kurtz, L. (2006). *Visual perception problems in children with AD/HD, autism, and other learning disabilities.* London: Jessica Kingsley Publishers.

London, E., & Etzel, R. A. (2000). The environment as an etiologic factor in autism: A new direction for research. *Environmental Health Perspectives, 108*(3), 401–404.

McGregor, E., & Campbell, E. (2001). The attitudes of teachers in Scotland to the integration of children with autism into mainstream. *The International Journal of Research and Practice, 5*(2), 189–209.

Muhle, R., Trentacoste, S. V., & Rapin, I. (2004). The genetics of autism. *Pediatrics, 113*(5), e472–e486.

National Autism Association (n.d.). All about autism: Definition. http://www.nationalautismassociation.org/definitions.php. Accessed Dec 2009.

Scheuermann, B., & Webber, J. (2002). *Autism: Teaching does make a difference.* Toronto: Wadsworth Thomson Learning.

Sze, S. (2009). A literature review: Pre-service teachers' attitudes toward students with disabilities. *Education, 130*(1), 53–56.

Chapter 5
Early Literacy

Connections and Disconnections Between Oral Language and Literacy

Susan Hill

Early language development (including the ability to communicate effectively with others and emergent literacy) has been identified as important for children's transitions between home, early care and education, and school (Kagan et al. 1995). In Australia, children's transition between home, early care and education, and formal schooling involves a complex set of interactions between individual children, their families, schools, and communities (Dockett and Perry 2009). Hay and Fielding-Barnsley (2009) write that children's oral language needs to be enhanced as a protective factor because oral language competencies underpin children's transitions to literacy.

This chapter explores the connections and disconnections between oral language and later literacy development. First, the chapter describes key studies into importance of aspects of oral language as a predictor of later literacy development in the first years of school and for later development. Next, four different Australian studies exploring language and literacy at home, in early education, and later school are described. These studies employ a range of sociocultural theoretical frameworks to explore emergent literacy (Crawford 1995). Finally, suggestions for innovative, play-based programs are suggested to enhance the continuities between oral language, literacy, as well as the diverse places and spaces in homes, early education and care, and the first year of school.

Oral Language as a Predictor of Early Literacy

Internationally, the development of children's oral language has long been regarded as the foundation for beginning reading as children draw on the meaning, syntax, and the phonology of spoken language as a bridge to emergent literacy (Saracho and Spodek 2007; NICHD (Early Child Care Research Network) 2005; Poe et al.

S. Hill (✉)
University of South Australia, Adelaide, SA 5001, Australia
e-mail: susan.hill@unisa.edu.au

D. M. Laverick, M. R. Jalongo (eds.), *Transitions to Early Care and Education,*
Educating the Young Child 4, DOI 10.1007/978-94-007-0573-9_5,
© Springer Science+Business Media B.V. 2011

2004; Menyuk and Chesnick 1997). Oral language and print knowledge are viewed as the two pillars of learning to read (Mol et al. 2009). When transitioning to school, children's language levels, in-class social behaviours, and initial reading development have been found to be closely interrelated (Hay and Fielding-Barnsley 2009).

Young children need to have control over several aspects of oral language prior to starting the beginning to read process—phonology, vocabulary, syntax, discourse, and pragmatics (Snow et al. 1998). In a review of research, the National Early Literacy Panel (2008) in the United States concluded that some aspects of oral language have substantial correlations with decoding and reading comprehension. There are several characteristics of oral language: sounds (phonology), sentence structure (syntax), word meanings (semantics), and word parts (morphology) (Richgels 2004). The quest for finding which aspects of oral language predict literacy development has created a large body of research.

Phonological awareness has been strongly linked to children's ability to learn to read and spell. Measures of preschoolers' level of phonemic awareness strongly predicts their future success in learning to read and "may be the most important core and casual factor separating normal and disabled readers" (Adams 1990, pp. 304–305). Children's awareness of phonology, particularly rhyme and alliteration, was found to have a powerful effect in their eventual success on learning to read (Bradley and Bryant 1983). Phonological skills, particularly rhyming, enable children to make analogies when learning to read and this is important in alphabetic literacy where there is a grapheme-to-phoneme relationship (Byrne 1998; Goswami and Bryant 1990). In learning to read, phoneme segmentation was also found important for the reading of sight words. Dixon et al. (2002) found that children's phoneme segmentation ability was related not only to learning new words quickly but also for building up a detailed representation of words useful for reading, proofreading, and eventually spelling.

The use of syntax or sentence structure in oral language has been identified as important for beginning reading comprehension and vocabulary development (Bowyer-Crane et al. 2008). Bishop and Snowling (2004) propose a two-dimensional model of reading difficulties with phonological skills lying on one dimension and non-phonological skills lying on the other. In this model, phonological skills are related to decoding and non-phonological skills, such as syntax and semantics, relate to reading comprehension. It is argued that children with a high competence in oral language sentence construction bring rich narrative language to the new task of reading and writing (Dickinson and Snow 1987; Roth et al. 2002).

Vocabulary development is closely tied to reading comprehension (Pearson et al. 2007). Children's vocabulary at age three is strongly associated with learning to read and reading comprehension at the end of third grade (Hart and Risley 2003). Dickinson and Tabors (2002) found the scores that kindergartners achieved on measures (receptive vocabulary, narrative production, and emergent literacy) were highly predictive of their scores on reading comprehension and receptive vocabulary in fourth and seventh grades. Once established, differences in vocabulary knowledge among children tend to persist (Biemiller 2001). However, Beck and McKeown (2007) report that reading aloud from children's literature and rich, focused instruction on sophisticated words enhanced children's vocabulary. The importance of reading books aloud is emphasized because everyday spoken language has fewer rare vocabulary encountered in books read aloud. Hayes and Ahrens (1988) state that the lexical input from conversations is a limited source of learning new words other than the most common terms. Young children's oral language vocabulary, when enhanced through the shared reading of picture books either in English or their primary language, has been shown to strengthen the vocabulary acquisition of English Language Learners (Roberts 2008).

This chapter now moves from the predictive nature of phonological awareness, syntax, and vocabulary for literacy development to describe several Australian studies which explored the connections between literacy development that occurs before school and during school experiences. These sociocultural studies cover a time span of 14 years and are described chronologically. All the studies explore transitions between home, preschool, and into the first years of school and all raise questions about the neat connections between oral language and later literacy development.

Prior-to-School, Home, and School Literacies

Literacy and Funds of Knowledge

A national Australian longitudinal study explored the connections and disconnections in literacy development of 100 children in diverse socioeconomic and geographic areas from the year prior to school through to the third year of school (Hill et al. 2000). This study examined literacy development in the preschool and first three years of school as well as in children's homes. Ethnographic research was employed with teacher-researcher and university researchers exploring the cultural and social patterns of literacy (Heath 1982) and the 'funds of knowledge' in local families and communities (Moll et al. 1992). In addition, the social and cultural capital in homes and communities based on Bourdieu (1986) was used to describe ways that language and literacy practices from home were incorporated into the preschool and school curriculum. This study analyzed children's literacy development using 14 different assessment items including: logographic knowledge with environmental print, concepts of print, letter identification, writing, and early book reading (Clay 2002; Goswami and Bryant 1990; Yopp 1995).

The findings of this study were similar to those of Heath (1982) regarding oral language and literacy in that most middle-class homes and school classrooms share some important practices. In middle-class homes and in classrooms, secondary sources were valued over information gained through spoken language in immediate social networks within communities. These secondary sources often took the form of print texts and these texts were understood as carrying authority because print-based sources were afforded greater status in formal school. However, in Australia, family practices did not fall out neatly along social–economic or cultural lines. There were examples of working-class families where parents employed school-like pedagogies in facilitating their children's learning and there were professional families in which parents allowed their children greater autonomy than they were granted in the classroom, and this disadvantaged these children.

The teachers in this longitudinal study found it difficult to draw on the children's community experiences to build a responsive curriculum and in many cases, the language and literacy curriculum themes and topics were already set before the children arrived in preschool and school. While the teachers found it difficult to redesign a more responsive curriculum to build on different home literacy experiences, they commented that the home visits conducted within the study improved the relationships with parents, therefore, making communication easier. This study focused on print-based literacy and the importance of oral language was only found by careful reading of the in-depth case studies of children in the form of teachers' comments about children talking or avoiding talk when retelling stories, telling news, or not responding to the question-and-answer format of teacher talk in the preschool and school.

Literacy Using a Range of Modalities

In another Australian longitudinal study into the connections among home, preschool, and school, the concept of literacy was broadened to a 'semiotic' orientation (Kress 1999, 2000). This study explored how meanings were made and goals accomplished using other 'semiotic resources' such as oral language, visual imagery, numerical symbols, and music (Hill and Nichols 2009). This meant understanding how children make meanings using a range of modalities, not just in the 'pre-literate' years but all through their learning. In both community and classroom settings, the use of print was accompanied with talk, gesture, and action (Dyson 1993; Heath, 1982). This semiotic definition of literacy enabled the researchers to think about how all these different representational resources are employed, even when the focus in school remained primarily on the production of print texts.

This research found that children drew on three worlds, each with its own set of participant practices involving language and behaviour: the official school world, the peer world, and the home world or the sociocultural community (Dyson 1993). Children were able to use a range of representational practices as a tool in their negotiations around social identities. For instance, chanting, drawing, writing, and performing as characters in their stories provide children with ways of establishing themselves as socially and academically adept. The children continually made connections between their multiple worlds bringing together languages, genres, and domains of knowledge in creative and unpredictable ways. Children were able to use a range of representational resources to please or to challenge a teacher, to win friends, or end an unpleasant social interaction (Hill and Nichols 2009).

This study found that when teachers and children explore the great wealth of texts present in children's worlds, the notion that the rules for producing different kinds of texts—whether spoken, written, or visual—is somehow natural, universal, and accessible to all was not substantiated. Rather, the arbitrary rules for reading and producing different genres are community-specific and situation-specific. Once this idea was taken on board by teachers, then all kinds of language could be analysed and explored and language could be treated as an 'object of contemplation' not just a tool for communication (Hemphill and Snow 1996). The development of this awareness that language is an 'object of contemplation' has further significance. It enables teachers and children to develop critical literacy with greater power for reflecting on social inequalities. Some cultural groups' ways of speaking may not be viewed or treated as legitimate in the classroom reflecting a minority status (McNaughton 2002).

New Literacies

In a study investigating children's use of new literacies, educators visited the homes and communities of focus children to gather data on each home's and community's 'funds of knowledge' (Hill 2007). In this case the 'funds of knowledge' were information and communication technologies used in homes and familiar to children—for example, mobile phones and mobile communication devices, written notes, audio and videos, computer programs, CD ROMS, the internet, and digital photographs and related editing programs (Marsh 2004). The teachers documented the children's funds of knowledge using learning stories (Carr 2004).

The teacher-researchers documented children's use of new literacies using video, digital photography, and written field notes and found that the use of new technologies by children that was far greater than teachers had anticipated. In most cases, the children had access to and could use information and communication technologies far in advance of the equipment in many of the schools and preschools. Computers, next to television, were the most popular form of entertainment and access to knowledge available in homes. Children as young as four years of age, with family members, went online to websites linked to television shows, used search engines to find information, and played interactive games online. Regardless of socioeconomic or geographic locations, most children also had regular access to computers, or were able to access them at friends' or other family members' houses.

The teacher-researchers wrote about how children were aware of an ever-increasing abundance of choice about ways to communicate information and increasing choice about how to access information. The researchers commented about the need for young children to be involved in more relevant tasks and in project-based (Vartuli and Rohs 2006) approaches to learning so that they learn to question information, pose problems, make decisions, and develop as critical and creative thinkers. In this study, building curriculum based on children's home knowledge of new literacies, which included oral language, music, and photography as well as print-based literacy, proved to be less problematic as the children often were more knowledgeable than the teacher about using different forms of new communication technologies (Hill 2010).

Oral Language and Literacy

The fourth and final study took place in a time of increasing accountability regarding educational outcomes and returns to the persistent problem about the connections between oral language and literacy in the first year of school. This study occurred in a predominantly low socio-economic area near a major city in Australia where children were entering school with huge discrepancies in their oral language development. The children at the school came from a range of cultural backgrounds (e.g., immigrants from Iraq, Afghanistan, Serbia, Sudan, and other African countries) as well as a small cohort of Aboriginal students. The teachers commented that some children were beginning school with relatively small vocabularies and some used forms of non-standard oral language. The teachers thought that children with non-standard forms of English syntax may have difficulty accessing the syntax of books or book language to aid their beginning reading; therefore, the teachers decided to develop an oral language intervention program, and then after the children had been engaged in the program for some months, measured the children's oral language and reading development.

The oral language intervention program was play-based as this was thought to be developmentally appropriate and intrinsically motivating as well as a means of enabling children to experiment with oral language and receive immediate feedback. The play-based activities also involve sustained symbolic thinking, use of narrative and a range of other vital early literacy skills (Dickinson et al. 2008; Stagnitti and Jellie 2006). It was thought that the use of language in context would lead to purposeful talk and allow for the development of vocabulary in rich contexts; this goal was further supported by authentic and relevant picture books. Oral language development in context rather than a series of isolated vocabulary, grammar, and phonological awareness drills, was thought to produce more robust oral language development.

The teachers created 15 themed play boxes with sets of levelled questions for teachers/adults to use to stimulate oral language. Each box contained play props, as well as fiction and non-fiction picture books, all based around a single theme. Oral language development was facilitated through structured and pretend play-based scenarios, levels of questioning to extend children's oral language, and reading stories related to the play scenarios. The teachers organized a combination of pretend play and organised play activities in the belief that pretend play is of particular importance to the development of higher-order skills, linguistic development, and academic success. Four classes participated in the program and the students were in mixed groups according to age/grade and oral language skills.

The use of narrative was encouraged in each play session with adults assisting students to formulate stories based around their play experiences. The adults worked with students to use the narrative genre framework to formulate charac-ters, set complications, events, resolutions, endings, and to make predictions about what would happen next. This essentially built on children's oral language skills, presenting them with different syntactic structures to everyday oral language and worked to scaffold children's learning for early writing and reading. The teachers photographed the play sessions and then students dictated their stories which were recorded onto PowerPoint slides and then replayed for the children to read. This lan-guage experience procedure enabled children to contemplate how spoken language can be represented in written form.

After several months of engagement in the play-based oral language program, the teachers collected data on the children's oral language, vocabulary, phonolo-gy, and book levels using the Peabody Picture Vocabulary Test-4 (Dunn and Dunn 2007) and the School-Based Phonological Awareness Screening Tool based on Gil-lon (2004). Reading performance based on accuracy of 90–95% on reading levels with benchmark, levelled books was also used (Brabham and Villaume 2002; Hill 2001; Pitcher and Fang 2007).

The data from the assessments of oral language and reading were collated and analysed. It was predicted that there would be a strong relationship between oral lan-guage and reading. This was not the case. The statistical analysis of the relationship between vocabulary, reading achievement, and phonological awareness revealed a very strong relationship between reading and phonological awareness. However, there was not a strong relationship between vocabulary and reading achievement. The study identified three distinct groups of children. In Group One, the children scored low on vocabulary and high on reading. The children who fit into this pattern were children with English as an additional language who spoke a dialect of English or Hindi at home. It was expected that this group of children, with low vocabulary, might have experienced difficulties with reading. Another group of children scored high on receptive vocabulary and low on reading and, with this group, it had been expected that oral language and reading would have been more closely linked. An-other group scored low on both oral language vocabulary and reading.

The findings were disappointing at first sight as there was not a neat relationship between various aspects of oral language and literacy development. The teachers commented on the diversity of children's home and prior to school experiences and how development varies widely within and across individual children. As Genishi and Dyson (2009) write, "like anything related to language and literacy, assessment timelines for individual children do not follow a straight line" (p. 136).

Discussion: Disconnections Between Oral Language and Learning to Read

Many studies have sought to identify a key aspect of oral language which may predict later literacy development; however, when reviewing the sociocultural stud-ies described here, there does not appear to be a narrow, hierarchical, step-by-step process from oral language to early reading. Disagreement persists about how the component skills of oral language and literacy relate to one another and to significant long-term outcomes. The NICHD (2005) study concluded that oral language is important in itself for 'learning to learn'. Snow and Van Hemel (2008) write that various oral language and literacy components are of obvious importance in their own right and that arguments about their predictive relationship to each other or to later developmental outcomes are unnecessary. Rather than identifying one, narrow aspect of oral language as being predictive of future literacy development, Roth et al. (2002) write that oral language is multidimensional in the way it contributes to early reading.

Oral language differs in very important ways from written language (Halliday 1975). Written language demands more conscious attention to form and this involves choices to do with semantics, syntax, and phonology. For example, a four-year-old beginning invented speller who wants to write 'I have a chair' has to consider word order and meanings, and when writing the word 'chair', the child needs to pay attention to phonemes in a way that is not required when he or she is speaking (Richgels 2004). Compared to spoken language, the act of writing takes more time. Readers find that the syntax of a sentence in written text contains more adjectival and adverbial clauses compared to spoken language which consists of more fragments and repetitions. Also, the vocabulary of written language reflects a greater range of vocabulary choice, perhaps because there is more time to choose words than when engaged in a spontaneous conversation. Purcell-Gates (2001) writes that teaching children to read and write should be concerned with the conceptual and procedural knowledge of how written language works and not with how children's standard or non-standard oral language constitutes the base upon which literacy develops. When comparing the acquisition of oral language and learning to read, reading is more like learning a second language or a secondary discourse for all children (Gee 1996).

Summary

Oral language and written language are different linguistic modes and are important in their own right and their predictive relationship to each other or to later developmental outcomes is less important. Young children are exposed to multiple linguistic modes in homes, early education and care, and schools and each of these contexts have their own set of participant practices including language and behaviour. Observational studies in school, homes, and in early education and care show that children are able to make connections between and among multiple worlds using language, genres, and knowledge domains in creative and unpredictable ways.

The idea that oral language has different features from written language is very critical for children who are dependent on school for learning how to read. Many children who grow up exposed to non-standard forms of English may be from low socio-economic areas and from minority groups. If educators tie children's home oral language to future success in school, this implies that whole groups of children and home environments need to change. When learning to read is viewed the same way as learning a secondary discourse, this enables teachers to focus on introducing a wide range of written language forms to consciously explore how written language works.

Finally, more collaborative school and university research is required to investigate the outcomes of practical, responsive, school-based interventions like the play-based program as discussed here. The play-based program provided opportunities for children to understand that language—whether written, spoken, visual, or multi-modal—is an object which can be explored within a particular situation and context. For example, in dramatic play children often take on the roles of talking like a baby, talking like a teacher or being a wild monster in a faraway place. After children see that language itself can be explored and this idea is taken on board, then all kinds of language can be investigated and language becomes an 'object of contemplation' not just a tool for communication. In addition, play in the form of literature boxes can be enriched when parents contribute artifacts and stories from their own cultural backgrounds, thereby building on and extending the notion that all forms of spoken and written language can be explored in a playful context in the home and in early education and care (Streelasky 2008).

References

Adams, M. J. (1990). *Beginning to read: Thinking and learning about print.* Cambridge, MA: Massachusetts Institute of Technology.

Beck, I. L., & McKeown, M. G. (2007). Increasing young low-income children's oral vocabulary repertoires through rich and focused instruction. *Elementary School Journal, 107*(3), 251–271.

Biemiller, A. (2001). Teaching vocabulary: Early, direct, and sequential. *American Educator, 25,* 24–28.

Bishop, D., & Snowling, M. (2004). Developmental dyslexia and specific language impairment: Same or different? *Psychological Bulletin, 130*(6), 858–886.

Bourdieu, P. (1986). *Distinction: A social critique of the judgment of taste.* (trans: R. Nice). London: Routledge & Kegan Paul.

Bowyer-Crane, C., Snowling, M., Duff, F., Fieldsend, E., Carroll, J., Miles, J. Götz, K., & Hulme, C. (2008). Improving early language and literacy skills: Differential effects of an oral language versus a phonology with reading intervention. *Journal of Child Psychology and Psychiatry, 49*(4), 422–432.

Brabham, E., & Villaume, S. (2002). Leveled text: The good news and the bad news. *The Reading Teacher, 55*(5), 438–441.

Bradley, L., & Bryant, P. E. (1983). Categorizing sounds and learning to read: A causal connection. *Nature 301,* 419–421.

Byrne, B. (1998). *The foundation of literacy: The child's acquisition of the alphabetic principle.* Hove: Psychology Press.

Carr, M. (2004). *Assessment in early childhood settings.* London: Sage.

Clay, M. M. (2002). *An observation survey of early literacy achievement* (2nd ed). Auckland: Heinemann Education.

Crawford, P. (1995). Early literacy: Emerging perspectives. *Journal of Research in Childhood Education, 10*(1), 71–86.

Dickinson, D., & Snow, C. (1987). Interrelationships among prereading and oral language skills in kindergartners from two social classes. *Early Childhood Research Quarterly, 2*(1), 1–25.

Dickinson, D., & Tabors, P. (2002). Fostering language and literacy in classrooms and homes. *Young Children, 57*(2), 10–18.

Dickinson, D., Darrow, C., & Tinubu, T. (2008). Patterns of teacher-child conversations in Head Start classrooms: Implications for an empirically grounded approach to professional development. *Early Education & Development, 19*(3), 396–429.

Dixon, M., Stuart, M., & Masterson, J. (2002). The relationship between phonological awareness and the development of orthographic representations. *Reading and Writing: An Interdisciplinary Journal, 15,* 295–316.

Dockett, S., & Perry, B. (2009). Readiness for school: A relational construct. *Australasian Journal of Early Childhood, 34*(1), 20–26.

Dunn, L., & Dunn, M. (2007). *Peabody picture vocabulary test.* (4th ed.). San Antonio: Pearson.

Dyson, A. H. (1993). *Social worlds of children learning to write in an urban primary school.* New York, TX: Teachers College Press.

Gee, J. P. (1996). *Social linguistics and literacies: Ideology in discourses.* London and White Plains, NY: Longman.

Genishi, C., & Dyson, A. H. (2009). *Children, language and literacy: Diverse learners in diverse times.* New York: Teachers College Press and National Association for the Education of Young Children.

Gillon, G. T. (2004). *Phonological awareness: From research to practice.* New York: Guilford Press.

Goswami, U., & Bryant, P. E. (1990). *Phonological skills and learning to read.* Mahwah, NJ: Lawrence Erlbaum.

Halliday, M. A. K. (1975). *Learning how to mean: Explorations in the development of language.* London: Edward Arnold.

Hart, B., & Risley, T. (2003). The early catastrophe: The 30 million word gap by age 3. *American Educator, 27*(1), 4–9.

Hay, I., & Fielding-Barnsley, R. (2009). Competencies that underpin children's transition into early literacy. *The Australian Journal of Language and Literacy, 32*(2), 148–162.

Hayes, J., & Ahrens, M. (1988). Vocabulary simplification for children: A special case of 'motherese'? *Child Language, 15,* 395–410.

Heath, S. B. (1982). What no bedtime story means: Narrative skills at home and school. *Language in Society, 11,* 49–76.

Hemphill, L., & Snow, C. (1996). Language and literacy development: Discontinuities and differences. In D. R. Olson & N. Torrance (Eds.), *The handbook of education and human development.* (pp. 173–201). Oxford: Blackwell.

Hill, S. (2001). Questioning text levels. *Australian Journal of Language and Literacy, 24*(1), 8–20.

Hill, S. (2007). Multiliteracies: Towards the future. In L. Makin, C. Jones Diaz, & C. McLachlan (Eds.), *Literacies in childhood: Changing views, challenging practices*, (2nd ed., pp. 56–70). Melbourne: Elsevier.

Hill, S. (2010). The millennium generation: Teacher-researchers exploring new forms of literacy. *Journal of Early Childhood Literacy, 10*(3), 314–340 (Special issue 'New Technologies in Childhood').

Hill, S., & Nichols, S. (2009). Multiple pathways between home and school literacy. In M. Fleer, A. J. E. Anning, & J. Cullen (Eds.). *Early childhood education*, (2nd ed., pp. 169–184). Thousand Oaks, CA: Sage.

Hill, S., Comber, B., Louden, W., Rivalland, J., & Reid, J. (2000). *100 Children go to school: Connections and disconnections in literacy development in the prior to school period and the first year of schooling.* Canberra: Commonwealth of Australia.

Kagan, S. L., Moore, E., & Bredekamp, S. (Eds.). (1995). *Reconsidering children's early learning and development: Toward shared beliefs and vocabulary.* Washington, DC: National Education Goals Panel.

Kress, G. (1999). Genre and the changing contexts for English language arts. *Language Arts, 76*(6), 461–469.

Kress, G. (2000). Design and transformation: New theories of meaning. In B. Cope & M. Kalantzis (Eds.), *Multiliteracies: Literacy learning and the design of social futures*, (pp. 153–161). Melbourne: Macmillan.

Marsh, J. (2004). The techno-literacy practices of young children. *Journal of Early Childhood Research, 2*(1), 51–66.

McNaughton, S. (2002). *Meeting of minds.* Wellington: Learning Media.

Menyuk, P., & Chesnick, M. (1997). Metalinguistic skills, oral language knowledge, and reading. *Topics in Language Disorders, 17*(3), 75–87.

Mol, S., Bus, A., & DeJong, M. (2009). Interactive book reading in early education: A tool to stimulate print knowledge as well as oral language. *Review of Educational Research, 79*(2), 979–1007.

Moll, L., Amanti, C., Neff, D., & Gonzalez, N. (1992). Funds of knowledge for teaching: Using a qualitative approach to connect homes and classrooms. *Theory into Practice, 31*(2), 13–41.

National Early Literacy Panel. (2008). *Developing early literacy: A scientific synthesis of early literacy development and implications for intervention.* Washington, DC: National Institute for Literacy.

NICHD (Early Child Care Research Network). (2005). Pathways to reading: The role of oral language in the transition to reading. *Developmental Psychology, 41*(2), 428–442.

Pearson, D., Hiebert, E., & Kamil, M. (2007). Vocabulary assessment: What we know and what we need to learn. *Reading Research Quarterly, 42*(2), 282–296.

Pitcher, B., & Fang, Z. (2007). Can we trust levelled texts? An examination of their reliability and quality from a linguistic perspective. *Literacy, 41*(1), 43–51.

Poe, M., Burchinal, M., & Roberts, J. (2004). Early language and the development of children's reading skills. *Journal of School Psychology, 42*(4), 315–332.

Purcell-Gates, V. (2001). Emergent literacy is emerging knowledge of written language not oral. In P. R. Britto, & J. Brooks-Gunn (Eds.), *Young children's emerging literacy skills in the context of family literacy environments* (pp. 7–22). San Francisco, CA: Jossey-Bass.

Richgels, D. (2004). Paying attention to language. *Reading Research Quarterly, 39*(4), 470–477.

Roberts, T. A. (2008). Home storybook reading in primary or second language with preschool children: Evidence of equal effectiveness for second-language vocabulary acquisition. *Reading Research Quarterly, 43*(2), 103–130.

Roth, F., Speece, D., & Cooper, D. (2002). A longitudinal analysis of the connection between oral language and early reading. *Journal of Educational Research, 95*(5), 259–272.

Saracho, O., & Spodek, B. (2007). Oracy: Social facets of language learning. *Early Child Development and Care, 177*(6–7), 695–705.

Snow, C., & Van Hemel, S. (2008). *Early childhood assessment: Why, what and how.* Washington, DC: National Academy Press.

Snow, C., Burns, S., & Griffin, P. (1998). *Preventing reading difficulties in young children.* Washington, DC: National Academy Press.

Stagnitti, K., & Jellie, L. (2006). *Play to learn: Building literacy in the early years.* Melbourne: Curriculum Corporation.

Streelasky, J. (2008). A collaborative approach to literacy: Inner-city preschool children, families and the school community. *Australian Journal of Early Childhood, 33*(3), 27–33.

Vartuli, S., & Rohs, J. (2006). Conceptual organizers of early childhood content. *Early Childhood Education Journal, 33*(4), 231–237.

Yopp, H. K. (1995). A test for assessing phonemic awareness in young children. *The Reading Teacher, 49*(1), 20–29.

Chapter 6
Teacher Outreach to Families Across the Transition to School

An Examination of Teachers' Practices and Their Unique Contributions to Children's Early Academic Outcomes

Annemarie H. Hindman, Lori E. Skibbe and Frederick J. Morrison

A substantial body of evidence demonstrates that partnerships between parents and teachers can promote children's learning throughout the elementary and secondary grades (Epstein 1995, 2001; Fan and Chen 2001; Izzo et al. 1999), and recent findings have established its importance during the early childhood years as well (Fantuzzo et al. 2004; Manz et al. 2004; McWayne et al. 2004). Yet the field knows very little about how teachers of young children reach out to parents across the school transition period or how particular outreach efforts are associated with children's learning of key early academic skills. Such information would help early childhood educators optimize the efficacy of their family outreach.

This exploratory, descriptive study examined the extent and nature of early childhood teachers' outreach to parents during one academic year, as well as its unique relations with children's early literacy, mathematics, and vocabulary outcomes, controlling for a series of covariates. Results inform our understanding of how teachers connect with families and how this outreach supports learning.

Teacher Outreach as an Asset for Child Development

Many children in the United States enter the early grades without the foundational academic skills that they will need to be successful in school (NAEYC/NCTM 2003; NRC 2001). Of particular import are early literacy skills, including alphabet

Reprinted from: Early Childhood Education Journal 38/4 (2010), Hindman et al.: "Teacher Outreach to Families Across the Transition to School: An Examination of Teachers' Practices and their Unique Contributions to Children's Early Academic Outcomes" (doi:10.1007/s10643-010-0410-4. Copyright 2010 by Springer Science+Business Media, LLC).

A. H. Hindman (✉)
Curriculum, Instruction, and Technology in Education, College of Education,
Temple University, Philadelphia, PA, USA
e-mail: ahindman@temple.edu

D. M. Laverick, M. R. Jalongo (eds.), *Transitions to Early Care and Education,*
Educating the Young Child 4, DOI 10.1007/978-94-007-0573-9_6,
© Springer Science+Business Media B.V. 2011

knowledge and sound awareness, which will later help children learn to decode (or sound out) novel words (Snow et al. 1998). In addition, early mathematics knowledge, such as concepts of number and shape as well as logical problem-solving skills, help children take advantage of later instruction in basic operations (NRC 2001, 2009). Finally, language (particularly vocabulary) enables children to make sense of instruction in literacy and mathematics, as well as to share and receive feedback on their own ideas (Catts and Kahmi 2005; Hindman et al. 2010).

While teachers can provide high-quality classroom instruction in each of these areas, children benefit from consistent or complementary experiences at home and school, nurtured by school–family partnerships (Bronfenbrenner 2005; Epstein 2001; Hoover-Dempsey and Sandler 2005). To date, the bulk of the research and popular literatures, especially in early childhood, has focused upon the family-involvement side of these partnerships (Fan and Chen 2001; Mattingly et al. 2002; PTA 2000), leaving the role of the teacher unexplored (Bronfenbrenner 2005; Pianta and Walsh 1998). More research on teachers' outreach practices is needed, particularly because parents of young children are generally very receptive to and trusting of their children's teachers (Adams and Christenson 2000; Pianta et al. 2001).

Teacher Outreach Practices of Import

Although teacher outreach has yet to be carefully studied, work on family involvement by Fantuzzo et al. (2000, 2004), building on the research of Epstein (1995, 2001), implies a collection of outreach practices oriented toward the home, school, or personal communication that may be particularly important for young children's development.

Frequency of Teacher Outreach

Teachers' outreach to families at home might include providing activities/homework for parents to use with children, as well as information about parenting or schooling that would support families' engagement with children (Epstein 2001). Evidence about the frequency of these events is quite sparse; one study (Pianta et al. 2001) suggests that more than two-thirds of kindergarten teachers send parents orientation materials about their child's classroom both before school begins and after the start of the year, but questions remain about how often teachers distribute activities and newsletters or other literature that provide specific links to the curriculum as it unfolds during the year. Such links could be uniquely important because they afford opportunities to address individual children's particular learning successes and difficulties with the classroom material.

A second cluster of teacher outreach activities, encouraging family involvement in school, might include inviting families to volunteer in the school, organizing workshops and trainings for families, or even hosting non-academic social events or performances (Epstein 2001; Fantuzzo et al. 2000; Hoover-Dempsey and Sandler 2005). At present, data about teachers' implementation of outreach of this nature are relatively limited. For example, of kindergarten teachers surveyed in two national school transition studies, more than 60% invited parents to open-house or orientation nights (Pianta et al. 1999; Schulting et al. 2005); as yet, however, similar information is not available for preschool and first grade. Further, a review of the literature found no research examining teachers' invitations to workshops or to volunteer, both of which may afford parents the opportunity to learn about the school curriculum and instructional methods. Similarly, no reports of data on social events and performances, which might allow parents to observe their children's development, are widely available in the field.

Finally, teachers might communicate with families through personal contacts such as conferences, home visits, phone calls, or written notes or emails (Epstein 2001; Rimm-Kaufman and Pianta 2005). Here, research is somewhat more abundant; conferences and/or home visits, mandated by school districts and early intervention programs, generally occur once or twice per year for each family (PTA 2000). Further, many kindergarten teachers (47.9%) talk with families at least once before the school year begins, and the overwhelming majority (94.7%) do so after school the year has commenced (Pianta et al. 1999; Rimm-Kaufman and Pianta 2005). However, information about all relevant practices for all three early grades of the school transition is needed. Building upon this patchwork research base, the current study examined the frequency of teachers' home-, school-, and communication-based outreach in preschool, kindergarten, and first grade.

Stability in Outreach over the School Transition

In addition, it remains unclear how outreach along each of these three dimensions is consistent or variable over the 3-year transition into formal schooling. One notable study (Rimm-Kaufman and Pianta 2005) identified decreases in teachers' communication with families from preschool to kindergarten, but no work has examined these trends among other outreach practices. Because understanding the stability of outreach across grades could inform pre- and in-service teacher training, as well as guidance to families, this study explored the nature and frequency of teacher outreach along all three dimensions from preschool to first grade.

Relations Between Outreach Practices

Further, it would be helpful for early childhood practitioners to understand whether teachers who use more of one practice necessarily use more of others, or whether implementation of one practice is relatively independent of the implementation of any other. At present, there is preliminary evidence among kindergarten teachers that most do not use all possible outreach practices; rather, they select a few from the universe of possibilities (Schulting et al. 2005). However, it remains unclear whether this trend characterizes preschool and first grade as well. Therefore, we examined correlations between these outreach practices across all 3 years of the transition to school.

Associations Between Outreach and Child Outcomes

Finally, as outreach efforts can be resource-intensive for both teachers and families, understanding their contributions to children's learning would help practitioners refine their practices. To date, very few studies have touched upon this issue. One recent project drawing on the ECLS-K dataset (Schulting et al. 2005) found that a composite measure of educator outreach (summing across the home-, school-, and communication-oriented practices described above) in kindergarten had small to moderate positive associations with children's early academic knowledge. However, this global outreach measure may well obscure nuanced differences between particular outreach practices. A few other studies have examined how specific outreach practices predict children's early academic learning, with several encouraging findings. For example, the dissemination of materials to the home and invitations for families to be involved in school can support children's academic and social development (e.g., Fantuzzo et al. 2000; Hoover-Dempsey et al. 2002; Stevenson and Baker 1987). Conversely, the contributions of communication-related practices appear somewhat more complex, as some data suggest that these interactions result in gains for children (Gomby 1999; St. Pierre and Layzer 1999), while other work (Eccles and Harold 1993) has found that school–family communication may negatively predict child outcomes in the primary and secondary grades. These results likely suggest that parents and teachers might communicate more often about children who are having trouble, but that these increased interactions do not necessarily result in gains in children's skills over the course of a school year. Additional research would help to untangle these conflicting results regarding this important issue.

As a final note, research on involvement and outreach has often utilized global measures of child skills, such as academic competence (spanning literacy and mathematics; Schulting et al. 2005), or a combination of literacy and vocabulary skills (Baker et al. 1999; Bradley and Gilkey 2002; St. Pierre and Layzer 1999; Wagner and Clayton 1999). Here too, more specific distinctions are needed; teacher outreach operates over and above the early childhood classroom curriculum, which research strongly suggests is heavily focused upon literacy (i.e., decoding) in the early childhood years (Al Otaiba et al. 2008; Pianta et al. 2007). Because children likely receive a heavy dose of decoding instruction in the classroom, it is plausible that teacher outreach would demonstrate stronger associations with skills that received more variable focus, such as vocabulary and early mathematics. The present study thus examines literacy, mathematics, and vocabulary skills, to isolate specific links between outreach and child learning in several key domains.

Research Questions

Two broad research questions guide this work:

1. How do teachers of young children reach out to families?

   (a) What is the frequency and nature of teacher outreach practices to families?
   (b) Is the frequency of outreach stable or variable across the 3-year school transition period (i.e., preschool, kindergarten, and first grade)?
   (c) How are these outreach practices correlated with one another?

2. How do teacher outreach practices predict children's early academic (literacy, mathematics, and language) outcomes, beyond the effects of other home and school covariates?

Method

Participants

Teachers

Participants, recruited from two contiguous school districts in a suburb of a major Midwestern city, included 16 preschool, 18 kindergarten, and 28 first-grade teachers. While all first-grade classes followed a full-day schedule, roughly half of the preschool teachers ($n = 7$) and two-thirds of the kindergarten teachers ($n = 12$) taught part-day classes. Classrooms were housed in 13 different schools across two districts serving similarly diverse populations.

Of the teachers, all but one was female, all but one was European-American, and all were native speakers of English. Overall, 14 teachers held bachelor's degrees and 38 held master's degrees, but these rates varied substantially by grade. Only 38% of preschool teachers held an advanced degree, as compared to 75% of kindergarten teachers and 90% of first-grade teachers. First-grade teachers were thus significantly more likely to hold master's degrees than preschool teachers ($p < 0.01$). Overall, teachers had 13.29 years of experience in teaching, although variability was notable ($SD = 10.12$).

Children and Families

Two hundred and ten children in these teachers' classrooms were included in the present study; on average, four children per classroom were involved. Children ranged in age from 3.31 to 6.99 years, with a mean age of 5.43 ($SD = 0.87$). The majority (76%) were identified by parents as Euro-American, although African-American (9%), Asian-American (7%), Arab/Middle-Eastern (5%), and Hispanic/Latino (3%) children also were represented. Most families (95%) spoke primarily English at home. Fifty-two percent of children were female. On average, mothers had 15.97 years of education (i.e., a Bachelor's degree) with little variability across the sample ($SD = 1.87$ years).

Measures

Academic Skills

In both fall and spring of the school year, basic literacy, mathematics, and vocabulary competence was assessed using the Woodcock-Johnson III (WJ) Tests of Achievement (McGrew and Woodcock 2001). Early literacy skills were measured using the Letter-Word subtest, while basic mathematics and reasoning skills were tapped with the Applied Problems subtest, and expressive vocabulary was gauged with the Picture Vocabulary subtest. Split-half reliability on all subtests was above 0.80 for children ages 3 through 7. W or Rasch scores, which account for item difficulty and, unlike standard scores, are designed to show growth across the year, were employed in analyses. A W score of 500 represents the average score of a 10-year-old.

Teacher Outreach

Teachers completed a School–Home Partnership Questionnaire adapted from the Family Involvement Questionnaire (Fantuzzo et al. 2000, 2004) and the Kohl et al. (2000) parent–teacher survey. Teachers reported on the frequency of nine outreach practices, including sending parents activities and newsletters (i.e., home-based outreach); inviting parents to volunteer in the classroom, attend workshops, and social/performance events (i.e., school-based outreach); and calling, writing, conferencing, and conducting home visits with families (i.e., conferencing and communicating). Teachers rated the frequency of each practice on a 7-point scale (0 = never, 1 = annually, 2 = two-three times per year, 3 = monthly, 4 = bi-weekly, 5 = weekly, and 6 = daily).

Classroom Instruction

Using the Pathways Teacher Questionnaire (Morrison 2003), teachers noted the number of minutes they devoted to 14 literacy, mathematics, and language (i.e., vocabulary) instructional practices each week. They also rated their warmth and sensitivity toward children on eight indicators (e.g., my students and I have happy moments together) and rated their management and discipline on 12 items (e.g., I have no trouble following through on rules). Reliabilities for the warmth and management scales were adequate ($\alpha > 0.70$).

Procedures

Data Collection

In fall, parents and teachers were mailed questionnaires about their demographic backgrounds that required approximately 5 minutes to complete. Children received the A version of the WJ in the fall and the B version in the spring.

In contrast to other studies, which have administered teacher outreach questionnaires at the beginning of the school year (see Pianta et al. 2001; Schulting et al. 2005), the School–Home Partnership Questionnaire was administered at the end of the year in order to capture practices from September through June. Teachers submitted one survey describing their average behaviors across the entire class, in line with previous work which has aggregated across the classroom (Pianta et al. 2001) or even the school (Schulting et al. 2005). The three preschool and three kindergarten teachers who taught multiple part-day classes completed only one form, averaging their outreach across classes. The decision to obtain one survey per teacher was rooted not only in respect for teachers' competing responsibilities, but also was informed by pilot research with this population, which indicated that preschool and kindergarten teachers ($n = 33$) who completed one outreach survey for each of their part-day classes reported no significant outreach differences across classes (Hindman and Morrison 2005).

Upon returning this and the other study-related questionnaires, teachers received a $ 20 gift card for a local bookstore. Eighty-seven percent of eligible teachers returned the School–Home Partnership survey. There were no significant differences in teacher education and experience between those who did and did not return the survey, nor were there differences by district or by half- versus full-day class schedules ($p > 0.15$ for all). There were only a few instances of missing data in the present study (i.e., less than 5% on teacher and family covariates); missing data were imputed using a single imputation with EM algorithms. Resulting means and standard deviations of the imputed data were equivalent to those in the observed data.

Results

Research Question 1

Extent, Nature, and Stability of Outreach Across the Transition to School

Regarding home-oriented outreach, on average, teachers reported sending newsletters approximately bi-weekly. However, Tukey post-hoc comparisons found that preschool teachers sent newsletters less frequently than either kindergarten teachers (mean difference = 1.36, $p < 0.001$) or first-grade teachers (mean difference = 0.83, $p = 0.014$). Similarly, activities were sent home about twice per month, but distribution was less frequent among preschool teachers than first-grade teachers (mean difference = 1.21, $p = 0.019$).

Regarding in-school involvement, teachers invited volunteers approximately twice per month, although invitations were less frequent in preschool than kindergarten (mean difference = 1.61, $p = 0.004$) and first grade (mean difference = 1.34, $p = 0.009$). Workshops were held infrequently—approximately once per year—and social events and performances took place approximately two to three times per year, with no differences between grades.

Finally, regarding communication-based outreach, teachers called the average child's family about three times per year, while personal notes or emails were sent monthly. Only one teacher—working in Head Start—engaged in home visits, performing two per year for each family. All teachers held two conferences per year. No differences between grades in these practices emerged.

With the exception of conferences and home visits, on which little variability was apparent, the range of implementation of all of the outreach practices spanned the entire possible range of responses, from never (0) to daily (6). Variables were normally distributed, although the workshop/training variable demonstrated some skew to the right (Table 6.1).

Correlations Among Teacher Outreach Practices

Relations among the teacher outreach practices were explored using zero-order correlations. Overall, few significant correlations emerged. Teachers who offered more opportunities for volunteering also disseminated more newsletters ($r = 0.26$, $p = 0.044$) and activities ($r = 0.44$, $p < 0.001$). In addition, teachers who offered more workshops and training opportunities also made more phone calls to families ($r = 0.34$, $p = 0.008$) and wrote more notes ($r = 0.40$, $p = 0.001$). Further, writing and calling were marginally linked ($r = 0.23$, $p = 0.074$). However, even these few significant correlations were small to moderate in size, indicating that many of teachers' choices about implementing outreach practices were relatively independent of their choices about any other.

Table 6.1 Descriptive statistics, teacher outreach

Grade	Teacher outreach practice M (SD)						
	Newsletter	Activity	Workshop	Volunteer	Social event	Call	Write
Preschool	3.31 (0.87)	3.12 (1.41)	1.13 (1.09)	3.05 (1.37)	2.12 (0.58)	2.50 (1.90)	2.65 (1.75)
Kindergarten	4.67 (0.69)	3.72 (1.18)	1.06 (1.31)	4.67 (1.14)	1.99 (0.56)	2.28 (1.53)	3.28 (1.64)
First grade	4.14 (1.04)	4.32 (1.04)	0.86 (0.76)	4.39 (1.55)	1.96 (0.66)	2.00 (0.77)	2.96 (1.13)
Total	4.08 (1.03)	3.84 (1.44)	0.98 (1.02)	4.13 (1.52)	2.01 (0.61)	2.21 (1.36)	2.97 (1.46)
ANOVA between groups	***	*	–	**	–	–	–

Variables were measured on a 7-point scale, where 0 = never, 1 = annually, 2 = two–three times per year, 3 = monthly, 4 = bi-weekly, 5 = weekly, and 6 = daily

*$p < 0.05$; **$p < 0.01$; ***$p < 0.001$

Research Question 2: Contributions of Teacher Outreach to Child Skills

Analytic Strategy

As children were nested within classrooms, preliminary analyses for each outcome employed fully unconditional multilevel models (FUMs) to determine what percent of the total variance in the outcome was between schools, between teachers within a school, and between children with the same teacher. In all cases, significant ($p <$ 0.05) variance was identified between teachers (ICC = 0.73 for decoding, 0.69 for mathematics, and 0.33 for vocabulary), but not between schools. Thus, two-level models were tested using the HLM 6.06 software (Raudenbush and Bryk 2002).

Level 2 included teacher outreach and other covariates such as grade level, teacher education (BA vs. MA), years of experience, class schedule (full- vs. half-day), and classroom instruction (i.e., minutes of literacy, mathematics, and vocabulary instruction, as well as warmth and management). At level 1, children's fall scores on the relevant assessment were entered, along with covariates such as child gender and ethnicity (minority vs. white), maternal education, and maternal employment. In the interests of parsimony, variables that did not make a significant ($p < 0.05$) contribution to the model were trimmed from final models; this trimming did not affect the pattern of significant effects. In the text below, we report the contributions of all predictors—including teacher outreach—to children's skill development over the course of the year and note the effect size for teacher outreach (Cohen 1988). Teacher outreach variables that predicted children's learning are summarized in Table 6.2.

Literacy

The strongest predictor of children's literacy (specifically, decoding) in spring was fall literacy skill ($B = 0.92$, $p < 0.001$). No child, family, or teacher covariates pre-

Table 6.2 Hierarchical linear model results: teacher outreach and early academic outcomes

Outcome	Teacher outreach predictor	Coefficient	p value	Variance explained (%)
Decoding	–	–	–	
Mathematics	Phone calls	−1.67	0.020	0.5
	Invitations for volunteers	1.77	0.004	0.6
Vocabulary	Phone calls	−1.67	<0.001	7.9
	Workshops	1.78	0.006	2.4

All variables were centered at the grand mean. The final model for decoding explained 90% of between-teacher variance in the outcome and 36% of the within-teacher variance. For mathematics, the final model explained 95% of between-teacher variance and 56% of the within-teacher variance. The final vocabulary model explained 29% of between-teacher variance and 50% of within-teacher variance

dicted this outcome. Finally, none of the teacher outreach practices predicted children's decoding.

Mathematics

Children with stronger fall mathematics skills had stronger skills in the spring ($B = 0.72$, $p < 0.001$). None of the child-level covariates explained variation in mathematical skill; however, skills were stronger among students of more experienced teachers ($B = 0.23$, $p = 0.039$), teachers with BAs rather than MAs ($B = -5.96$, $p = 0.016$), and in full-day classrooms ($B = 7.06$, $p = 0.001$). In addition, opportunities for classroom volunteering were positively associated with mathematics skills ($B = 1.77$, $p = 0.004$), while phone calls were inversely related of these skills ($B = -1.67$, $p = 0.020$). Together, these outreach variables explained 1.1% of the variance in the outcome, an association of small magnitude.

Vocabulary

Fall vocabulary skills predicted spring skills ($B = 0.67$, $p < 0.001$). None of the child-level covariates were significantly related to vocabulary learning. However, across grades, children in full-day classrooms outperformed their peers in the spring, controlling for everything else in the model ($B = 3.32$, $p = 0.017$). Of teacher outreach variables, workshops and trainings were positively associated with children's vocabulary learning over the course of the year ($B = 1.78$, $p = 0.006$), explaining 2.4% of the variance in spring skills, a small relation. Further, phone calls were inversely related to children's growth on this measure ($B = -1.67$, $p < 0.001$), accounting for 7.9% of the outcome variance, a small to moderate association.

Discussion

This descriptive, exploratory study revealed that teachers in preschool, kindergarten, and first grade used a variety of family outreach strategies. Outreach to the home, including distributing activities and newsletters, took place approximately twice per month. Invitations for volunteering were offered about as often, while social events were staged several times per year and workshops or trainings took place annually. Regarding communication, phone calls were made to each family approximately three times per year, with notes and emails sent home monthly. Teachers varied substantially in the frequency of implementation of most practices. Over the three grades, no systematic declines in the frequency of outreach were observed; rather, significant increases were apparent in some practices. Moreover, teachers generally implemented each practice independently of any other, as correlations between these kinds of outreach were low.

In addition, these outreach practices uniquely contributed to children's early learning, over and above the effects of child, family, and classroom factors; however, relations between teacher outreach and child skills were selected and more pronounced for skills that typically received less focus in early childhood classrooms. Specifically, teachers' invitations for volunteers were linked to children's mathematical problem solving, while providing workshops was associated with children's vocabulary development. Phone calling was inversely linked to vocabulary and mathematics. As in previous studies, these factors uniquely explained a small portion of the variance in child skills.

Several findings warrant additional discussion. First, in contrast to previous work (Rimm-Kaufman and Pianta 1999), the frequency of outreach from teachers to families was relatively stable over these three school transition grades and, in some cases, increased over time. This divergence from prior findings may suggest that there is a good deal of variability across programs (e.g., Head Start, public preschool) and communities in outreach practices. Future research might examine how factors such as teachers' ideas and goals, or policies of schools and districts, shape change in outreach across the school transition period (Graue and Brown 2003).

Second, teachers' reports of frequency of their outreach spanned the entire distribution of possible responses for nearly all variables, with few significant correlations between practices, suggesting that different teachers employed this body of practices in different ways. Future work might investigate how teachers think about outreach, including (a) how they evaluate what is necessary and effective, and (b) which school, family, or community factors promote or impede outreach. Studies might focus particularly upon outreach practices that uniquely explain variance in children's skills.

However, even with this variability, on average, outreach happened rather infrequently, relative to children's daily transitions between the home and the school. Thus, there may be opportunities to increase teacher–parent partnership, particularly around practices linked to child outcomes.

Select associations between outreach and child skills were observed, over and above covariates attendant to children, families, and teachers. That vocabulary learning was greater in classrooms where teachers provided more workshops/trainings for families suggests that (a) teacher outreach is more strongly associated with content that typically receives less focus in the earliest of years of school, and (b) outreach practices that personally provide families with information might have stronger relations to child skills than simply sending activities home. Specifically, workshops may provide information about development and learning that families later use with young children. Although the variance explained by this association is small, it is notable that this link emerges after accounting for the effects of a collection of home- and classroom-based covariates related to children's language development.

In addition, the frequency of invitations to volunteer in the school was related to children's mathematical problem solving. It is unlikely that teachers who provide more volunteering opportunities also teach more mathematical reasoning (and, in fact, analyses held classroom instruction constant). Instead, this result likely suggests that, at least in this community, volunteering provides families with information related to mathematical skills and logical thinking to which they would otherwise not be introduced, which in turn informs their subsequent work with children (NRC 2001). For example, parent volunteers in the classroom or school may witness problem-solving activities such as puzzles, mathematics instruction, or even discussion of complicated storybook plots. Indeed, in light of increasingly demanding and sophisticated standards for early learning, the modern classroom may look very different from what parents remember, and they may learn new skills that they then can share with children.

Finally, children whose teachers made more phone calls to parents had slower growth in vocabulary and mathematical problem solving. Although attributions of causality are inappropriate with these correlational data, this study supports previous research (see Eccles and Harold 1993; Hoover-Dempsey and Sandler 2005) indicating that parents and teachers sometimes communicate more about children who are struggling, but that this communication does not ultimately raise children's scores during the school year. Future work might examine precisely what content phone calls address and how teachers and families could better capitalize on efforts to raise child skills.

It is also important that parent volunteering did not predict child vocabulary, and that teacher workshops did not predict mathematics. These null findings suggest that the role of teacher outreach in child outcomes—over and above classroom and home instruction—is content-specific. The absence of effects for home instruction raises qualitative questions about precisely what activities/information teachers sent to families and how families used this to educate themselves and their children.

Limitations and Future Research Directions

Many aspects of teacher outreach are translated to children through family involvement, although it was beyond the scope of this study to collect data on this involvement. Future work might simultaneously examine the nature and extent of teacher outreach and family involvement, as related to child outcomes. Further, this study included a single measure of outreach, and subsequent research might collect multiple, brief teacher surveys or interviews across the year, or use an ongoing diary method (see Rimm-Kaufman and Pianta 1999) to collect richer data about day-to-day outreach.

Implications for Practitioners

The high variability in outreach across teachers suggests that administrators and teachers might collaborate to ensure that outreach is frequent and consistent across classrooms. Second, encouragement to continue focusing on outreach can be inferred from these data, but given their specific and modest benefits, such outreach strategies might best be considered as a support for a larger instructional program.

Third, the inverse associations between communication and children's vocabulary and mathematical problem solving indicate that simply addressing a matter with families, even in the highly intimate context of a personal conversation, will not necessarily lead to gains in children's skills. Rather, teacher outreach may be the first step of many on the part of parents, teachers, and children themselves to build knowledge in children as well as the adults who strive to help them.

References

Adams, K. S., & Christenson, S. L. (2000). Trust and the family–school relationship: Examination of parent–teacher differences in elementary and secondary grades. *Journal of School Psychology, 38*(5), 477–496.

Al Otaiba, S., Connor, C., Lane, H., Kosanovich, M. L., Schatsneider, C., Dyrlund, A. K., et al. (2008). Reading First kindergarten classroom instruction and students' growth in phonological awareness and letter naming-decoding fluency. *Journal of School Psychology, 46,* 281–314.

Baker, A. J. L., Piotrkowski, C. S., & Brooks-Gunn, J. (1999). The Home Instruction Program for Preschool Youngsters (HIPPY). *Future of Children, 9*(1), 116–133.

Bradley, R. H., & Gilkey, B. (2002). The impact of the Home Instructional Program for Preschool Youngsters (HIPPY) on school performance in 3rd and 6th grades. *Early Education and Development, 13*(3), 301–311.

Bronfenbrenner, U. (2005). *Making human beings human: Bioecological perspectives on human development.* Thousand Oaks, CA: Sage.

Catts, H., & Kahmi, A. (2005). *The connection between language and reading disabilities.* Mahwah, NJ: Erlbaum.

Cohen, J. (1988). *Statistical power analysis for the behavioral sciences.* Hillsdale, NJ: Erlbaum.

Eccles, J. S., & Harold, R. S. (1993). Parent–school involvement during early adolescent years. *Teacher's College Record, 94*(3), 568–587.

Epstein, J. L. (1995). School/family/community partnerships. *Phi Delta Kappan, 76*(9), 701–712.

Epstein, J. L. (2001). *School, family, and community partnerships.* Boulder, CO: Westview.

Fan, X., & Chen, M. (2001). Parental involvement and students' academic achievement: A meta-analysis. *Educational Psychology Review, 13*(1), 1–22.

Fantuzzo, J. F., McWayne, C., Perry, M. A., & Childes, S. (2004). Multiple dimensions of family involvement and their relations to behavioral and learning competencies for urban, low-income children. *School Psychology Review, 33*(4), 467–480.

Fantuzzo, J. F., Tighe, E., & Childes, S. (2000). Family involvement questionnaire: A multivariate assessment of family participation in early childhood education. *Journal of Educational Psychology, 92*(2), 367–376.

Gomby, D. S. (1999). Understanding evaluations of home visitation programs. *Future of Children, 9*(1), 27–43.

Graue, M. E., & Brown, C. P. (2003). Pre-service teachers' notions of families and schooling. *Teaching and Teacher Education, 19,* 719–735.

Hindman, A. H., & Morrison, F. J. (2005). *Family involvement in early childhood education: Teacher and parent partnership practices.* Paper presented at the annual meeting of the American Educational Research Association, Montreal, Canada.

Hindman, A. H., Skibbe, L. E., Miller, A., & Zimmerman, M. (2010). Ecological contexts and early learning: Contributions of child, family, and classroom factors during Head Start to literacy and mathematics growth through first grade. *Early Childhood Research Quarterly, 25,* 235–205.

Hoover-Dempsey, K. V., & Sandler, H. M. (2005). *The social context of parental involvement: A path to enhanced achievement* (No. R305T010673). Nashville, TN: Vanderbilt University.

Hoover-Dempsey, K. V., Walker, J. M. T., Jones, K. P., & Reed, R. P. (2002). Teachers Involving Parents (TIP): Results from an in-service teacher education program for enhancing parental involvement. *Teaching and Teacher Education, 18*(7), 843–867.

Izzo, C. V., Weissberg, R. P., Kasprow, W. J., & Fendrich, M. (1999). A longitudinal assessment of teacher perceptions of parent involvement in children's education and school performance. *American Journal of Community Psychology, 27*(6), 817–839.

Kohl, G. O., Lengua, L. J., & McMahon, R. J. (2000). Parent involvement in school: Conceptualizing multiple dimensions and their relations with family and demographic risk factors. *Journal of School Psychology, 38*(6), 501–523.

Manz, P. H., Fantuzzo, J. W., & Power, T. J. (2004). Multidimensional assessment of family involvement among urban elementary students. *Journal of School Psychology, 42*, 461–475.

Mattingly, D. J., Prislin, R., McKenzie, T. L., Rodriguez, J. L., & Kayzar, B. (2002). Evaluating evaluations: The case of parent involvement programs. *Review of Educational Research, 72*(4), 549–576.

McGrew, K. S., & Woodcock, R. W. (2001). *Woodcock Johnson-III.* Itasca, IL: Riverside.

McWayne, C., Hampton, V., Fantuzzo, J. W., Cohen, H. L., & Sekino, Y. (2004). A multivariate examination of parent involvement and the social and academic competencies of urban kindergarten children. *Psychology in the Schools, 41*, 363–377.

Morrison, F. J. (2003). *Pathways teacher questionnaire.* Ann Arbor, MI: University of Michigan.

NAEYC/NCTM. (2003). *Early childhood mathematics: Promoting good beginnings.* www.naeyc. org/about/positions/pdf/psmath. Accessed 1 Dec 2008.

NRC. (2001). *Adding it up: Helping children learn mathematics.* Washington, DC: National Academy Press.

NRC. (2009). *Mathematics learning in early childhood: Paths toward excellence and equity.* Washington, DC: The National Academy Press.

Pianta, R. C., & Walsh, D. J. (1998). Applying the construct of resilience in schools: Cautions from a developmental systems perspective. *School Psychology Review, 27*(3), 407–417.

Pianta, R. C., Cox, M. J., Taylor, L. C., & Early, D. (1999). Kindergarten teachers' practices related to transition to school: Results of a national survey. *Elementary School Journal, 100*(1), 71–86.

Pianta, R. C., Kraft-Sayre, M., Rimm-Kaufman, S. E., Gerke, N., & Higgins, T. (2001). Collaboration in building partnerships between families and schools: The NCEDL kindergarten transition study. *Early Childhood Research Quarterly, 16*, 117–132.

Pianta, R. C., Belsky, J., Houts, R., & Morrison, F. J. (2007). Opportunities to learn in America's elementary classrooms. *Science, 315*(5820), 1795–1796.

PTA. (2000). *Building successful partnerships.* Bloomington, IN: Solution Tree.

Raudenbush, S. W., & Bryk, A. (2002). *Hierarchical linear models: Applications and data analysis methods* (2nd ed.). Thousand Oaks, CA: Sage.

Rimm-Kaufman, S. E., & Pianta, R. C. (1999). Patterns of family–school contact in preschool and kindergarten. *School Psychology Review, 28*(3), 426–438.

Rimm-Kaufman, S. E., & Pianta, R. C. (2005). Family–school communication in preschool and kindergarten in the context of a relationship-enhancing intervention. *Early Education and Development, 16*(3), 287–316.

Schulting, A. B., Malone, P. S., & Dodge, K. A. (2005). The effect of school-based kindergarten transition policies and practices on child academic outcomes. *Development and Psychopathology, 41*(6), 860–871.

Snow, C. E., Burns, M. S., & Griffin, P. (1998). *Preventing reading difficulties in young children.* Washington, DC: National Academy Press.

St. Pierre, R. G., & Layzer, J. I. (1999). Using home visits for multiple purposes: The comprehensive child development program. *Future of Children, 9*(1), 134–151.

Stevenson, D. L., & Baker, D. P. (1987). The family-school relation and the child's school performance. *Child Development, 58*, 1348–1357.

Wagner, M. M., & Clayton, S. L. (1999). The Parents as Teachers program: Results from two demonstrations. *Future of Children, 9*(1), 91–115.

Part II
Policies and Issues

Chapter 7
Critical Perspectives on Transition to School

Reframing the Debate

Anne Petriwskyj and Susan Grieshaber

Effective transition to school is a valuable contributor to children's sense of confidence in the school setting and to improving children's academic outcomes. However, traditional understandings of school entry have focused on children's readiness as a set of normative characteristics, rather than on the shared processes that support the change experience of children and families. A shift toward considering school transition as a procedural question in the late 1990s and early 2000s focused on narrow approaches involving preparation of children and on school structural provisions such as age of entry. Such approaches support binary constructions of children and rely on theories that draw from Western normative understandings of child development. The alternative use of critical theory offers opportunities to reframe transition as a more equitable process, by drawing attention to more complex inter-relationships between stakeholders and more respectful power dynamics. This chapter considers alternate ways of thinking about transition based on critical theory. It focuses on recent Australian research examples but also draws from the international literature base on transition to school. The chapter begins by discussing the terminology used to talk about school entry and then considers the implications of binary constructions such as "ready" and "unready". A brief outline of the limited way in which approaches to transition have been conceptualized is followed by an analysis of theories and pedagogies that promote effective transition. The chapter concludes with some suggestions for beginning to rethink practices that concern transition to school.

A. Petriwskyj (✉)
School of Early Childhood, Queensland University of Technology, Victoria Park Road,
Kelvin Grove, QLD 4059, Australia
e-mail: a.petriwskyj@qut.edu.au

D. M. Laverick, M. R. Jalongo (eds.), *Transitions to Early Care and Education,*
Educating the Young Child 4, DOI 10.1007/978-94-007-0573-9_7,
© Springer Science+Business Media B.V. 2011

Terminology

The way entry to school is named frames thinking about whether it is a question of children's normative characteristics (readiness for school), a set of characteristics of a school (the ready school), or a shared characteristic of varied stakeholders (pre-paredness). Despite inclusive educational policies, the titles of some initial school classes (e.g. preparatory) have continued to emphasize children's preparation or readiness for existing school circumstances, rather than change within schools to include all children and to support their school entry. A focus on children's readiness as normative developmental or academic characteristics is incompatible with contemporary policies of inclusion. In contrast, transition to school denotes a dynamic process of change involving multiple settings and stakeholders. Thus, transition is a broader construct accommodating a more diverse range of children and other stakeholders such as teachers, families, and communities.

The way in which diverse abilities and cultural background in young children are named also serves to frame thinking about children's characteristics, adjustment, and achievement as they enter school. Narrow attention to children experiencing transition difficulties has been supported by a continuing emphasis on need terminology (e.g. special or additional needs) rather than participation rights. Terminology such as "disabled", "at risk", and "minority group" frames a deficit image of children with non-prototypical abilities or backgrounds, instead of an image of competent and resourceful children. Using critical theory as a frame, Hyun (2007) contends that separate categorical labelling of children for service access (e.g. autistic, non-English speaker) serves to reinforce traditional group stereotypes and power differences. Separate categorical labels also fail to recognize multiple exceptionalities in individuals (e.g. giftedness in Indigenous children, Cronin and Diezmann 2002). Thus, policies on transition to school continue to focus on singular constructs such as age of school entry and processes for children with disabilities (e.g. Education Queensland 2007).

Binary Constructions

Simple binary divisions of "ready" and "unready" have been adopted as a means of identifying support program requirements of children with developmental delays associated with organic disabilities or diverse cultural experience. The outcome of such binary understandings of readiness is that its converse, unreadiness, is constructed as deficit, and grade retention as one solution. The concept of child readiness incorporates adjustment by children to the expectations of schools, and, once in the school setting, academic achievement (Dockett and Perry 2007). Normative constructions of children's abilities and cultural resources also support a simplistic binary division of children into typical and atypical. Differences from the norm are constructed as child-related deficits requiring a remedial solution (Davis et al.

2007). Thus, programs to support school entry in the past have often been specifically remedial in orientation, particularly for children from social, economic, and culturally diverse backgrounds or for children with developmental delays. However, such approaches are incompatible with contemporary views of diversity as a resource, and of children and families as competent co-contributors to learning (e.g. cultural resources children bring from home, individual strengths of children with disabilities) (Kilderry 2004).

The persistence of readiness notions signals reliance on traditional developmental stage theories, despite the lack of evidence of their relevance to non-European cultures (Grieshaber 2008). Stage theories imply deficits in children with delayed developmental progress or culturally diverse experience, and a lack of need for gifted children to receive any support or pedagogic variation. In recent studies of transition to school in Australia, teachers consistently emphasized children's readiness for school, and reported continued use of retention in grade or the use of remedial services for children who were deemed "unready" (Dockett and Perry 2007; Petriwskyj 2005). Such constructions have been actively supported by government literature for families, which used the title "preparatory" and discussed the role of kindergarten in children's readiness for school (Department of Education and Training [DET] 2007). Thus, it is not surprising that O'Gorman (2008) found that some parents expressed a preference for school-like or formal teacher-directed kindergarten activities to enhance children's preparation for school. This conceptualization of the year prior to Year 1 of elementary education is at odds with the play-based yet focused approach of contemporary Australian early childhood curricula, such as the *Early Years Curriculum Guidelines* (Queensland Studies Authority 2006) and the national birth-5 curriculum: *Belonging, Being & Becoming: The Early Years Learning Framework for Australia* (Department of Education, Employment and Workplace Relations [DEEWR] 2009).

Narrow Approaches to Transition

There has been a gradual shift towards broader understandings of school entry that go beyond children's normative development to consider the role of the school. However, this move initially resulted in narrow approaches to transition focused on structural provisions by schools, and preparatory practices prior to school to enhance children's school adjustment. Structural provisions include raising the age of school entry, introducing special transition classes or curricula, and providing support programs for children deemed unready. Changes to the age of school entry have included accelerated entry for gifted children or delayed entry for children with disabilities. Some Australian research continues to indicate the value of delaying the school entry age, particularly for boys (Boardman 2006). However, there is international evidence that children whose home environment is challenging may progress more quickly if school entry is not delayed, particularly if they gain access to a more enriched academic environment (Stipek and Bylar 2001). Therefore,

Australian schools have introduced reception classes based in schools to support transition (e.g. kindergarten, transition, pre-primary), transition curricula (e.g. *Early Years Curriculum Guidelines*) and specialized programs for groups whose progress has been an ongoing concern (e.g. Indigenous children, McCrea et al. 2000).

Following the Preparing for School study in the state of Queensland, Australia (Thorpe et al. 2004), the age of school entry was raised by six months. A transition class called "preparatory" was introduced, and a new early years' curriculum was developed to bridge prior-to-school and early elementary school programs. While the value of full time play-based yet focused programs located at a school was shown to support children's progress, there were concerns in relation to children from equity groups (Thorpe et al. 2004). For example, evaluation of classroom practice using the Classroom Observation Scoring Manual found that recognition of difference, particularly incorporation of cultural knowledges, was low (Thorpe et al. 2004). In a follow-up study (Petriwskyj 2010), schools were found to use structural changes to manage extreme class complexity (e.g. class streaming, in-class ability grouping, withdrawal classes). Teachers reported that they relied on cultural teaching assistants for cultural and linguistic knowledge, as access to professional education on culture was limited.

Preparatory practices have also been a valued strategy for improving children's sense of confidence at school entry (Dockett and Perry 2007). However, a simple binary division of responsibilities has placed emphasis on the sending setting, such as the family home or the preschool, rather than on the receiving setting, such as the school, or on shared responsibility. Approaches such as priming for a single change event of school entry and preparation practices to orient children to the school culture, environment, and expectations (Corsaro and Molinari 2000; Pianta and Kraft-Sayre 2003) have a demonstrated value in assisting children to adjust to school cultures and facilities. However, orientation practices alone fail to take account of children's prior experiences of learning, the differences between prior experiences and institutional settings such as schools, and children's trajectories over time. They frame transition as a single change event requiring the child to adjust, rather than transition as a lengthy and dynamic change process involving a range of stakeholders. Thus, difficulties in adjustment are deemed to be problems of the child or the family rather than an indication that school processes or pedagogies need to change. In a longitudinal study in an area of Australia characterized by economic and social diversity (Raban and Ure 2000), parents reported that ongoing adjustment difficulties arose from rigid expectations by the school, inexperience or frequent changes in teachers, and child boredom related to low teacher expectation. Teachers, in contrast, perceived difficulties in adjustment as lack of readiness. This emphasis on readiness is also supported by statutory assessment pressures in schools that promote a normative achievement focus. Teachers face a tension between achieving set learning milestones at prescribed time markers and providing for variations in children's learning speed.

In the context of inclusion, there has been some questioning of these narrow approaches to transition, resulting in a shift to considering longer term transition processes, readiness of schools, and shared responsibilities of stakeholders (Graue

2006). Contemporary classrooms and schools are complex contexts, which require a more sophisticated process to address the range of learners, adult stakeholders, teacher relationships, the contexts that are involved, and pedagogies that consider diversity. Structural provisions (e.g. support programs, ability grouping, additional resourcing) enhance opportunities to teach but do not necessarily enhance opportunities to learn for school entrants with diverse abilities and/or from diverse backgrounds (Hamre and Pianta 2007). Preparatory practices contribute to children's sense of confidence in entering an unfamiliar setting, yet such practices contain an assumption that children remain in the same area and system to begin school. Contemporary changes in family structure and family mobility together with policies of inclusion have increased the complexity of class groups and the demands on teachers (Henderson 2004). This requires change in pedagogies to support all children.

Theories and Pedagogies for Transition to School

Relationships between stakeholders (e.g. between children, children and teachers, families and teachers, teachers in different settings) offer a secure base for effective transition of children (Niesel and Griebel 2007). Thus, models of transition to school have adopted ecological theoretical perspectives (Dockett and Perry 2007; Rimm-Kaufmann and Pianta 2000). Although ecological systems theory considers children within the context of their family and community, it does not account well for the diversity of children's circumstances. Transition models based on ecological theory offer limited consideration of children's progress over time, which is highlighted in transition literature that considers trajectories over extended periods (Burchinal et al. 2002). The assumption that the central place of the child in ecological theory is universally appropriate is questionable, as it overlooks the multiple priorities in families and communities, and diverts attention from the role of culture in mediating experience (Vogler et al. 2008). This is a key consideration for Australian Indigenous children, families, and communities whose cultural perspectives have not been accorded sufficient priority (Frigo and Adams 2002).

Socio-cultural perspectives take into account the influence of the cultural context on children (Corsaro and Molinari 2000). Reduction in the philosophical contrasts between cultural contexts (home and school, early childhood setting and school) could enable greater continuity of experience and enhance children's sense of confidence during school transition (Raban and Ure 2000). Continuity between early childhood education settings and schools may be seen as more structured lessons in classes for younger children (e.g. in preschool or kindergarten), the establishment of learning outcomes in play programs for younger children (e.g. DEEWR 2009), or incorporation of learning-oriented guided play in lower primary (Brostrom 2005). Links among teachers to share information about children and on teaching are needed to ensure continuity and graduated change.

Continuity of learning also involves home-school links, including use of home languages in schools and incorporation of culturally valued practices. This is particularly relevant in Australia for migrant, refugee, and Indigenous children; and children from economically and socially diverse backgrounds whose home and school experience may contrast (Frigo and Adams 2002; McCrea et al. 2000; Raban and Ure 2000; Sanagavarapu and Perry 2005). Therefore, partnerships between families and communities and schools are essential to ensure that children's prior experience is taken into consideration in their school program. An Australian study of impacts on children's outcomes found that improved adjustment and achievement were associated with high levels of family and community engagement (Thorpe et al. 2004). However, teachers focused on internal relationships within the school amongst children's peers, within the school staff, and between teachers and children. Relationships with families emphasized parents and other community volunteers engaging in classroom assistance tasks, rather than negotiation of transitions between teachers and families. Thus, teachers were unaware that some children from South-East Asian backgrounds were experiencing peer related difficulties and internalizing behaviours at school entry and throughout Year 1.

In studies of Australian Indigenous children's school transition, lack of family consultation and low expectations meant that teachers failed to capitalize upon strengths of Indigenous children such as responsibility or resilience (Cronin and Diezmann 2002; Dockett and Perry 2007). Interviews with Bangladeshi families in Australia identified a concern that children's school adjustment was hampered not only by their limited English proficiency, but also by school expectations of independence that were at odds with valued socialization practices at home (Sanagavarapu and Perry 2005). Further, narrow traditional constructions of family fail to capitalize on the potential involvement in transition of fathers, working parents, extended family members, and non-traditional families. Closer partnerships between teachers, families, and communities would offer opportunities to communicate more effectively about such concerns, alert adults to the complexities of children's lives, link learning more closely to children's experiences, and assist children to feel more confident during school transition.

Transitions are complex, and involve multiple, overlapping changes that are both vertical (from year to year) and horizontal (within the day or week). Some children may attend more than one setting (e.g. outside-school-hours care, specialist classes, English language classes, or learning support). For some children, there may be multiple transitions between locations or schools within a short space of time (e.g. children from geographically mobile families, Indigenous travel for cultural events) (Frigo and Adams 2002; Henderson 2004). Thus, children may experience confusion about behaviour expectations, or may resist changes about which they feel uncertain. Teachers need to take the added pressures of multiple transitions into account and minimize overlapping transitions within the school day. In a study of inclusive transition in Australia, teachers explored pedagogic continuity between year levels through teacher discussion, and minimized horizontal transitions by adopting more in-class support rather than withdrawing children for assistance (Petriwskyj 2010). However, an observed reliance on unqualified teaching assistants to provide support programs indicated that teachers were still negotiating ways to balance the demands of the whole class and the learning of individuals. This indicates that more extensive and pro-active reform of transition approaches, framed by critical perspectives, may be required. Teachers also need to be more aware of the theories that underpin their practice and that of colleagues, in order to enhance continuity for children during transition (Wood and Bennett 2001).

In contrast to ecological theory and sociocultural perspectives, critical theory (Giroux 2006) attends to the unequal distribution of power according to social class, gender, race, disability, culture and language, and to the ways structural factors (e.g. low funding) and low expectations can impede the achievement of some groups. Critical theory moves away from normative ideas that underpin categorizations of children to recognize the right to participation of all individuals (Woodhead 2006) and the role of social institutions such as schools in creating circumstances that enable or disable children (McLaren 2007). Pedagogy based on critical theory breaks from past blaming of children for educational failure. It re-focuses on more socially just teaching approaches based on teachers' critique of normative assumptions, and of the hidden curriculum of unequal power relationships (Davis et al. 2007).

Critical pedagogy has drawn attention to the agency of children, through which children feel empowered to value themselves and others (Kilderry 2004; McLaren 2007) and to the need for broader educational reforms that reflect equitable and respectful relationships (Giroux 2003). Such reconsideration is particularly relevant in Australia as the definition of inclusion has been extended to consider the sense of belonging of children from varied social, economic, cultural or family structure backgrounds, as well as gifted children and those with disabilities and varied learning styles (DEEWR 2009). Early childhood education in Australia has been challenged to reframe practice around theories that go beyond traditional Western developmentalism, and to transform pedagogies such that the participation rights of all children are considered (Grieshaber 2008). Australian transition studies have drawn attention to diversity considerations such as gender, disability, cultural and linguistic experience, social circumstances, and giftedness (Nyland 2002; Raban and Ure 2000; Whitton 2005). Therefore, inclusive transition processes need to take into account a range of variations within a class, and the multiple forms of diversity existing within any individual child. They need to be non-stigmatizing, yet provide support to individual children and families in negotiating their changing circumstances and roles.

These are pedagogic concerns, rather than issues that can be addressed through structural change such as altering the age of school entry, or through pragmatic additions to repertoires of practice such as orientation programs. Critical pedagogies prompt teachers to name a perceived problem, reflect critically on the circumstances, and to act pedagogically in ways that are more respectful and inclusive. Pro-active transition reforms are needed to enhance opportunities for all children both prior to school and in early elementary contexts, and to balance continuity between settings with challenges to children to engage with new learning. Such reform would include more equitable relationships with families and community that consider power dynamics. Areas for potential attention include assessment and non-stigmatizing transition processes.

Assessment of learning or development through tests that may be used to retain children in grade is inconsistent with contemporary policies of inclusion. In Australia, inclusion goes well beyond full or partial inclusion placement to mean a deeper pedagogic practice of differentiating learning to enhance the participation and sense of belonging of all children (DEEWR 2009). Assessment that relies on Western normative development (e.g. checklists, readiness tests) fails to take the range of young children's experience into account, is de-contextualized, and constructs diversity as deficit (Ryan and Grieshaber 2005). The use of such assessment strategies for decisions about the timing or location of school entry for children with diverse abilities or backgrounds will necessarily place them at a disadvantage. Further, they offer teachers little information on which to make pedagogic decisions to support continuity of learning. If assessment focused more on continuous assessment for learning, rather than assessment for school placement or statutory reporting, the form of documentation and analysis of assessment data could be framed more strongly by individual learning and influences on learning. Documenting observations of the group, not just the individual, takes into account the role of social influences in children's learning. If this documentation (e.g. digital images, narratives) is shared with children and family members, additional insights from the whole community of learners can support learning (Hatherly and Richardson 2007). This approach not only adds richness to pedagogic decision-making but also capitalizes on prior experience and on relationships supporting the child during school transition.

Transition strategies that take a more inclusive approach incorporate relationships and continuity of experience as well as preparatory practices that orient children to school. Stigmatizing strategies such as grade retention or targeted transition support programs need to be minimized. Critically aware teachers trying to incorporate a range of strategies into their transition processes also need to be vigilant and insightful regarding the hidden curriculum, which involves the unintended consequences of pedagogic decisions (Kilderry 2004). Hidden curriculum often refers to non-subject-related learning, such as learning about expected school behaviours, and the way this may disadvantage some children (e.g. by gender, ethnicity, socioeconomic status, ability category) in standardized learning situations (McLaren 2007). Giroux (2003) and McLaren (2007) identify resistance to rigid behaviour expectations and even academic learning by some children as being a reasonable rejection of undue repression, or of a struggle to have their own lives visible in their school experience.

Differentiated transition processes and ongoing pedagogic provision that capitalize on the life experience and strengths of all school entrants, offer opportunities for all children to feel valued and develop a sense of belonging. There is emerging Australian research evidence of tentative reforms to transition in some schools that have a high proportion of children with diverse abilities and cultural backgrounds (Petriwskyj 2010). At one school, teachers incorporated children's friendships and individual response patterns into differentiated transition planning (e.g. co-location of friends in the same Year 1 class). This illustrated ways of re-focusing on child agency and children's transition capital (Dunlop 2007) to utilize the personal and cultural resources that they bring to school.

Strategies that teachers could adopt to assist their progress towards more equitable transition approaches include critical reflection on practice and re-conceptualization of pedagogic planning as action research (MacNaughton et al. 2007). Critical reflection implies that teachers give deep consideration to questions of power dynamics in relationships, the inclusive and non-stigmatizing nature of their practices, and the degree to which they listen respectfully to a range of stakeholders regarding transition. Teachers in an Australian action research study of school transition (Petriwskyj 2005) found that external facilitation assisted them to negotiate ideas, undertake critical reflection, and intellectualize their work by moving discussion from narratives of practice to broader pedagogic issues. Deep negotiation of meanings is required for reforming transition pedagogies, since the complexities inherent in education need to be acknowledged, together with reflection on the ethics of interactions with the diversity of children, families, and communities. This suggests that the approach to teacher preparation and in-service professional development may need to change, to enable teachers to move beyond surface additions to practice and to engage more deeply with negotiation of understandings about inclusion and transition.

Conclusion

The development of more sophisticated multi-level strategies for supporting transitions of children and families requires a theoretical shift, changes in the terminology used to name and frame approaches, and the use of pedagogies that ensure transition processes are inclusive. Critical theoretical framing of transition can facilitate deeper pedagogical reflection about equity in relationships with families and children. But theorizing alone is insufficient. As well as changes in terminology and pedagogies, theorizing needs to be accompanied by support mechanisms such as school change, ongoing professional learning opportunities for teachers and significantly, time for teachers to understand, reflect, and change their ideas about transition to school. These approaches would support a shift in ways teachers think about transition as a professional responsibility towards all children, and about the input of stakeholders including children, families, and communities. We conclude with some recommendations for teachers, teacher educators, and policy makers, which are not exhaustive.

Suggestions for Teachers

- Recognize and acknowledge that diversity exists in any group.
- Focus on strengths and abilities that children and families bring so that they are seen as resourceful rather than as deficient.
- Recognize and acknowledge that multiple categories of diversity may be represented within an individual.

- Make differences and similarities an explicit part of the daily curriculum.
- Learn about deficit theories and how they position difference of any sort.
- Expect all children to learn and achieve.
- Recognize that categorical labelling of children for service access reinforces power differences and traditional stereotypes.
- Learn about your own biases and those of the children in your class, and work conscientiously against them on a daily basis.
- More equitable approaches come from reflecting critically on power dynamics and unexamined assumptions about neediness.
- Recognize that teachers can be subject to excessive demands, especially in with competing demands of international equity and inclusion trends and national testing and accountability measures.
- Identify children's learning preferences and use them pedagogically.
- Take up relevant professional development opportunities.
- Share what works with other practitioners.
- Involve and consult meaningfully with parents about their practices.
- Develop long-term transition processes that take into account current understandings of transition as a multi-year, multi-faceted process.

Suggestions for Teacher Educators

- Teach about the most recent theoretical perspectives that are being used in research about transition and inclusive educational practices.
- Make critical theory and other theoretical perspectives that challenge the dominant power relationships in society integral parts of pre-service teacher education courses.
- Make diversity a central part of curriculum in teacher education courses.
- Encourage student teachers to think beyond simple modifications to everyday practice to reflect deeply about the theories that underpin their decision-making and the lenses they use for decisions.
- Teach about both overarching pro-active pedagogies that attend to the realities of diversity in school entrants, and strategies for differentiated responses to individual children's reactions as they enter school.
- Explicitly link pedagogies of prior to school and early elementary education to assist student teachers in considering pedagogical continuity.

Suggestions for Policy Makers

- Re-write policies on transition to school so that they focus on pedagogical processes supporting a range of children (instead of singular constructs such as age of school entry, readiness, or risk).

- Provide opportunities for regular, ongoing professional development.
- Incorporate policy on family and community involvement, to reinforce the importance of broader stakeholder participation in transition.

References

Boardman, M. (2006). The impact of age and gender on prep children's academic achievements. *Australian Journal of Early Childhood, 31*(4), 1–6.

Brostrom, S. (2005). Transition problems and play as a transitory activity. *Australian Journal of Early Childhood, 30*(3), 17–26.

Burchinal, M., Peisner-Feinburg, E., Pianta, R., & Howes, C. (2002). Development of academic skills from preschool through to second grade: Family and classroom predictors of developmental trajectories. *Journal of School Psychology, 40*(5), 415–436.

Corsaro, W., & Molinari, L. (2000). Priming events and Italian children's transition from preschool to elementary schools: Representations and action. *Social Psychology Quarterly, 63*(1), 16–33.

Cronin, R., & Diezmann, C. (2002). Jane and Gemma go to school: Supporting young gifted Aboriginal children. *Australian Journal of Early Childhood, 27*(4), 12–17.

Davis, K., Gunn, A., Purdue, K., & Smith, K. (2007). Forging ahead: Moving towards inclusive and anti-discriminatory education. In L. Keesing-Styles & H. Hedges (Eds.), *Theorising early childhood practice: Emerging dialogues* (pp. 99–117). Sydney: Pademelon.

Department of Education and Training (2007). Preparing for enrolment in the preparatory year. http://education.qld.gov.au/studentservices/inclusive/prep/docs/prep_info_sheet.pdf. Accessed 12 Nov 2009.

Department of Education, Employment and Workplace Relations (DEEWR) (2009). *Belonging, being & becoming: The early years learning framework for Australia.* Canberra: Commonwealth of Australia.

Dockett, S., & Perry, R. (2007). *Transitions to school: Perceptions, expectations, experiences.* Sydney: University of New South Wales Press.

Dunlop, A.-W. (2007). Bridging research, policy and practice. In A.-W. Dunlop & H. Fabian (Eds.), *Informing transitions in the early years: Research, policy and practice* (pp. 151–168). Maidenhead: Open University Press.

Education Queensland (2007). Variation to school age entry enrolment. http://www.education.qld.gov.au/strategic/eppr/students/smspr007. Accessed 22 Oct 2008.

Frigo, T., & Adams, I. (2002). Diversity and learning in the early years of school. Paper presented at the Australian Association for Research in Education (AARE) Conference, Brisbane, December.

Giroux, H. (2003). Critical theory and educational practice. In A. Darder, M. Balodano, & R. Torres (Eds.), *The critical pedagogy reader* (pp. 27–56). New York: Routledge Falmer.

Giroux, H. (2006). *The Giroux reader.* Boulder: Paradigm.

Graue, E. (2006). The answer is readiness—Now what is the question? *Early Education and Development, 17*(1), 43–56.

Grieshaber, S. (2008). Interrupting stereotypes: Teaching and the education of young children. *Early Education and Development, 19*(3), 505–518.

Hamre, B., & Pianta, R. (2007). Learning opportunities in preschool and early elementary classrooms. In R. Pianta, M. Cox, & K. Snow (Eds.), *School readiness and transition to kindergarten in the era of accountability* (pp. 49–83). Baltimore: Brookes.

Hatherly, A., & Richardson, C. (2007). Building connections: Assessment and evaluation revisited. In L. Keesing-Styles & H. Hedges (Eds.), *Theorising early childhood practice: Emerging dialogues* (pp. 51–70). Sydney: Pademelon.

Henderson, R. (2004). Educational issues for the children of itinerant seasonal farm workers: A case study in an Australian context. *International Journal of Inclusive Education, 8*(3), 293–310.

Hyun, E. (2007). Cultural complexity in early childhood: Images of contemporary young children from a critical perspective. *Childhood Education, 83*(5), 261–266.

Kilderry, A. (2004). Critical pedagogy: A useful framework for thinking about early childhood curriculum. *Australian Journal of Early Childhood, 29*(4), 33–37.

MacNaughton, G., Hughes, P., & Smith, K. (2007). Re-thinking approaches to working with children who challenge: Action learning for emancipatory practice. *International Journal of Early Childhood, 39*, 39–57.

McCrea, D., Ainsworth, C., Cummings, J., Hughes, P., Mackay, T., & Price, C. (2000). *What works: Explorations in improving outcomes for Indigenous students.* Canberra: Australian Curriculum Association.

McLaren, P. (2007). *Life in schools: An introduction to critical pedagogy in the foundations of education* (5th ed.). Boston: Pearson.

Niesel, R., & Griebel, W. (2007). Enhancing the competence of transition systems through co-construction. In A.-W. Dunlop & H. Fabian (Eds.), *Informing transitions in the early years: Research, policy and practice* (pp. 21–32). Maidenhead: Open University Press.

Nyland, B. (2002). *Language, literacy and participation rights: Factors influencing educational outcomes for Australian boys.* Paper presented at the Australian Association for Research in Education conference, Perth, December.

O'Gorman, L. (2008). The Preparatory year in a Queensland non-government school: Exploring parents' views. *Australian Journal of Early Childhood, 33*(3), 51–58.

Petriwskyj, A. (2005). Transition to school: Early years teachers' roles. *Australian Research in Early Childhood Education, 12*(2), 39–50.

Petriwskyj, A. (2010). Diversity and inclusion in the early years. *International Journal of Inclusive Education 14*(2), 195–212.

Pianta, R., & Kraft-Sayre, M. (2003). *Successful kindergarten transition.* Baltimore: Brookes.

Queensland Studies Authority (2006). Early Years Curriculum Guidelines. Brisbane: Queensland Studies Authority.

Raban, B., & Ure, C. (2000). Continuity for socially disadvantaged school entrants: Perspectives of parents and teachers. *Journal of Australian Research in Early Childhood, 7*(1), 54–65.

Rimm-Kaufmann, S., & Pianta, R. (2000). An ecological perspective on the transition to kindergarten: A theoretical framework to guide empirical research. *Journal of Applied Developmental Psychology, 21*(5), 491–511.

Ryan, S., & Grieshaber, S. (2005). Shifting from developmental to post-modern practices in early childhood teacher education. *Journal of Teacher Education, 56*, 34–45.

Sanagavarapu, P., & Perry, R. (2005). Concerns and expectations of Bangladeshi parents as their children start school. *Australian Journal of Early Childhood, 30*(3), 45–51.

Stipek, D., & Bylar, P. (2001). Academic and social behaviour associated with age of entry to kindergarten. *Applied Developmental Psychology, 22*, 175–189.

Thorpe, K., Tayler, C., Bridgstock, R., Grieshaber, S., Skoien, P., Danby, S., & Petriwskyj, A. (2004). *Preparing for school: Report of the Queensland preparing for school trials 2003/2004.* Brisbane: Queensland University of Technology.

Vogler, P., Crivello, G., & Woodhead, M. (2008). *Early childhood transitions research: A review of concepts, theory and practice.* Working paper No. 48. The Hague: Van Leer Foundation.

Whitton, D. (2005). Transition to school for gifted children. *Australian Journal of Early Childhood, 30*(3), 27–31.

Wood, E., & Bennett, N. (2001). Early childhood teachers' theories of progression and continuity. *International Journal of Early Years Education, 9*(3), 229–243.

Woodhead, M. (2006). Changing perspectives on early childhood: Theory, research and practice. UNESCO Strong Foundations background paper. http://unesdoc.unesco.org/images/0014/001474/147499e.pdf. Accessed 28 Nov 2008.

Chapter 8
Transition in the Classroom

The Teacher

Margaret A. King

Introduction

Many children spend significant amounts of time participating in group care—child care centers, family child care homes, and schools—away from the comfort of their homes. The manner in which they transition into group care contributes to their sense of safety and security. The child's home provides the foundation for the development of relationships, interactions, and ways of being. As children leave their home environments and enter groups that are different from these early experiences, they have to make adjustments and find new ways of interacting. Much of the research about transitions and children focuses on the preparation between the home and the group setting and the role of the teacher and parent in helping the child to adjust to the new environment (Dockett and Perry 2004; Laverick 2008). Another focus is the transition from preschool to kindergarten (Gill et al. 2006; Rimm-Kaufman and Pianta 2000; Yeboah 2002).

Teachers bring to the transitioning situation their histories, beliefs, and concepts about transitions and how they should occur. At the core of meeting the transitional needs of children is the teachers' ability to understand what they feel and know about transitions.

Teachers' Transition Histories

Understanding oneself is considered an element in teaching and teacher development (Bullough and Gitlin 2001; Freese 2006; Kelchtermans 2009). The exploration of the self is continuous throughout a teacher's career and self-understanding impacts decision-making in the classroom. In the case of transitions, teachers' understand-

M. A. King (✉)
Ohio University, W324 Grover Center, Athens, OH, USA
e-mail: kingm@ohio.edu

D. M. Laverick, M. R. Jalongo (eds.), *Transitions to Early Care and Education*, Educating the Young Child 4, DOI 10.1007/978-94-007-0573-9_8,
© Springer Science+Business Media B.V. 2011

ing of their transitional histories influence how they handle transitions, and how responsive they are to modifications of their behavior based on new information.

Teachers' transition histories are reflected in how and what they do to encourage successful transitions for children. Teachers must first look at themselves and think about what they believe about transitions; how they should behave; and how children should behave. The foundation of their transitional histories come from three sources: The experiences they bring from their personal experiences with transitions; the experiences they have helping children transition; and what they have learned about transitions using content knowledge from the field of early childhood education. It is important for teachers to reflect on these areas of their personal and professional development as they create strategies to support successful transitions for children.

Personal experiences with transitions are the first step in the teachers' understanding their transitional history. Teachers can begin by asking themselves:

- What is my transitional history?
- Were transitions easy or difficult for me?
- How did the adults in my life help me to deal with transitions?
- Were the adults helpful or supportive or did they leave me to work out the transitions on my own?

These questions help teachers to understand the emotions that they associate with transitions; thus providing insight about how they might view transitions.

Second, prior experiences handling transitions with young children help the teacher determine how she will handle future transitions. The earliest professional experiences with children's transitions begin in their preservice preparation and continue throughout their careers. These experiences impact practice; therefore, the teacher will need to reflect on these experiences. Asking questions such as:

- How did I plan for transitions?
- What worked when I implemented the transitions?
- What did not work when I implemented transitions?
- How did individual children respond?
- How did the group respond?
- What would I change?
- What would I do again?

Answering these questions will help teachers to identify how they handled transitions in the past. Moreover, these experiences coupled with their personal experiences contribute to the development of a belief system about transitions.

Third, the teacher uses evidence-based knowledge about transitions and children to add to her personal experiences and her experiences handling transitions to develop new ways of thinking about transitions. The evidence-based knowledge can come from a variety of sources: journals, books, and courses. It is the evidence-based knowledge the teacher integrates that provides an opportunity for the teacher to begin to critically examine her practice and to implement best practices related to transitions. It is at this point the teacher can begin to ask questions such as:

- How does what I am learning relate to what I know?
- How can I integrate this new information to what I do?
- Will this new knowledge change what I am doing or does it affirm what I am doing?

It is important that teachers use all three pieces of information to make decisions and to improve their understandings and practices in regard to transitions in the classroom. Considering teachers' transitional histories in the context of new knowledge offers an opportunity for teachers to change practices.

Transitional Strategies

Engaging parents in the process of transitioning children into any early care and education environment is the key to making the transition work for the child (Dockett and Perry 2004; King 1988; Laverick 2008). However, we believe that, even when children have support at home, the transition into the classroom may be difficult because the burden for a successful transition is the responsibility of the child and family. There may be a disconnect between what the child needs and what the early care and education environment is offering; therefore, the proposed strategies represent what should happen within the early care and education environment to support the child.

The transitional needs of children in early care and education programs are many. Most often concern is given to their cognitive needs or their ability to adjust to the pedagogical differences between group settings (Gill et al. 2006; Pianta et al. 1999). We must also consider the socio-emotional needs of the child as a significant factor in transitioning children into early care and education group settings. School adjustment is tied to creating a safe secure learning environment; therefore, the strategies need to support the emotional well being of children based on best practice (Janson and King 2006; Lumpkin 2007). The strategies are ones that may or may not be easily implemented depending on the teachers' transitional histories and their willingness to change or modify their beliefs.

Know Children's Transitional Histories

Knowing children involves understanding their developmental and sociocultural backgrounds but it also means knowing their transitional histories. It seems that a great deal of time is spent understanding what they know cognitively and to some extent what they know socially. Less attention is given to how children handle and respond to change within the classroom environment. Attention to children's transitional histories is important because these experiences may affect children's responsiveness to subsequent transitions. Children's transitional histories are not as complex as teachers' but are equally important. Even though much of the research focuses on transitioning from preschool to kindergarten, in fact, children have many opportunities to transition in and out of group settings during the first eight years of life.

For some children, their first experience transitioning into a group care environment is when they enter early care and education center as an infant, toddler, or preschooler. For example, the child who has slept on his mom's stomach and now must sleep in a crib; the toddler who spent most of his time playing alone with his Mom and Dad but now must share the adults with eight or ten children; the two-year-old who spent time playing alone and now must share with other children; or the three-year-old who carries his special teddy bear with him everywhere he goes entering group care for the first time and now must leave the toy at home are all examples of children entering groups where the values of the system are different from the child's prior experiences. It is this transitional history that children often bring to group settings. We believe that one factor that influences the manner in which children transition to the new setting is related to the "good fit" between the child, teacher, and environment (Churchill 2003). Teachers need to be aware of children's transitional histories to support a goodness of fit between the child and the environment.

Respond to Differences

The differences that children bring into the classroom need a response and acknowledgement by the teacher. In teaching, sometimes teachers' believe that it is important to treat all children the same to achieve equity in the classroom. A common belief is that teachers should not see differences. However, each child is unique and in order to create equity, teachers must look at each child as an individual.

Acknowledging that each child has a specific way to deal with separations and transitions and respecting the transitioning patterns of the child allows the child to create a pattern of security in an unfamiliar environment. Each time a child changes a school, classroom, or teacher, it is a new and unfamiliar experience for the child. Some children easily make the transition while others feel insecure and disconnected. Either way, it is important for the teacher to understand the child's pattern of transitioning and adjustment.

Robert is a child who appears to transition easily into the group. He comes into the classroom, goes to the reading area, takes a book, and begins to read. After many days entering the classroom with no problems, Robert becomes anxious and irritable as he enters the classroom. The teacher is concerned with the change in Robert's behavior and believes that there must be problems at home. Both the teacher and parents begin to work out a plan to handle Robert's behavior. The one factor that the teacher did not consider is that she changed the daily schedule; so, instead of Robert having the opportunity to go to the reading area to read, he was required to go to group meeting. Since the teacher was unaware of Robert's transition pattern, she was unable to prepare him for the change. As teachers examine their own transitional histories, they may need to think about their need to start the day with a cup of coffee or a newspaper in order to have a good day. Therefore, recognizing and acknowledging patterns of transitions help both children and teachers form positive relationships.

Allow Transitional Objects

Some children need to transition into classrooms using objects brought from home. Transitional objects are important because they provide comfort to children when they are transitioning into group settings (Winnicott 1953). Transitional objects may be the expected objects such as teddy bears or blankets or less expected items such as a picture of a parent, a favorite toy, or a cereal box (King 1988). A five-year-old attending kindergarten often took her favorite blanket, now in tatters, with her to school. Each morning she carefully placed it in the bottom of her backpack. When she became stressed with the daily activities of the classroom, she would return to her cubby and reach into the bottom of her backpack to be able to touch the blanket. This was not easy to do because the teacher frequently scolded her for always being in the cubby area of the classroom. A preschool boy often brought the same empty cereal box to school day after day. The teacher frequently talked with his Mom about leaving the cereal box at home because it was a distraction in the classroom. The boy frequently protested when the teacher took it away or made him put it away. Unaware that the child was using the empty cereal box as a transitional tool, the teacher added to the child's stress and discomfort. In both cases, the teacher was unaware of the child's need to maintain a connection with the home environment, the familiar, by using transitional objects.

In many classrooms the transitional object is not allowed or if it is allowed, it must remain in the child's cubby except during rest or naptime. It is important that children be allowed to use transitional objects as they wish since for many children the transitional object creates a sense of safety and security.

Foster Caring and Supportive Relationships

The caring relationship that children have with their teachers is an important factor in school success (Lumpkin 2007). The connection that children develop with teachers as they transition into the classroom may impact their engagement with learning (Protheroe 2007). For example, John had difficulty transitioning into his first grade classroom. Each day he would cry and stand by the door. Frustrated by John's refusal to join the group and stop crying, his teacher ignored the behavior and told the children in the classroom to do the same. Eventually, John would find his way to his desk but he spent most of the day disengaged from the daily classroom activities.

Children who are having difficulty transitioning into the classroom need to have teachers who are willing to respond to them using empathy and caring. The teachers' interactions either help the child to feel connected to the classroom or tell the child that his feelings are not important. Full engagement and participation in the classroom environment occurs when children feel emotionally safe and secure (Janson and King 2006; Sylwester 1994; Zull 2004).

Conclusion

The way teachers teach is based on multiple factors including beliefs, experiences, and what they know. To meet the needs of children and provide safe and secure transitional experiences, teachers must consider their personal transitional experiences; their transitional experiences with children; and their knowledge of appropriate transitions. Several appropriate transitional strategies are identified in this chapter. It is important for teachers to consider how these strategies can be integrated into their practice by examining their belief systems and deciding how these new practices fit.

References

Bullough, R. V., Jr., & Gitlin, A. (2001). Becoming a student of teaching: Knowledge production and practice. (2nd ed.). New York: Routledge.

Churchill, S. (2003). Goodness of fit in early childhood settings. *Early Childhood Journal, 33*(2), 113–118.

Dockett, S., & Perry, B. (2004). What makes a successful transition to school? Views of Australian parents and teachers. *International Journal of Early Years Education, 12*(3), 217–230.

Freese, A. (2006). Reframing one's teaching: Discovering our teacher selves through reflection and inquiry. *Teaching and Teacher Education, 22,* 100–119.

Gill, S., Winters, D., & Friedman, D. (2006). Educators' views of pre-kindergarten and kindergarten readiness and transitional practices. *Contemporary Issues in Early Childhood. 7*(3), 213–227.

Janson, G., & King, M. (2006). Emotional security in the classroom: What works for young children. *Journal of Family and Consumer Sciences, 98*(7), 70–74.

Kelchtermans, G. (2009). Who I am in how I teach is the message: Self-understanding, vulnerability and reflection. *Teachers and Teaching: Theory and Practice, 15*(2), 257–272.

King, M. (1988). Making arrival time easier. *Day Care and Early Education, 16*(2), 18–20.

Laverick, D. (2008). Starting school: Welcoming young children and families into early school experiences. *Early Childhood Education Journal, 35*(4), 321–326.

Lumpkin, A. (2007). Caring teachers: The key to student learning. *Kappa Delta Pi Record, 43*(4), 158–160.

Pianta, R., Cox, M., Taylor, L., & Early, D. (1999). Kindergarten teachers' practices related to transition to school: Results of a national study. *The Elementary School Journal, 100*(1), 71–86.

Protheroe, N. (2007). Emotional support and student learning. *Principal, 86*(4), 50–54.

Rimm-Kaufman, E., & Pianta, R. (2000). An ecological perspective on transition to kindergarten: A theoretical framework to guide empirical research. *Journal of Applied Developmental Psychology, 21*(5), 284–298.

Sylwester, R. (1994). How emotions affect learning. *Educational Leadership, 52*(2), 60–62.

Winnicott, D. (1953). Transitional objects and transitional phenomena. *International Journal of Psychoanalysis, 34,* 89–97.

Yeboah, D. (2002). Enhancing transition from early childhood phase to primary education: Evidence from the research literature. *Early Years, 22*(1), 51–68.

Zull, J. (2004). The art of the changing brain. *Educational Leadership, 62*(1), 68–74.

Chapter 9
Preparing Preschoolers for Kindergarten

A Look at Teacher Beliefs

Sandraluz Lara-Cinisomo, Allison Sidle Fuligni and Lynn A. Karoly

Introduction

Children from low-income and linguistic minority families may attend a variety of different types of early care and education (ECE) programs during their preschool years. Some programs meet their working parents' need for child care and others are targeted early childhood learning programs, such as Head Start or state preschool (Barnett and Yarosz 2007). The nature of the early learning programs these children experience varies by program type, intensity, and overall setting, as well as by the belief systems and curriculum practices offered by classroom staff (Rimm-Kaufman and Pianta 2000). Prior research suggests that ECE teachers' beliefs about how best to prepare children for formal schooling are likely to influence their classroom practices and therefore children's experiences in early learning programs (Duncan et al. 2007; Fang 1996; Kagan 1992; Pajares 1992; Stipek and Byler 1997; Vartuli 1999).

However, it is unclear whether early learning educators' belief systems about the skills children should have when they begin kindergarten vary across ECE settings and the extent to which there is agreement between the belief systems of ECE educators and their counterparts who teach at the kindergarten level. There is also little information about how teacher belief systems vary with the amount of education the educator has obtained. Therefore, an examination of teacher belief systems and practices by program type, teacher education, and teaching level can help us better understand how early learning programs vary in their approach to preparing children for the transition to formal schooling and whether there is a correspondence in belief systems between ECE and kindergarten educators.

S. Lara-Cinisomo (✉)
College of Education, Child and Family Studies, University of North Carolina,
9201 University City Blvd., Charlotte, NC, USA
e-mail: slaracin@uncc.edu

D. M. Laverick, M. R. Jalongo (eds.), *Transitions to Early Care and Education,*
Educating the Young Child 4, DOI 10.1007/978-94-007-0573-9_9,
© Springer Science+Business Media B.V. 2011

To examine these issues, we use data from a diverse set of programs serving preschool children from low-income and linguistic minority backgrounds. These data were collected as part of the Los Angeles: Exploring Children's Early Learning Settings (LA ExCELS) study in Los Angeles County. We explore how early education teachers' beliefs about preparing children for kindergarten may vary in different types of early education settings, namely public centers, private centers, and licensed family child care (FCC) homes, and for different levels of teacher education. In addition, since children in our study were followed from their ECE settings to their kindergarten program, we are also able to consider differences in educators' belief systems by teaching level, i.e., ECE program teachers versus kindergarten teachers.

Specifically, we seek to answer the following research questions:

1. What are the beliefs of early educators in public centers, private centers, and family based programs about how best to prepare children for kindergarten?
2. Are there differences in beliefs between early childhood educators and kindergarten teachers?
3. Is teacher education associated with differences in beliefs about kindergarten preparation and do patterns related to education vary when teaching level (ECE versus kindergarten) is taken into account?

To set the stage for our study, in the next section we briefly review relevant prior research on the role of teacher belief systems in preparing children for kindergarten entry. We then describe our data and methods and present our results. We conclude the chapter with a discussion of the implications of our findings.

The Role of Teacher Belief Systems in Preparing Children for Formal Schooling[1]

Numerous studies have shown the cognitive and emotional benefits of preschool attendance for kindergarten readiness and later school success (e.g., Gormley 2007; Shonkoff and Phillips 2000). However, relatively few studies have focused on the role of teacher belief systems in helping children prepare for kindergarten. Teacher beliefs about the important elements of school readiness are critical to the structure of the program and are believed to be associated with quality of care and children's subsequent academic performance (Duncan et al. 2007; Fang 1996; Kagan 1992; Pajares 1992; Stipek and Byler 1997; Vartuli 1999).

Previous studies show a range of belief systems exist among teachers about what children need to have to get ready for school (Lee and Ginsburg 2007; Rimm-Kaufman and Pianta 2000). These beliefs vary among preschool and kindergarten teachers about *what* children need to get ready for school and *how* to teach children

---

[1] This section draws on previously published studies by Lara-Cinisomo et al. 2008, 2009.

those skills (Foulks and Morrow 1989; Hains et al. 1989; Piotrkowski et al. 2000). For example, early childhood educators are more likely to report problem solving as a key feature of school readiness, while kindergarten teachers more often emphasize appropriate school behavior (Lin et al. 2003). Interestingly, both groups of teachers consistently place academic skills at or near the bottom of their readiness priorities (Currie 2001; Lin et al. 2003; Wesley and Buyusse 2003). Hains et al. (1989) found that, across academic and socioemotional domains, preschool teachers have significantly higher expectations for school readiness than do kindergarten teachers.

Given the breadth of research on teacher belief systems, there is surprisingly little information on belief systems among teachers from different early childhood education settings (e.g., private, public, and family-based programs). The research on belief systems among early childhood educators often examines center-based care alone, and studies that include family-based care lump all caregivers into a single category (NICHD Early Child Care Research Network 2002; Stipek and Byler 1997).

However, three recent studies based on data from the LA ExCELS study add to the limited literature (Fuligni et al. 2009; Lara-Cinisomo et al. 2008, 2009). In a qualitative study based on focus-groups discussions, Lara-Cinisomo et al. (2008) examined belief systems of educators from a range of early learning settings including from public and private preschools and home-based programs. The investigators found numerous commonalities across settings. Their study showed that teachers believed that an ecological approach to preparing a child for school is necessary. Additionally, teachers believed that children need to be ready emotionally (confident, motivated), physically (healthy with good motor skills), and cognitively (alphabet, numbers and problem-solving skills), and have good social skills that will allow the child to get along with others. At the parent level, teachers noted that parents need to provide a stimulating home environment that promotes learning and that parents need to prepare the child for the transition from home to school. At the teacher level, participants said that teacher–parent relationships were also important in preparing a child for kindergarten. This ecological approach supports previous work by Rimm-Kaufman and Pianta (2000), which acknowledges the various factors needed to help the child transition successfully to formal schooling.

A second study highlighted the specific teaching domains that teachers believed to be important when preparing preschoolers for kindergarten (Lara-Cinisomo et al. 2009). The study revealed great variation within center-based programs and across center and family-based care. Teachers from private, public, and family-based programs were equally aware of the key early learning experiences that are important to children's school readiness—the same kinds that have been found to predict high-quality care (Maxwell et al. 2001; McMullen et al. 2006; Stipek and Byler 1997), such as positive caregiver-child interactions; safety within the learning environment; and stimulating learning opportunities (Adams and Rohacek 2002; Magnuson et al. 2004).

Furthermore, the study identified three dimensions of classroom experiences as important for children getting ready for kindergarten: teacher–child interactions, learning environment, and learning opportunities. However, when looking at factors that make up these three dimensions, variation within and across program types was revealed. The authors suggest that personal attributes, such as attitudes about child development, may be more likely to generate differences between the philosophies of family- and center-care providers than would differences in education and training. In fact, others have found that teacher attitudes, rather than training, were related to teacher behaviors, such as encouraging children and providing indirect guidance (Berk 1985; Kontos et al. 1996), although those with more formal training are more likely to both endorse and engage in more developmentally appropriate practice (Bredekamp and Copple 1997; File and Gullo 2002; McMullen 1999; McMullen and Alat 2002; Snider and Fu 1990; Vartuli 1999).

A third study used quantitative teacher questionnaires about teachers' education, professional development, and mentoring to explore the effects of different patterns of training in diverse early educators (Fuligni et al. 2009). That study used a person-centered approach to identify patterns of education, training, and mentorship to illustrate how early educators may vary not only with respect to levels of education, but also with respect to the amount of supervision and monitoring they receive to support their educational practice. The study identified four groups of professional development patterns (low professional development and low monitoring, low professional development with high monitoring, college level education with no child development training, and bachelor's level education with monitoring) and found that the most highly trained group was made up of educators in all three program types (public, private, and FCC). Educators in the two highest professional development groups held beliefs about children that were most "modern" or democratic, espousing beliefs such as "Children should be allowed to disagree with their parents," and disagreeing with statements like "The major goal of education is to put basic information into the minds of children." These types of beliefs could be considered to be more child-centered and suggest that higher levels of teacher education may influence beliefs.

What early childhood educators believe has important implications for children's early learning experiences, including classroom climate and quality and ultimately children's transitions into kindergarten. Given that children may experience a range of early learning settings, it is important that we understand what caregivers in those various settings believe about what children should experience prior to entering kindergarten.

A number of studies have examined the successful transition from ECE programs to kindergarten (Ramey et al. 1998; Meisels and Liaw 1993; NICHD Early Child Care Research Network 2003; Ladd and Price 1987), with a small number focusing on teachers' perspectives on children's readiness to transition to kindergarten (Birch and Ladd 1998; Rimm-Kaufman et al. 2000) and practices teachers implement to help children transition to kindergarten (Early et al. 1999; Pianta et al. 1999). Our study considers the transition to kindergarten in the context of the beliefs of the teachers of a set of children at risk in their progression from diverse ECE programs into kindergarten. By comparing the belief systems of these educators, we can consider how children's educational experiences may be affected as they encounter the different educational settings.

Data and Measures

The LA ExCELS study is a longitudinal study designed to assess the early education experiences of 3- to 5-year-old children from low-income families in Los Angeles County, California. Children were recruited at the start of the academic year when the child was 3 years old or turning age 4 (i.e., two years prior to kindergarten eligibility) in three types of ECE settings—public center-based programs such as Head Start (Public); private center-based programs including church-based programs (Private); and licensed home-based family child care programs (FCC). Participating children were followed for three years, until the spring of their kindergarten year, and the early education programs they attended were observed each year. In addition, a comparison group of children not enrolled in any formal type of care was recruited (not presented here).

This study is based on 103 ECE teachers and 57 kindergarten teachers. The vast majority of teachers were female (94%). The ECE teachers come from 42 public, 44 private, and 17 family child care programs. Eighty-five percent of ECE teachers possessed at least an associate's degree and 93% of kindergarten teachers had at least a bachelor's degree.

ECE and kindergarten teachers responded to a self-administered questionnaire that included questions about their personal backgrounds and training, as well as their beliefs about the work they do. We were interested in analyzing teacher beliefs about how children should be taught and teacher practices in preparing children for schooling. To assess these beliefs, we relied on two scales described below.

Beliefs About Early Childhood Education We used a nine-item scale designed to assess teachers' beliefs about how young children should be taught including items regarding child-centered approaches (e.g., "Children should be allowed to select many of their own activities from a variety of learning areas that the teacher has prepared") and teachers' beliefs about using more academic practices (e.g., "Children should learn to form letters correctly on a printed page"). This scale has been used by others including the Head Start Family and Child Experiences Survey (FACES) and in other research by the authors using data from LA ExCELS (Fuligni et al. 2009; Zill et al. 2003). Scoring was based on a 5-point scale ranging from "strongly disagree" to "strongly agree." Items were summed, with five items reverse coded so a higher score indicates agreement with child-directed and developmentally appropriate practices. After averaging across the nine items, scores ranged from 2.33 to 4.89 ($M=3.57$, $SD=56$). Cronbach's alpha indicated reasonable internal consistency at 0.63.

Beliefs About Preparation for School This eight-item scale measured teachers' beliefs about practices in preparing children for elementary school. Questions focused on a range of settings including home activities and preschool activities, such as "Parents should make their children know the alphabet before they start kindergarten" and "Attending preschool (for example, nursery or pre-kindergarten) is very important for success in kindergarten." This scale has also been previously reported by the authors from this study (Fuligni et al. 2009). Responses based on a 5-point scale were averaged for a total score. Average scores ranged from 2.38 to 5.00 (M=4.03, SD=0.64), with higher scores indicating more agreement with beliefs about the importance of school preparation prior to entering kindergarten. Cronbach's alpha indicated acceptable internal consistency at 0.74.

Results

The following analyses employ teachers' scores on the two beliefs scales described above—beliefs about early childhood education and beliefs about school preparation—as outcomes. To address our research questions, we compared the average scores for the two beliefs scales by ECE program type and across teacher type defined by teaching level and education. We also conducted analyses of variance to compare averages on each of our outcomes using SPSS.

What Are the Beliefs of Early Educators in Public, Private, and Family-Based Programs About How Best to Prepare Children for Kindergarten?

Table 9.1 reports means on the two belief scales for ECE teachers in total and separately for the three program types. In general, ECE teachers held beliefs about ECE that tended toward favoring child-directed activities over more structured teacher-directed activities. However, averages indicated beliefs only slightly above a neutral attitude toward a mild agreement with child-centered statements. Means on the beliefs about school preparation scale tended to be higher, indicating stronger beliefs among all teachers in the importance of early academic activities and preparation before kindergarten. No significant differences in beliefs were found between ECE teachers in the three different program types for either of the belief scales. A two-group comparison between public and family child care teachers on the ECE scale where the gap is the largest also did not yield a significant difference.

Table 9.1 Teacher beliefs among ECE teachers by program type

Program type	Belief scale mean (*SD*)	
	Early childhood education	School preparation
Public (*n*=42)	3.81 (0.52)	3.95 (0.74)
Private (*n*=44)	3.72 (0.60)	4.05 (0.55)
Family (*n*=17)	3.56 (0.52)	3.99 (0.66)
Total (*n*=103)	3.73 (0.56)	4.00 (0.64)

Table 9.2 Teacher beliefs by teaching level

Teaching level	Belief scale mean (SD)	
	Early childhood education	School preparation
ECE (n=103)	3.73 (0.56)	4.00 (0.64)
Kindergarten (n=57)	3.27 (0.44)	4.08 (0.62)
Total (n=160)	3.56 (0.56)	4.03 (0.64)

Are There Differences in Beliefs Between Early Childhood Educators and Kindergarten Teachers?

Table 9.2 compares ECE teachers to kindergarten teachers in their belief systems. The results indicate that ECE teachers hold more child-centered beliefs about early childhood education than kindergarten teachers do. Furthermore, kindergarten teachers reported slightly higher beliefs about the importance of school preparation than ECE teachers. To determine whether these differences were significant, we also conducted an analysis of variance to compare means by teaching level (ECE versus kindergarten). The results indicate that these differences are statistically significant for beliefs regarding early childhood education by teaching level (F (1, 158)$=29.29$, $p<0.001$) but not for the school preparation belief scale (results not shown).

Is Teacher Education Associated with Differences in Beliefs about Kindergarten Preparation and Do Patterns Related to Education Vary When Teaching Level (ECE Versus Kindergarten) is Taken into Account?

To answer this question, we first explored averages in the two belief scales by highest level of education for all teachers, ECE and kindergarten, combined. With regard to ECE beliefs, as shown in Table 9.3, teachers with an associate's degree

Table 9.3 Teacher beliefs by teacher education

Teacher education	Belief scale mean (SD)	
	Early childhood education	School preparation
Highest education level		
No degree (n=33)	3.56 (0.57)	4.10 (0.63)
AA (n=30)	3.83 (0.64)	3.99 (0.65)
BA (n=58)	3.49 (0.55)	3.98 (0.66)
Master or higher (n=35)	3.50 (0.48)	4.04 (0.63)
Other (n=4)	3.33 (0.40)	4.34 (0.45)
Total (n=160)	3.56 (0.56)	4.03 (0.64)

tended toward more child-centered beliefs compared to teachers with less or more formal education. An analysis of variance on averages indicated that none of these differences were statistically significant at the 0.05 level or lower, however. In contrast, teachers at all education levels highly endorsed more early academic activities and preparation before kindergarten; no significant differences related to teachers' education level were found for this scale.

Finally, we explored whether teacher education effects were similar or different when teaching level was included in the analysis. That regression analysis showed no independent effect of teacher education after controlling for the teaching level (results not shown). Teaching level is significant only for the early childhood education scale, similar to what we find when we separately examine these two stratifying variables in Tables 9.2 and 9.3. Thus, the finding of higher scores for ECE teachers on beliefs about early education is consistent across levels of teacher education.

Discussion

This analysis has examined differences in educators belief systems about approaches to early childhood education and the importance of providing early learning opportunities before children enter kindergarten. Using data from the LA ExCELS study, we have considered differences among ECE teachers based upon their setting, finding no significant differences in the belief systems that guide teachers based on whether they are based in public or private center-based settings or in family child care home-based settings. In terms of preparation for elementary schooling, we found that, in general, these early childhood educators strongly endorse the importance of multiple sources of school preparation including preschool and parenting engagement in providing children with academic activities. Furthermore, these ECE teachers believe to a moderate degree that early learning experiences should be child-directed and contextualized. These results contribute to what is otherwise a sparse literature base examining the differences in belief systems across ECE settings and are consistent with prior research by the authors using qualitative and quantitative data on other dimensions of belief systems from LA ExCELS (Fuligni et al. 2009; Lara-Cinisomo et al. 2008, 2009).

Because children in LA ExCELS are followed into their kindergarten program and data were collected from those teachers as well, we have an opportunity to contrast the belief systems for ECE teachers serving a group of children primarily from low-income and linguistic minority backgrounds with those of the kindergarten teachers that subsequently served the same children. Here we find that there is a significant difference in the orientation of these two groups of teachers, notably with respect to their views regarding *how* children should be educated before they enter formal schooling. In particular, according to the early childhood education scale, the ECE teachers adopt a more child-directed approach in their beliefs regarding early education, whereas the kindergarten teachers share a more structured and teacher-centered approach. Note that teachers at both levels are responding to questions about approaches to early education which suggests that kindergarten teachers would apply the approach they likely use in a kindergarten classroom to a classroom serving children one or two years younger.

The differences observed in belief systems between ECE and kindergarten teachers, especially regarding approaches to early childhood education, may stem from differences in their education levels as kindergarten teachers typically are required to have a bachelor's degree, whereas in California, as in many other states, teachers in early education programs do not have any specific degree requirement beyond a high school diploma according to state licensing requirements and only Head Start, among publicly subsidized programs in the state, requires any type of post-secondary degree (Karoly et al. 2007). However, our analysis shows that there are no significant differences in either of the belief scales we examined related to teacher education level. Moreover, when we controlled for educational differences, the contrast between ECE and kindergarten teachers in the early childhood education scale remained significant.

The difference found in the orientation of ECE teachers versus kindergarten teachers on the early childhood education scale merits further exploration. To do so, we examined the mean scores by teacher level for each of the nine items that make up the early childhood education belief scale (see Table 9.4). A test of the differences in the two groups on each item shows that there are significant differences in five items, with differences as large as a scale point on the five-point scale. This more detailed analysis highlights the ways in which ECE teachers more strongly

Table 9.4 Item-level mean scores for ECE beliefs scale by teaching level

ECE beliefs items	Teaching level		
	ECE	Kindergarten	F
Children should be allowed to select many of their own activities from a variety of learning areas that the teacher has prepared (writing, science center, etc.)	4.70	4.02	22.32***
Children should be allowed to cut their own shapes, perform their own steps in an experiment, and plan their own creative drama, art, and writing activities	4.60	4.23	8.88**
Children should be involved in establishing rules for the classroom	4.51	4.35	1.26
Children should be instructed in recognizing the single letters of the alphabet, isolated from words	3.51	4.07	6.69*
Children should learn to color within predefined lines[a]	2.57	3.56	22.55***
Children should learn to form letters correctly on a printed page[a]	2.74	4.46	72.65***
Children should dictate stories to the teacher[a]	4.26	4.25	0.01
Children should know their letter sounds before they learn to read[a]	4.03	3.81	1.27
Children should form letters correctly before they are allowed to create a story[a]	1.65	1.54	0.38

*$p<0.05$; **$p<0.01$; ***$p<0.001$
[a] Items reverse coded in ECE belief scale

advocate for children to guide their own learning experiences and to be exposed to academic content through meaningful activities rather than in abstract formats. For example, ECE teachers more strongly endorse the view that "children should be allowed to select many of their own activities from a variety of learning areas that the teacher has prepared" and "children should be allowed to cut their own shapes, perform their own steps in an experiment, and plan their own creative drama, art, and writing activities," whereas kindergarten teachers feel more strongly that "children should be instructed in recognizing the single letters of the alphabet, isolated from words." Kindergarten teachers also place more emphasis on performing tasks the "right way" such as coloring within predefined lines and correctly forming letters on a printed page, rather than allowing more freedom of expression.

These differences in orientation suggest that children making the transition from early education programs to kindergarten will face differences in the orientation their teachers have toward learning. Children are likely to be experiencing more teacher-directed activities as they move into kindergarten classrooms and to be engaged in more academic learning that may be separated from content and experiential connections. Considering these differences in teaching orientation, we may question whether children are ready to make this transition in learning approaches at this age. In particular, this transition may be more challenging for subgroups of children whose learning styles and degree of school readiness are less compatible with this decontextualized approach.

Additional research is needed to connect these findings with children's actual experiences in ECE and kindergarten programs. Connecting teachers' reported beliefs to their observed teaching practices could provide further insight into just how similar or different these educators are. For instance, we might predict that endorsement of child-centered beliefs may more readily translate into child-centered practices in some settings (possibly family child care programs) than others (such as public kindergarten classrooms) depending on the autonomy of the teacher within the program.

Another question that could be addressed through further analysis of this data set is how individual children's experiences with different ECE and kindergarten teachers holding similar or different belief systems may affect those children's experiences in the transition to kindergarten. Analysis of children's trajectories of learning and adjustment over this period could provide additional insight into the role of these teacher beliefs in supporting consistent learning experiences across the school transition.

We must note some limitations to our findings. In particular, although the study is groundbreaking in its inclusion of diverse types of ECE programs, the sample size is relatively small, particularly with respect to the family child care providers. Although all ECE programs recruited in the first year of the study served families from low-income backgrounds, the family child care providers who volunteered to participate represent a relatively professional group of educators. They do not accurately represent the population of family child care providers in the Los Angeles area. Furthermore, the study sample as a whole reflects the great diversity of early childhood education and care options in the Los Angeles area but may not generalize to other regions of the United States. Nevertheless, the longitudinal study procedures resulted in the sampling of increasingly large numbers of teachers each year, resulting in a diverse group of early educators contributing to these findings.

Ultimately, since we did not find strong associations between teacher education and their belief systems, we may want to ask whether the education setting (ECE versus kindergarten) influences beliefs about early education approaches, or whether teachers' belief systems actually guided their career choices into particular early education settings. Although we are unable to answer this question with the current data, our findings should be used to inform discussions about when children are developmentally ready to encounter decontextualized learning, and to guide approaches to supporting children's transitions from various early learning settings into kindergarten.

Acknowledgments The authors are grateful to the National Institute of Child and Human Development (R01 HD046063-01) for their support of this research. The authors would also like to thank Carollee Howes, Principal Investigator of the LA ExCELS, for her support of this research.

References

Adams, G., & Rohacek, M. (2002). More than a work support? Issues around integrating child development goals into the child care subsidy system. *Early Childhood Research Quarterly, 17*(4), 418–440.

Barnett, W. S., & Yarosz, D. J. (2007). *Who goes to preschool and why does it matter? Preschool Policy Matters, 15*. New Brunswick, NJ: National Institute for Early Education Research, policy brief 15, November.

Berk, L. E. (1985). Relationship of caregiver education to child-oriented attitudes, job satisfaction, and behaviors toward children. *Child Care Quarterly, 14*(2), 103–129.

Birch, S. H. & Ladd, G. W. (1998). The teacher-child relationship and children's early school adjustment, *Journal of School Psychology, 35*(1), 61–79.

Bredekamp, S., & Copple, C. (Eds.) (1997). *Developmentally appropriate practice in early childhood programs* (revised edn.). Washington, DC: National Association for the Education of Young Children.

Currie, J. (2001). Early childhood education programs. *Journal of Economic Perspectives, 15*(2), 213–238.

Duncan, G. J., Dowsett, C. J., Claessens, A., Magnuson, K., Huston, A. C., Klebanov, P., Pagani, L., Feinstein, L., Engel, M., Brooks-Gunn, J., Sexton, H., Duckworth, K., & Japel, C. (2007). School readiness and later achievement. *Developmental Psychology, 43*(6), 1428–1446.

Early, D. M., Pianta, R. C., & Cox, M. J. (1999). Kindergarten teachers and classrooms: A transition context. *Early Education and Development, 10*(1), 25–46.

Fang, Z. (1996). A review of research on teacher beliefs and practices. *Educational Research, 38*(1), 47–65.

File, N., & Gullo, D. F. (2002). A comparison of early childhood and elementary education students' beliefs about primary classroom teaching practices. *Early Childhood Research Quarterly, 17*(1), 126–137.

Foulks, B., & Morrow, R. D. (1989). Academic survival skills for the child at risk for school failure. *Journal of Educational Research, 82*(3), 158–165.

Fuligni, A. S., Howes, C., Lara-Cinisomo, S., & Karoly, L. (2009). Diverse pathways in early childhood professional development: An exploration of early educators' in public preschools, private preschools, and family child care homes, *Early Education & Development, 20*(3), 507–526.

Gormley, W. T. (2007). Early childhood care and education: Lessons and puzzles. *Journal of Policy Analysis and Management, 26*(3), 633–671.

Hains, A. H., Fowler, S. A, Schwartz, I. S., Kottwitz, E., & Rosenkoetter, S. (1989). A comparison of preschool and kindergarten teacher expectations for school readiness. *Early Childhood Research Quarterly, 4,* 75–88.

Kagan, D. M. (1992). Implications of research on teacher belief. *Educational Psychology, 27*(1), 65–90.

Karoly, L. A., Reardon, E. & Cho, M. (2007). *Early care and education in the Golden State: Publicly funded programs serving California's preschool-age children.* Santa Monica, CA: RAND Corporation.

Kontos, S., Howes, C., & Galinsky, E. (1996). Does training make a difference to quality in family child care? *Early Childhood Research Quarterly, 11*(4), 427–445.

Ladd, G. W. & Price, J. M. (1987). Predicting children's social and school adjustment following the transition from preschool to kindergarten. *Child Development, 58*(5), 1168–1189.

Lara-Cinisomo, S., Fuligni, A. S., Ritchie, S., Howes, C., & Karoly, L. (2008). Getting ready for school: An examination of early childhood educators' belief systems. *Early Childhood Education Journal, 35*(4), 343–349.

Lara-Cinisomo, S., Fuligni, A. S., Daughtery, L., Howes, C., & Karoly, L. (2009). A qualitative study of early childhood educators' beliefs about key preschool classroom experiences. *Early Childhood Research & Practice, 11*(1).

Lee, J. S., & Ginsburg, H. P. (2007). What is appropriate mathematics education for four-year-olds? *Journal of Educational Research, 5*(1), 2–31.

Lin, H., Lawrence, F. R., & Gorrell, J. (2003). Kindergarten teachers' views of children's readiness for school. *Early Childhood Research Quarterly, 18,* 225–237.

Magnuson, K. A., Meyers, M. K., Ruhm, C. J., & Waldfogel, J. (2004). Inequality in preschool education and school readiness. *American Educational Research Journal, 41*(1), 115–157.

Maxwell, K. L., McWilliam, R. A., Hemmeter, M. L., Ault, M. J., & Schuster, J. W. (2001). Predictors of developmentally appropriate classroom practices in kindergarten through third grade. *Early Childhood Research Quarterly, 16*(4), 431–452.

McMullen, M. B. (1999). Characteristics of teachers who talk the DAP talk and walk the DAP walk. *Journal of Research in Childhood Education, 13,* 216–230.

McMullen, M. B., & Alat, K. (2002). Education matters in the nurturing of the beliefs of preschool caregivers and teachers. *Early Childhood Research & Practice, 4*(2). http://www.ecrp.uiuc.edu/v4n2/mcmullen.html

McMullen, M. B., Elicker, J., Goetze, G., Huang, H. H., Lee, S. M., Mathers, C., et al. (2006). Using collaborative assessment to examine the relationship between self-reported beliefs and the documentable practices of preschool teachers. *Early Childhood Education Journal, 34*(1), 81–91.

Meisels, S. J. & Liaw, F. R. (1993). Failure in grade: Do retained students catch up? *Journal of Educational Research, 87*(2), 69–77.

NICHD Early Child Care Research Network (2002). Early child care and children's development prior to school entry: Results from the NICHD study of early child care. *American Educational Research Journal, 39,* 133–164.

NICHD Early Child Care Research Network (2003). Does quality of child care affect child outcomes at age 4 ½? *Developmental Psychology, 39,* 451–469.

Pajares, M. F. (1992). Teachers' beliefs and educational research: Cleaning up a messy construct. *Review of Educational Research, 62*(3), 307–332.

Pianta, R. C., Cox, M. J., Taylor, L., & Early, D. (1999). Kindergarten teachers' practices related to the transition to school: Results of a national survey. *Elementary School Journal, 100,* 71–86.

Piotrkowski, C. S., Botsko, M., & Matthews, E. (2000). Parents' and teachers' beliefs about children's school readiness in a high-need community. *Early Childhood Research Quarterly, 15*(4), 537–558.

Ramey, S. L., Lanzi, R. G., Phillips, M. M., & Ramey, C. T. (1998). Perspectives of former Head Start children and their parents on school and the transition to school. *Elementary School Journal, 98*(4), 311–327.

Rimm-Kaufman, S. E., & Pianta, R. C. (2000). An ecological perspective on the transition to kindergarten: A theoretical framework to guide empirical research. *Journal of Applied Developmental Psychology, 21,* 491–511.

Rimm-Kaufman, S. E., Pianta, R. C., & Cox, M. J. (2000). Teachers' judgments of problems in the transition to kindergarten. *Early Childhood Research Quarterly, 15,* 147–166.

Shonkoff, J. P., & Phillips, D. A. (Eds.) (2000). *From neurons to neighborhoods: The science of early childhood development.* Washington, DC: National Academy Press.

Snider, M. H., & Fu, V. R. (1990). The effects of specialized education and job experience on early childhood teachers. *Early Childhood Research Quarterly, 5*(1), 69–78.

Stipek, D. J., & Byler, P. (1997). Early childhood education teachers: Do they practice what they preach? *Early Childhood Research Quarterly, 12*(3), 305–325.

Vartuli, S. (1999). How early childhood teacher beliefs vary across grade level. *Early Childhood Research Quarterly, 14*(4), 489–514.

Wesley, P. W., & Buyusse, V. (2003). Making meaning of school readiness in schools and communities. *Early Childhood Research Quarterly, 18*(3), 351–375.

Zill, N., Resnick, G., Kim, K., O'Donnell, K., Sorongon, A., McKey, R. H., et al. (2003). *Head Start FACES 2000: A whole-child perspective on program performance.* Washington, DC: Department of Health and Human Services.

Chapter 10
The School Readiness of Preschoolers from Urban Backgrounds

Regena F. Nelson

Introduction

Recent studies on the school readiness of urban preschoolers have focused on racial differences in performance on standardized assessments. A critical factor in the performance gap between children from different racial backgrounds is a teacher's ability to work effectively with families from racially diverse backgrounds. In this study, three veteran preschool directors in programs that serve children from minority and low-income backgrounds in an urban area will share their perceptions of this problem and ways to address it. This study used a focus group method to determine: (1) the issues teachers from White, middle-class backgrounds face when working with children from economically and racially diverse backgrounds; (2) the professional development models that are most effective in addressing these issues and changing teachers' practices; and (3) the impact of changes in teachers' practices on the school readiness of preschoolers from urban backgrounds.

Background

Barbarin and Crawford (2007) described a troubling dynamic between boys from African-American backgrounds and teachers from white backgrounds in preschool. Observers on their research team shared concerns about interactions they frequently witnessed in the classrooms. African-American boys were being isolated from group activities and labeled as "bad" by teachers and their peers. The boys' response to this stigmatization was to act out more, thus validating the label they had been given. The observers noted that as their behavior problems increased, their school performance decreased.

R. F. Nelson (✉)
Department of Teaching, Learning & Educational Studies, Western Michigan University, 1903 W. Michigan Avenue, Kalamazoo, MI, USA
e-mail: nelsonr@wmich.edu

D. M. Laverick, M. R. Jalongo (eds.), *Transitions to Early Care and Education*, Educating the Young Child 4, DOI 10.1007/978-94-007-0573-9_10,
© Springer Science+Business Media B.V. 2011

The authors also shared that the observers visited other multiracial classrooms where all children were engaged in group activities and no one was isolated. The teachers valued everyone's contributions and unique qualities. This led them to believe that the difference in classrooms was due to the teachers, not the children. They wondered what caused the differences in how the white teachers interacted with their multiracial students:

> Why are these teachers so successful at treating all children in their classes equitably? Is it solely their personal qualities that make the difference? Did these teachers graduate from a teacher education program that prepared them to work with children from a wide range of cultural backgrounds? How might administrative supports be playing a role? These are questions worth pursuing in the future. (p. 24)

Statistics state that minority children comprise approximately 30% of all children in US schools and are projected to increase to over 50% by the year 2050 (Banks 2001). As an early childhood teacher educator, I also wondered if we were preparing White female teachers in our program to interact positively with all children. Throughout our program they have field experiences in urban, multiracial, and economically mixed school districts. They discuss and debate the effects of poverty, gender, and ethnicity on educational opportunities and performance. They develop individualized behavior plans during their internships. Overall, they graduate feeling positive about working in urban schools. My belief is that we are preparing them well. This study examined the influence of personal experiences, professional development, and administrative support on how teachers prepare preschoolers in urban schools for the transition to kindergarten.

Literature Review

As stated earlier, an important exercise in pre-service teacher programs is to provide opportunities for students to learn about other cultures and how cultural differences influence educational opportunities and expectations for academic performance.

Pappamihiel (2004) describes how she works with preservice teachers to increase their understanding of cultural differences and how to address them in the classroom. She found that preservice teachers focused on finding the similarities among cultures and minimizing the differences among them. However, children from other cultures may see this approach as ignoring the uniqueness they bring to the classroom. Therefore, she proposes that teachers affirm children's culture by increasing their awareness of different cultures and using the information to teach children how to interact with each other in culturally appropriate ways.

Helping teachers feel comfortable and confident with this approach requires a large amount of support. Jacobson (2000) described how she developed an anti-bias support-supervision group for teachers of young children. In this group, teachers examined their racial beliefs, and how their beliefs influenced their practice. The ten teachers who participated in the group for 20 weeks found it extremely helpful. They were able to able to see how some of their personal issues about race affected how they viewed children of color. The group provided a place for them to resolve these issues so they could improve their interactions with the children. Teachers who participated in the group were more likely to accept long-term teaching positions in programs that serve children of color.

Grieshaber and Cannella (2001) report that many teachers in multicultural classrooms choose these settings because of their experiences in multicultural communities. Teachers in multicultural settings shared that they have had internship, work, and educational experiences in programs with people of color. These experiences had a significant impact on how they viewed themselves and other people. Once they learned the culturally appropriate ways to interact in these communities, they were able to form relationships that helped them feel a part of the community.

It is important to note that each culture has different norms and ways of interacting with each other. Therefore, teachers must gather resources on the cultures of all the children in their programs. This information can be found in books, the Internet and people in the community.

The Assembly of Alaska Native Educators (2001) created a handbook for teachers at all grade levels to guide them on how to understand and value native Alaskan traditions and culture. The handbook addresses curriculum issues and how to integrate cultural information into the classroom. Information on communication and parenting styles is explained so educators can provide a welcoming environment and encourage parent participation in the school. Teachers are urged to get involved in community events and learn more about the culture and invite people from the community into the classroom to explain cultural traditions.

Barbarin et al. (2005) conducted interviews with African-American families. The families emphasized that they value education. They understand the importance of engaging their children through written and spoken language and hold high expectations for academic success. However, as with all cultures, the stress and challenges of poverty have a negative effect on some African-American families' ability to fully participate in school activities and programs. African-American families are more involved in their children's school when barriers to participation (e.g., transportation, child care, and inconvenient meeting times) are removed. Teachers can enhance parent involvement by understanding parenting styles and how to increase continuity between home and school cultures.

Fuller et al. (1996) studied how families from Latino backgrounds use child care to understand how they prepare their children for school. The researchers reported that Latinos value continuity between home and school culture. Latino families have strong kin networks. They prefer to use relative care for child care rather than center-based child care programs. They view relative care as a way to support their cultural connections. Schools can increase Latino family engagement by acknowledging the importance of communicating in a family's native language.

A successful transition from preschool to kindergarten is a complex process. Parents need information on how to choose a school, set up times to visit schools, and what to ask during the visits. This process requires a high level of family engagement (Halladay 2009). Therefore, it is vitally important that schools use culturally sensitive methods to help parents with the process (Rous et al. 2010).

Kolozak (2004) describes a process that programs can use to determine if they are engaging diverse families in culturally sensitive ways. Educators are advised to first assess the strengths and weaknesses of their program in engaging diverse families. Then develop a plan to address the weaknesses. The steps of the plan should include (1) discussing the issues that caused the problem; (2) gathering resources to address the problem; (3) implementing a new process or program; and (4) evaluating the child care program's progress toward resolving the problem. This is a process that preschool directors can use to improve how they engage diverse families and prepare children for the transition to kindergarten.

Methods

Sample

The sample for this study is three White, female preschool center directors who have partnered with the local university to work with early childhood interns. Their centers serve economically and racially diverse populations. Director A works at the university's child care center. She has been a director for 22 years. The center enrollment is 45 toddler and preschool children. Director B works at a private child care center that has three locations. She has been a director for 31 years. The center enrollment is 80 infant, toddler, and preschool children. Director C works in a center that serves the community and residents of the local women's shelter. She has been a director for 9 years. The center enrollment is 36 infant, toddler, and preschool children.

Instrument

The focus group questions are adapted from the Sanders et al. (2007) study on how child care directors from African-American backgrounds view the use of developmentally appropriate practice (DAP) with children of color.

Part 1: Personal Background Information

- Where were you born?
- How did you come to be in Kalamazoo?
- How did you end up working in child care/preschool?

Part 2: Questions About School Readiness

- Could you please describe your beliefs about school readiness?
- What do you think is the one most important thing that should happen in your center/program every day to prepare children for school?

- How do you determine if you have prepared children for school?
- Does your program prepare all children for school?

Part 3: Questions About Professional Development

- Think of a good day at your center and a bad day at your center. What makes the difference between a good and bad day in terms of what you and the teachers do with children and families?
- What professional development opportunities do you provide for your staff to help them be effective in preparing all children for school?

Part 4: Questions About Race and Culture

- Your center/program contains children from different cultures. Do you think that what happens at this center/program, e.g., the way teachers and you relate to the kids, the way the kids are taught and cared for here is similar or different from what happens at home? How similar, how different?
- What are the challenges in educating children of color? How do you deal with the challenges?
- Is there anything you can think of that makes it beneficial to work with such a diverse group of children and families?

Procedures

All directors in the study gave their consent to participate in the focus group and have their responses analyzed and shared. The participants met for one 90-minute focus group. The researcher gave the directors questions in advance to review. The researcher asked the questions in order and allowed each person to respond. The researcher recorded the interview and took notes.

Data Analysis

The researcher reviewed the notes and highlighted responses that fit into the following categories:

- Directors' background information
- School readiness and the transition to kindergarten
- Cultural conflict issues
- Teacher attributes that are needed for working with children of color
- Professional development techniques for helping staff work well with children of color

Results

The general results of the content analysis of the directors' responses are provided below. Directors' specific responses during the focus group interviews follow.

Background

The focus group interview revealed that the directors had similar upbringings. They were all White women who grew up in mid-size towns in the Midwest. The directors had undergraduate degrees in education and chose positions in early childhood education rather than in elementary schools because there were more employment opportunities in early childhood when they graduated. The directors represent professionals at the beginning, middle, and end of their careers.

School Readiness Skills and the Transition to Kindergarten

Next, the directors shared their views about school readiness and the transition to kindergarten. They all endorsed the view that all children are ready to learn and kindergarten programs should support the development of all types of learners. In their preschool programs they reported an emphasis on developing social skills, positive approaches to learning new things, independence, initiative, and following directions.

Cultural Conflict Issues

The directors admitted that their White, Midwestern backgrounds were much different from the cultural backgrounds of the families at their centers. As a result, there were differences in behavioral expectations for routines, disciplines, and meal times. They also discussed that in some cases, the differences among family behaviors are also due to the impact of poverty and racism. In other words, some families developed certain behaviors as an adaptive response to the stressors of racism and poverty.

Positive Approaches and Strategies for Working with Children of Color

The directors agreed that the challenges that arise because of cultural conflicts can be overcome by focusing on best practices for all children. The directors believed it was important for their staff to be positive role models for children and develop nurturing relationships with each child. Although each center used a different curriculum model, the models all emphasized developmentally appropriate practices, teaching life skills and exposing children to places and events in the community.

Professional Development Techniques for Helping Staff Work Well with Children of Color

The directors believed that they were responsible for helping their staff become more effective with working with children of color. They discussed general professional development techniques, such as providing training on best practices for early childhood education and working individually with staff to improve their interactions with children. In addition, they mentioned specific training that relates to cultural conflict issues, such as attending anti-racism seminars and multicultural events in the community.

The directors' specific responses were analyzed in order to address the following research questions.

What Are the Issues White, Middle-Class Teachers Face When Working with Children from Economically and Racially Diverse Backgrounds?

The directors discussed culture conflict issues in the classroom. They acknowledged that teachers and students come from different cultural and economic backgrounds:

> African-American boys are dramatic, show-offy, and want to be center stage. That can be a problem. However, if you understand that they are imitating preachers in their community, you see it as a positive thing. (Director B)

> When I see a child acting out [I think] what is not being met? Where are they coming from? It's different for each culture. How can I relate to them and create an environment to share our cultures, so we can understand? (Director C)

Overall they were concerned about teachers' lack of knowledge about cultural traditions, norms, and parenting styles. Increasing teachers' understanding of different cultures was a top priority for the directors.

What Are the Professional Development Models That are Most Effective in Addressing These Issues and Changing Teachers' Practices?

The directors discussed the various professional development opportunities they offer their staff to improve their instruction and interactions with children. The offerings include workshops, conferences, feedback on observations, discussion at staff meetings, and on-site training sessions. One director described the anti-racism workshop she is attending with her staff and the impact it has had on their interactions with the families at her center:

> I'm lucky that we talk about [racism] openly. We are learning about it and we always bring it to the table as an issue at the center and how it affects others. I'm trained as a trainer to do anti-racism training. I'm excited that other staff are thinking about becoming trainers, too. (Director C)

Another director shares what she has learned about the effects of poverty on behavior and attempts to separate poverty issues from race issues:

> Understanding what poverty does to families [and what] living in certain communities does to families. It creates behaviors that can be criticized. We need to understand the underlying issues. These are challenges. (Director B)

What is the Impact of Changes in Teachers' Practices on Urban Preschoolers' School Readiness?

The directors in this study have programs that are accredited by NAEYC and agreed that they focus on maintaining the integrity of their program curriculum and philosophy. They believed if they are successful in accomplishing this goal then all children who leave their programs should be ready. They also voiced concerns about pressure to change their program goals to meet developmentally inappropriate expectations in the local kindergarten programs:

> We do best with staying true to the philosophy of the program and how we interact with the children. That's all we can do. We do what's best for children, not inappropriate standards. The question should be "Is school prepared for our children"? (Director A)

Another director shared that attending a center with a population that is racially diverse can also enhance school readiness skills:

> We are teaching life skills. How to get along with people who aren't like you, the children, the staff and the parents benefit. (Director C)

Recommendations and Conclusions

In conclusion, the directors believed that centers with children from culturally diverse backgrounds face challenges due to cultural conflicts. However, these challenges can be overcome through staff development and partnerships with families. Using these approaches, they have experienced many social and academic benefits of having students in their programs from diverse backgrounds.

They recommend the following approaches to other programs that want to engage families from diverse backgrounds and have a positive school transition experience for their children:

1. Hire teachers and staff that have a disposition for understanding and respecting cultural differences.

2. Implement a developmentally appropriate curriculum and continually work on improving teacher–child interactions.
3. Work with families to incorporate cultural traditions and daily practices into the curriculum.

References

Assembly of Alaska Native Educators. (2001). *Guidelines for nurturing culturally healthy youth.* Fairbanks, AL: Alaska University.

Banks, J. A. (2001). *Cultural diversity and education: Foundations, curriculum and teaching.* Boston: Allyn & Bacon.

Barbarin, O. A., & Crawford, G. M. (2007). Acknowledging and reducing stigmatization of African-American boys. *Early Developments, 11*(2), 21–24.

Barbarin, O. A., McCandies, T., Coleman, C., & Hill, N. E. (2005). Family practices and school performance of African-American children. In V. C. McLoyd, N. E. Hill, & K. A. Dodge (Eds.), *African American family life: Ecological and cultural diversity* (pp. 227–244). New York, NY: Guilford.

Fuller, B., Eggers-Pierola, C., Holloway, S. D., Liang, X., & Rambaud, M. F. (1996). Rich culture, poor markets: Why do Latino parents forgo preschooling? *Teachers College Record, 97*(3), 403–418.

Grieshaber, S., & Cannella, G. S. (2001). Personal stories: Early childhood educators and re-conceptualized identities. In S. Grieshaber & G. S. Cannella (Eds.), *Embracing identities in early childhood education: Diversity and possibilities.* (pp. 23–42). New York, NY: Teachers College Press.

Halladay, J. (2009). Our journey to kindergarten. *Teaching Tolerance, 36,* 19–22.

Jacobson, T. (2000). *Prod and pry from inside out: Ethnography of anti-bias support-supervision group for teachers of young children.* Proceedings of the Lillian Katz Symposium, Champaign, IL, 171–179.

Kolozak, K. S. (2004). Assessing your center to create a diverse staff. *Exchange, 158,* 55–58.

Pappamihiel, N. E. (2004). Hugs and smiles: Demonstrating caring in a multicultural early childhood classroom. *Early Child Development and Care, 174*(6), 539–548.

Rous, B., Hallam, R., McCormick, K., & Cox, M. (2010). Practices that support the transition to public preschool programs: Results from a national survey. *Early Childhood Research Quarterly, 25*(1), 17–32.

Sanders, K. E., Deihl, A., & Kyler, A. (2007). DAP in the 'hood: Perceptions of child care practices by African-American child care directors for children of color. *Early Childhood Research Quarterly, 22*(3), 394–406.

Chapter 11
Culture, Health, and School Readiness

An Integrated Approach to Transition

Suzanne M. Winter

Theory and Approaches for Integrating Culture, Health, and School Readiness

No Universal Definition

Currently, there is no universally accepted definition of school readiness to guide communities, teachers, and parents to ensure that children enter school prepared to achieve academic success (Dockett and Perry 2009). School readiness, from a global perspective, is a concept that begs for a comprehensive definition that can be widely embraced. Expectations for children's academic readiness and early education practices that are culturally acceptable and recommended by professionals to achieve the goal of school readiness for young children can vary from one nation to another. To examine the intersections of culture, health, and school readiness, it is critical to first examine the theoretical approaches currently in use and those with potential for creating strong foundations for effective school readiness programs and transition practices worldwide.

Academic Emphasis

With rapid globalization, nations are placing greater emphasis on academic readiness earlier in a child's life as a preparation for school. In the United States, for instance, No Child Left Behind policies have targeted early literacy and academic skills as a primary emphasis toward improving school readiness and promoting higher academic achievement (US Department of Health and Human Services 2003). Evidence does substantiate the importance of high quality environments and

S. M. Winter (✉)
Child and Adolescent Policy Research Institute, The University of Texas at San Antonio,
501 W. Durango Blvd., San Antonio, TX 78249, USA
e-mail: suzanne.winter@utsa.edu

D. M. Laverick, M. R. Jalongo (eds.), *Transitions to Early Care and Education*,
Educating the Young Child 4, DOI 10.1007/978-94-007-0573-9_11,
© Springer Science+Business Media B.V. 2011

rich experiences to promote children's language and cognitive processing skills (Lonigan et al. 2007; Mashburn 2008; Mashburn et al. 2009). However, the push toward early reading and academic skills has seemed to eclipse efforts to promote development in other critical domains, such as physical motor, social, and emotional.

Some experts have cautioned that undue emphasis on academic performance is transforming the westernized concept of "childhood" and the reality of childhood for many children as nations push to compete in the global marketplace (Ruddick 2003; Stearns 2005). Others warn that standards driven education can have unintended consequences, such as widening achievement gaps between children who are economically advantaged and disadvantaged (Darling-Hammond 2004; Kagan et al. 2005).

Balanced Curriculum

Standards driven, academically oriented approaches to school readiness have yielded little progress toward ensuring all children are prepared for formal schooling and a healthy, productive life. The result has been a push down of academic curricula to increasingly younger children who would benefit from a balanced approach to the curriculum. The overemphasis on academics has led to movement away from developmentally appropriate practices in early childhood education and the elimination of play, a key process known to facilitate children's learning. Some experts warn of an imminent crisis as children are forced into academic curricula too early. They point to research substantiating that early exposure to academic curricula does not lead to positive results. Overemphasis on academics can result in children lacking rich play and social experiences that result in important skills that are foundational for academic success. These experiences are vital to reading comprehension because vocabulary and language learned through such experience bring understanding to the meaning of written language. Lack of rich play opportunities may cripple children's creativity and problem-solving abilities. Moreover, play is essential to the development of critical social and emotional skills necessary for successful human relationships (Bodrova and Leong 2003a; Lloyd 2003; Miller and Almon 2009).

Burgeoning research is building a compelling case for the relationship between health, physical and emotional, and the cognitive aspects of children's development (Carlson et al. 2008; Webster-Stratton and Reid 2004). Such research suggests children are likely to fail to achieve academic goals unless educators actively promote children's development across all domains. Unfortunately, three recent university research studies commissioned by the Alliance for Children provide evidence suggesting that children in kindergartens across the United States are not receiving a balanced curriculum. These studies found that the curriculum for kindergartens in New York and Los Angeles study sites was overwhelmingly academic in content. On typical days, kindergartners in New York spent an average of 150 minutes daily in literacy and academic instruction. In Los Angeles, 62% of the kindergartners in the study engaged in literacy instruction over 90 minutes per day (Miller and Almon

2009). These studies substantiate that children have few opportunities for play in kindergarten, despite studies that link engagement in play to the development of thinking skills (Bodrova and Leong 2003b; Lloyd 2003).

Interdisciplinary Approaches

To ensure that culture and health have a rightful place in the school readiness paradigm, it is essential to adopt an interdisciplinary approach. Reviews of bodies of research informed by various disciplines and fields of study are needed to provide a firm foundation for understanding children's early development and learning. Broad perspectives, rather than narrow views, are critical to properly support children during formative years. Commitment to an interdisciplinary approach requires willingness to step beyond the confines of a single discipline and examine theory and practice in another. It takes firm resolve and serious commitment not only to delve into the research bases of other disciplines but also to gain a thorough understanding of discipline specific tenets and perspectives. Such a commitment is necessary to guarantee broad, balanced, and multilevel support for children's development. Interdisciplinary approaches span a range of disciplines to identify and address a full spectrum of variables that might influence school readiness. Rather than focusing narrowly on the attainment of a vertical acquisition of academic and reading skills, interdisciplinary approaches to school readiness promote a broad range of experiences and attention to enriching children's environments to stimulate optimal development and learning during preschool years.

Convergent Theoretical Perspective

The diversity of children and the worldwide obesity epidemic affecting young children necessitate careful re-evaluation of the theoretical underpinnings of early education and school readiness programs. Working from an interdisciplinary approach presents an interesting conundrum. Does one accept all theories, in total, from across the multiple disciplines informing early education and school readiness efforts? Such a broad, eclectic approach may impede arriving at consensus in the international community about core principles for improving school readiness practices, internationally. Adopting a convergent theoretical perspective may be particularly important when interdisciplinary approaches are used to inform theory and school readiness practice. Rather than simply blending theories across disciplines which results in an eclectic theoretical foundation, a convergent perspective is drawn differently. A convergent perspective seeks commonalities or points of agreement or consensus that can bridge theoretical foundations across disciplines. The resulting theoretical foundation represents a convergence of theoretical tenets drawn from across disciplines and fields of study. A convergent approach has been suggested for programs serving diverse groups of children. A convergent theoretical perspective is respectful of diversity. It is derived from multiple theories and this is thought to enhance widespread application. Yet, the consonance resulting from this convergence creates unity that facilitates consensus in thought and action. Common tenets drawn from across disciplines synthesize research and practice in school readiness. Application of convergent theory appears to have potential to enhance collaboration across fields to improve the school readiness of children worldwide. Further, application of a convergent perspective fits well with the current trend toward interdisciplinary research, problem solving, and policymaking (Mallory 1994; Winter 2007).

Ecological Approaches

A common theoretical plank that can be identified across several disciplines is ecological thinking. Ecological perspectives offer many points of convergence in thinking across fields. In education and the social sciences, an ecological model posited by Urie Bronfenbrenner has been widely embraced to explain child development and undergird practice (Bronfenbrenner and Morris 1998). An advantage of the ecological theory Bronfenbrenner posits is that it acknowledges that children are in constant interaction with different layers of sociocultural contexts that surround them, beginning with influences in the home and neighborhood. Factors in the community and beyond, while less direct, can, nevertheless, exert an impact on children's development and school readiness. The idea underlying application of ecological approaches is that school readiness strategies can be targeted to affect different layers of factors where additional resources and support might improve children's school readiness (Dockett and Perry 2008, 2009).

In public health and the medical community, ecological models are also familiar and widely used to support pragmatic efforts to improve the health of children and families. Moreover, some researchers in public health have taken the ecological approach a step further to examine the dynamics between societal systems in each sociocontextual layer of influence surrounding individuals in a population. The advantage this extension of the approach offers is that researchers can investigate the nature of the interactions between various systems and study the impact of the presence or absence of interactions among systems on specific groups or individuals (Trochim et al. 2006).

In summary, ecological approaches seem congruous with current school readiness goals in the United States and across the globe. According to the National Institutes of Health and Human Development, research is needed to examine school readiness and health promotion strategies in tandem. The major goal of this approach is to improve the trajectories of children, especially children at high risk of school failure (Eunice Kennedy Shriver National Institute of Child Health and Human Development 2009). Ecological approaches appear to have potential for providing a common framework of thought to promote an integrative stance toward culture, health, and school readiness. These approaches can serve as common ground to facilitate collaboration across fields and disciplines. The remainder of this chapter will examine the interplay of these constructs and draw implications for practice.

Culture and School Readiness

Impact of Sociocultural Contexts

From an international perspective, a critical area of research is examining the role culture plays in understanding and conceptualizing the construct of school readiness. Families from different racial and cultural backgrounds have similarities and differences in the socialization goals they set for children and their expectations about school readiness. Awareness and acknowledgement of the goals and expectations of parents is essential to ensure that school readiness programs and policies are culturally responsive to diverse families (Achhpal et al. 2007). The ecology surrounding children and influencing their growth, development, and behavior varies from one society to another across the globe. Moreover, few cultural environments are static. Stability often gives way to instability as cultures react to internal and external changes. Changes to the political, economic, and social fabric of societies can affect child rearing, schooling, and other cultural patterns. Conflict, environmental disasters, immigration, and urbanization can result in major changes for children and their families. Rapid globalization is also changing the landscape of the world's population. Demographic shifts and technological advances are resulting in children being reared in more diverse populations. Increasingly, societal modernization occurs as previously less-developed countries move toward industrialization. Undeniably, the sociocultural context for many children is shifting and some believe that the ecology of childhood itself is changing in response to the myriad of social and cultural changes occurring (LeVine 2002; Marsella 2009).

Yet, little is known about the effects that living in dynamic sociocultural contexts might have on children's development and school readiness. Cross-cultural studies are essential for gaining insight into the impact of culture on children (LeVine 2002). Some researchers suggest examining childhood as a dynamic process that is influenced by multiple factors, including the phenomenon of globalization (Ruddick 2003). Other investigators suggest that a sociohistorical approach also is necessary to bring a full understanding to cross-cultural research. Such an approach would examine current sociocultural contexts of children's development enlightened by an understanding of historical circumstances and influences (Gauvain and Munroe 2009; Stearns 2005).

Contextual influences on various aspects of culture are known to influence children's development. Although improved communication, commerce, and technology are increasingly bringing nations together into a growing global economy, cultural differences still exist and must be understood by early childhood educators. Individual nations and communities within those nations present unique cultural contexts for children's growth and development. Consequently, cross-cultural studies, undertaken from various perspectives, are necessary to help educators understand cultural nuances affecting children's behavior and school readiness. Cross-cultural studies and research conducted in various countries of the world can provide insight into various aspects of children's development and societal phenomena and changes that might impact children's school readiness.

Cognitive Development

Studying children's cognitive development from a sociocultural perspective is essential to inform school readiness efforts worldwide. The culture of communities includes accepted modes of social interaction, the organization of communities, and available methods of educating children and providing formal schooling. All of these sociocultural factors are known to influence children's cognitive development. However, less is known about the impact of social change in societies transitioning from traditional to modern, industrialized nations. This phenomenon, referred to as "modernization," can have widespread effects to the nurturing environments of children. As societies change from traditional to modern, changes occur in the number and types of resources available to families, modes of communication, technological advances, and quality of healthcare. A study of four cultural communities in Belize, Kenya, Nepal, and Samoa, suggested that as modernization occurs, it changes the ecology in which children grow and develop. Children who lived in modernized communities were observed to have more sophisticated play and had better cognitive skills, in particular, those related to academic achievement. The investigators concluded that societal changes precipitated by modernization appeared to positively impact the cognitive development of children (Gauvain and Munroe 2009).

Social and Emotional Development

The social and emotional development of children is critical to their school readiness. Children's social skills and their dispositions toward learning can affect their adjustment to schooling in formal settings. There is evidence that children's social skills and emotional development are also culturally influenced by the contexts of societies in which they live. While some cultural differences are very subtle, others can be quite dramatic. Children acquire behaviors that are encouraged and rewarded by parents and other authority figures within the sociocultural context of their society. The behaviors children learn and the effects certain behaviors have can be strikingly different from one cultural group to another. For example, a study of Chinese two-year-olds found evidence of differences in behaviors and outcomes for Chinese toddlers compared to children in Western societies. Investigators examined behavioral inhibition, a cluster of behaviors including wariness and anxiety that young children may exhibit in new and unfamiliar situations. Behavioral inhibition is commonly associated with problematic behavior and linked to poor academic outcomes in studies of children in Western societies such as the United States and Canada. In contrast, the study of behavioral inhibition in Chinese toddlers found behavioral inhibition predicted positive behaviors such as cooperation, peer acceptance, and social integration. Additionally, behavioral inhibition resulted in positive developmental outcomes including better social skills and adjustment to school for Chinese children. These children also had attitudes and competencies related to successful school performance and were less likely to experience learning problems. The findings suggested that differences in parenting reactions to children exhibiting behavioral inhibition might account for the contrasting outcomes found in Chinese children. The investigators noted that Chinese mothers reacted more supportively when their children displayed behavioral inhibition characteristics compared to Western mothers who tended to view their child's inhibition with disdain (Chen et al. 2009). Different sociocultural contexts can influence the social and emotional characteristics children bring to their palette of school readiness skills and abilities. The social skills they acquire are, in part, a function of the environments they experience and the kinds of social interactions they have with family in their homes and with people in their communities.

Measuring Children's School Readiness

To understand school readiness from an international perspective, investigators have examined children's school readiness across diverse groups of children. However, patterns of providing preschool education and the ages of children upon entry into school readiness programs vary across different geographical areas (de Lemos 2008). Consequently, these factors must be taken into account when comparing the school readiness of children from different countries. Diverse groups of children residing in the same locale may also have different characteristics that can affect the measurement of their school readiness. In addition to the cultural diversity of groups being compared, another vital consideration is the linguistic diversity of children. Children's ability to effectively use the language of instruction can impact their school readiness and adjustment to school settings. Instruments have been developed and used to measure the school readiness of culturally and linguistically diverse children. Rather than using assessments for individual screening of children, tools providing group level data can be useful in guiding the development of programs for populations of children. The results of these measurements also facilitate the evaluation of various types of preschool programs to determine their effectiveness in preparing young children for school (de Lemos 2008; Janus et al. 2009).

Access to School Readiness Programs

Whether the sociocultural contexts allow preschoolers access to early educational opportunities or not can also affect children's school readiness. Unfortunately, some children are afforded greater access to early childhood education than others. Global poverty keeps millions of children from receiving the education they need to be successful in life. According to the World Bank, half the children in developing nations will lack access to even fundamental levels of education. It has been estimated that approximately 125 million children worldwide do not have access to a primary school program and this lack of education further perpetuates the cycle of poverty. Providing a primary education for all children was one of the goals targeted by the World Bank and the United Nations in the year 2000 to help reduce global poverty (Young 2002).

When children do have access to school readiness programs, there is evidence that children are better prepared and attain greater academic success in school. For instance, in some Australian communities, low-income, indigenous children enter school lacking fundamental mathematical concepts and skills. There is some evidence to suggest that entering preschool programs a year earlier at four years of age might help improve language and early numeracy understanding necessary for success in school (Warren et al. 2008). A Cambodian study examined the results of an intensive two-month intervention intended to compensate for the lack of preschool education available to children before they entered formal schooling. The findings of the study revealed that children who participated in the school readiness program were able to acquire fundamental school readiness skills in the short term. Later school performance of children who participated in the school readiness program exceeded those of peers who did not participate in the program. These findings suggest that school readiness programs can make a difference in countries where access to early education programs is limited (Nonoyama-Tarumi and Bredenberg 2009). However, providing access to school readiness programs for all children is a daunting task and reaching children in poverty and those in rural areas can prove especially difficult. For example, the country of Jordan has launched widespread school reform efforts that include focusing on poor, rural areas for improvement to children's school readiness. Subsequently, a large, national study in Jordan found evidence that more affluent children in urban areas were better prepared for school compared to children in lower income families residing in rural areas. A specific set of demographic characteristics were associated with higher levels of school readiness in children entering school. Assessments revealed that male children living in urban areas with smaller families had better school readiness skills. Higher levels of parental education were also related to higher levels of school readiness among Jordanian children (Al-Hassan and Lansford 2009).

Community Involvement

Overcoming the effects of poverty and promoting school readiness can be difficult to achieve despite high motivation and widespread reform efforts. Programs to reduce poverty and improve school readiness have been tried in various countries, including the United States. Community collaboration and the integration of services are strategies that have been tried in the United States to improve the quality of care and education for young children (Brauner et al. 2004). The trend toward community collaboration is strong, and community involvement is considered an efficient use of resources that can result in a better system of support and services for families with young children. Strengthening families by ensuring access to critical community services has potential for exerting a positive impact on children's school readiness (Weigel and Martin 2006). Establishing policies and creating relationships between local government agencies and early childhood programs has been recommended to improve the quality of early care and education. Community participation and public investment in school readiness efforts has shown promise as a strategy for achieving better child outcomes (Kagan and Neuman 2003). Yet, despite the struggle to overcome the deleterious effects of poverty and insufficient resources for promoting school readiness, many children enter school ill-prepared and at serious risk of school failure. The achievement gap continues to widen between economically advantaged and disadvantaged children (Currie 2005; Mashburn 2008). From an international perspective, it has been suggested that community involvement strengthens relationships between families and schools as well as other services available in the community aimed toward improving the health and school readiness of children. Community involvement can increase successful lobbying for resources. The pooling of available resources can result in more efficiency, especially when resources are scarce (Dockett and Perry 2009).

Health and School Readiness

Health and Transition to School

Health as foundational to school readiness is not a new idea, although concentration on pre-academic preparation has seemed to take center stage in recent years. The National Goals Panel recommended this approach and Head Start has traditionally provided health services to children (Boyer 1991). However, few programs have truly integrated health into the curriculum for children, as well as training for parents and teachers. Yet, a variety of health conditions can affect children worldwide and place children at risk of school failure and interfere with their smooth transition to school. Diseases and chronic conditions, such as diabetes, intestinal parasite infections, cardiac deficits, sickle cell anemia and other health issues, are known to affect academic performance (Taras and Potts-Datema 2005a). Consequently, it seems incumbent upon the research community to place greater emphasis on the examination of child health in relation to school readiness.

Obesity in Young Children

Obesity is currently one of the most troublesome global concerns. Obesity rates are rising worldwide and a global epidemic has been declared (World Health Organization 2004). Childhood obesity has afflicted increasingly younger children requiring professionals to address this health issue before and during a child's transition to school (Centers for Disease Control and Prevention 2009b, 2009d). Nearly 10% of infants and toddlers are already overweight by two years of age (National Center for Health Statistics 2007). One in four US children are either overweight or at risk of becoming overweight and obesity rates for preschoolers have doubled in a single generation (Centers for Disease Control and Prevention 2008b; Ogden et al. 2008).

Obesity substantially increases the risk of health consequences during childhood and as an adult. Obesity is strongly associated with the development of cardiovascular disease and cancer (Polednak 2008). In addition, Type 2 diabetes, orthopedic problems, sleep apnea, psychosocial dysfunction, and other serious health problems can occur as a result of childhood obesity (Centers for Disease Control and Prevention 2008a; Wang and Dietz 2002). Obesity, and the health conditions obesity precipitates, can interfere with children's transition into school and their future academic achievement.

Obesity Widens Achievement Gaps

Compelling evidence suggests that obesity in children is associated with poor school performance (Taras and Potts-Datema 2005b). When children transition into kindergarten lacking fundamental school readiness skills and, also at risk for obesity and other health problems, achievement gaps can widen (Centers for Disease Control and Prevention 2009a). Health and educational disparities must be recognized and simultaneously addressed if these serious gaps are to be reduced for children prior to school entry (Currie 2005; Datar et al. 2004; National Institutes of Child Health and Human Development 2000). Health and educational disparities increase achievement gaps, especially for minority children who are disproportionately at risk of health problems and educational inequities (Centers for Disease Control and Prevention 2009c; National Institutes of Child Health and Human Development 2000). Cultural and language barriers can have a negative impact on low-income, minority children. These issues can impede their access to healthcare and quality early educational programs (Collins and Ribeiro 2004; Pianta et al. 2007). Increasing evidence corroborates to the detrimental effects of obesity on the school readiness of children. Research consistently associates school failure and lack of academic achievement with childhood obesity. Consequently, poor health and lack of school readiness place many children across the globe in double jeopardy (Centers for Disease Control and Prevention 2008a; Taras and Potts-Datema 2005b). Given this information, it seems imperative to study health, especially childhood obesity, as a major health condition with potential to influence children's school readiness.

Early Prevention

Few studies have reported success in reversing obesity in children or adults. Consequently, the US Surgeon General, Centers for Disease Control, and other experts in the medical profession have recommended a focus on prevention beginning early in a child's life. These experts believe it is critical for families, preschools, and community agencies to use comprehensive strategies to help children establish a healthy lifestyle of nutritious eating and physical activity to promote optimal growth, development, and learning (American Medical Association 2009). Children who develop healthy lifestyles early before school entry may be better prepared to withstand future pressures to engage in unhealthy eating and activities in later childhood. The early grades of formal schooling may be a particularly important time for children to have well-established eating and physical activity habits. An analysis of the Early Childhood Longitudinal Study (ECLS-K) found that children who became overweight between kindergarten and third grade showed poorer school performance compared to children with normal weight. Girls were particularly at risk, scoring lower on mathematics and reading achievement and exhibiting more behavioral and social adjustment problems compared to boys (Datar and Sturm 2006).

Teachers and Parents as Models

Teacher professional development and parent education components of programs may be especially important to early prevention of obesity in school transition programs. Modeling of healthy behaviors and the interaction styles adults use with preschool children have an impact on children's health and school readiness. While culture influences interactions and behaviors of adults with children, Baumrind identified four basic interaction styles used by parents, teachers, and other adults: authoritarian, authoritative, indulgent, and uninvolved. Using the ideal style, authoritative, adults respond to children and make appropriate demands on children (Baumrind 1991). These interaction styles are used by adults across cultures and have been useful in studying the promotion of healthy habits in children. Research studies have found that parents and teachers who adopt the authoritative style with children promote children's self-regulation, a skill that has important ramifications for healthy eating habits. The authoritative style was also found to help build children's competence and self-esteem which may help children resist temptations to engage in unhealthy eating or risky health behaviors in the future. Authoritative teachers and parents offered children healthy choices of foods and activities rather than restricting children's choices. This style of interaction used positive approaches to discipline rather than rewarding children with food. Supervision of eating and physical activities encouraged children without coercion. Children were encouraged to respond to their own natural cues, such as feelings of satiety, when eating. Supervision of physical activity focused on facilitation of child initiated activities and social interactions toward building skills and competence (Patrick et al. 2005; Rhee et al. 2006).

Preschool-aged children learn through good modeling by adults who are influential in their lives. Studies have revealed that teachers can apply social and cognitive behavioral modeling techniques based on Social Cognitive Theory (SCT) to promote healthy eating and physical activity. Children's physical activity was found to increase when teachers encouraged participation in non-competitive physical activities, especially when these activities involved social interactions with peers. When teachers modeled eating healthy meals and snacks, children who observed these behaviors were more likely to make healthier food choices (Cole et al. 2006).

Children acquire preferences for foods very early and, once established, these preferences are very persistent and difficult to change. Moreover, maternal food preferences are known to influence and sometimes limit the variety of foods mothers offer their children. Cultural heritage is a major influence on patterns of eating and varieties of food offered to children. Consequently, transition to school programs can respect the cultural patterns of families and may extend the range of nutrient-rich foods children have an opportunity to eat for optimal growth and development during their preschool years (Briefel et al. 2006).

Cultural Responsiveness

To combat obesity, the US National Summit on Obesity issued recommendations emphasizing the use of culturally sensitive practices that meet the Culturally and Linguistically Appropriate Services (CLAS) standards of the Office of Minority Health of the US Department of Health and Human Services. The CLAS standards recommend use of ethnically sensitive assessments and culturally sensitive educational strategies. These guidelines call for promotion of strategies that involve the community as a whole and are integrated into the policies of schools and community agencies. For example, cultural preferences should be a prime consideration when establishing policies regarding nutritional and physical activity programs for children (American Medical Association 2004).

Cultural responsiveness is particularly important when school readiness efforts address the transition of children from home to school. Abundant research substantiates the critical role of parents and teachers as models who influence children's behaviors in regard to health and school readiness. Adults are gatekeepers for food access and opportunities for physical activity available to young children. These are two critical influences on both the health and school readiness of children. The quality of home and school environments is critical to children's school readiness and their later successful performance in school. The examples of adults in these environments help to establish and sustain physical activity habits, food preferences, and engagement in sedentary activity (Centers for Disease Control and Prevention 2008a). Experts recommend using an ecological approach aiming strategies for improving children's health and reducing the risk of obesity at multiple sociocontextual layers of influence in society, including homes and schools (Campbell and Hesketh 2007).

Implications

Cross-cultural studies of child development are essential to ensure that young children of all cultural heritages and backgrounds have the best opportunities to be prepared for school. The study of cultural patterns and the stability or instability of those trends enhances our understanding of children's development (LeVine 2002). Another important implication of cultural research for school readiness is the importance of diversity education (Marsella 2009). Beginning early, diversity education can help preserve the cultural identity of individuals and encourage children to appreciate and understand the cultural diversity in their community. As children and families come into contact with people representing an increasing diversity of cultures, a focus on developing cultural competence can help them interact with the widening circle of culture in which they will live as a result of globalization (Gudykunst and Kim 1992). It is imperative that findings from cross-cultural studies be accessible to educators and be used to inform practice. Integrating this body of research into teacher education and professional development for teachers in service is critical to improve the cultural responsiveness of teachers to children and families.

Establishing theoretical foundations for international perspectives on school readiness based on Bronfenbrenner's widely accepted ecological model (Bronfenbrenner 1986) could be useful to guide research and practice in the international arena. Rather than narrow academic approaches, ecological thinking might encourage respect for ways cultures differ in parental expectations for children and cultural preferences for creating smooth transitions for children from home to school. For example, a study comparing preschool transition in two countries on opposite sides of the globe, Iceland and Australia, found similarities and differences in accepted practices. While preschool teachers in both nations recognized the importance of preserving continuity between home and preschool, their practices reflected the different contexts and cultural expectations of families and teachers' own interpretations of acceptable practices in their countries (Einarsdottir et al. 2008). Clearly, the implication of studies of cultural differences in family expectations and teachers' school readiness practices is that cultural responsiveness is paramount. Recognition of cultural context in policymaking and program development will be critical to improving the school readiness of all children. Most important, cultural responsiveness appears especially critical to reduce the gap in school readiness and health for children in poverty (National Institutes of Child Health and Human Development 2000).

Finally, experts believe that efforts to improve children's health and prevent childhood obesity can complement existing school transition programs. However, few programs have been developed and tested to establish the effectiveness of programmatic strategies. There is a need for further research to develop approaches and to study implementation of recommended strategies in school readiness programs. Research is needed to ensure optimal transitions for children to school that take into account the culture, health, and school readiness of children. The goal of such an integrated approach is to ensure children are well prepared and preschool programs are ready to provide the necessary support for children and their families.

References

Achhpal, B., Goldman, J. A., & Rohner, R. P. (2007). A comparison of European American and Puerto Rican parents' goals and expectations about the socialization and education of preschool children. *International Journal of Early Years Education, 15*(1), 1–13.

Al-Hassan, S. M., & Lansford, J. E. (2009). Child, family and community characteristics associated with school readiness in Jordan. *Early Years: An International Journal of Research and Development, 29*(3), 217–226.

American Medical Association (2004). *National summit on obesity: Executive summary*. Chicago, IL: Author.

American Medical Association (2009). Obesity. http://www.ama-assn.org/ama/pub/physician-resources/public-health/promoting-healthy-lifestyles/obesity.shtml. Accessed 11 Dec 2009.

Baumrind, D. (1991). The influence of parenting style on adolescent competence and substance use. *Journal of Early Adolescence, 11*(1), 56–95.

Bodrova, E., & Leong, D. J. (2003a). Chopsticks and counting chips: Do play and foundational skills need to compete for the teachers' attention in an early childhood classroom? *Young Children, 58*(3), 10–17.

Bodrova, E., & Leong, D. J. (2003b). The importance of being playful. *Educational Leadership, 60*(7), 50–53.

Boyer, E. L. (1991). *Ready to learn: A mandate for the nation*. Princeton, NJ: The Carnegie Foundation for the Advancement of Teaching.

Brauner, J., Gordic, B., & Zigler, E. (2004). Putting child back into child care: Combining care and education for children ages 3–5. *Social Policy Report, 18*(3), 3–15.

Briefel, R., Ziegler, P., Novak, T., & Ponza, M. (2006). Feeding infants and toddlers study: Characteristics and usual nutrient intake of hispanic and non-hispanic infants and toddlers. *Journal of the American Dietetic Association, 106*(1, Supplement 1), 84.e1–84.e14.

Bronfenbrenner, U. (1986). Ecology of the family as a context for human development: Research perspectives. *Developmental Psychology, 22*(6), 723–742.

Bronfenbrenner, U., & Morris, P. A. (1998). The ecology of developmental processes. In R. M. Lerner (Ed.), *Handbook of child psychology: Theoretical models of human development* (5th ed., Vol. 1, pp. 993–1028). New York: Wiley.

Campbell, K. J., & Hesketh, K. D. (2007). Strategies which aim to positively impact on weight, physical activity, diet and sedentary behaviours in children from zero to five years. A systematic review of the literature. *Obesity Reviews: An Official Journal of The International Association For The Study of Obesity, 8*(4), 327–338.

Carlson, S. A., Fulton, J. E., Lee, S. M., Maynard, M., Brown, D. R., Kohl, H. W., et al. (2008). Physical education and academic achievement in elementary school: Data from the Early Childhood Longitudinal Study. *American Journal of Public Health, 98*(4), 721–727.

Centers for Disease Control and Prevention (2008a). Contributing factors. Overweight and Obesity. http://www.cdc.gov/nccdphp/dnpa/obesity/contributing_factors.htm. Accessed 16 July 2008.

Centers for Disease Control and Prevention (2008b, May 22, 2007). Overweight prevalence. Overweight and Obesity. http://www.cdc.gov/nccdphp/dnpa/obesity/childhood/prevalence.htm. Accessed 16 July 2008.

Centers for Disease Control and Prevention (2009a). Childhood overweight and obesity: Contributing factors. http://www.cdc.gov/obesity/childhood/causes.html. Accessed 18 Aug 2009.

Centers for Disease Control and Prevention (2009b). Data and statistics: U.S. Obesity Trends 1985–2008. http://www.cdc.gov/obesity/data/index.html. Accessed 18 Aug 2009.

Centers for Disease Control and Prevention (2009c). Obesity prevalence among low-income, preschool-aged children-United States, 1998–2008. *MMWR, 58*(28), 769–773.

Centers for Disease Control and Prevention (2009d). Trends in childhood obesity. Accessed from http://www.cdc.gov/obesity/childhood/trends.html. Accessed 29 Aug 2009.

Chen, X., Chen, H., Li, D., & Wang, L. (2009). Early behavioral inhibition and social and school adjustment in Chinese children: A 5-year longitudinal study. *Child Development, 80*(6), 1692–1704.

Cole, K., Waldrop, J., D'Auria, J., & Garner, H. (2006). An integrative research review: Effective school-based childhood overweight interventions. *Journal for Specialists in Pediatric Nursing, 11*(3), 166–177.

Collins, R., & Ribeiro, R. (2004). Toward an early care and education agenda for Hispanic children. *Early Childhood Research and Practice, 6*(2). http://ecrp.uiuc.edu/v6n2/collins.html

Currie, J. (2005). Health disparities and gaps in school readiness. *The Future of Children, 15*(1), 117–138.

Darling-Hammond, L. (2004). Standards, accountability, and school reform. *Teachers College Record, 106*(6), 1047–1085.

Datar, A., & Sturm, R. (2006). Childhood overweight and elementary school outcomes. *International Journal of Obesity, 30*(9), 1449–1460.

Datar, A., Sturm, R., & Magnabosco, J. L. (2004). Childhood overweight and academic performance: National study of kindergartners and first-graders. *Obesity Research, 12*, 58–68.

de Lemos, M. (2008). Assessing development and readiness for school across different cultural and language groups. *Australian Journal of Learning Difficulties, 13*(2), 73–98.

Dockett, S., & Perry, B. (2008). Starting school: A community endeavor. *Childhood Education, 84*(5), 274–280.

Dockett, S., & Perry, B. (2009). Readiness for school: A relational construct. *Australasian Journal of Early Childhood, 34*(1), 20–26.

Einarsdottir, J., Perry, B., & Dockett, S. (2008). Transition to school practices: Comparisons from Iceland and Australia. *Early Years: An International Journal of Research and Development, 28*(1), 47–60.

Eunice Kennedy Shriver National Institute of Child Health and Human Development (2009). *Child Development and Behavior Branch (CDBB), NIHCD, Report to the NACHHD Council.* Washington, DC: Author.

Gauvain, M., & Munroe, R. L. (2009). Contributions of societal modernity to cognitive development: A comparison of four cultures. *Child Development, 80*(6), 1628–1642.

Gudykunst, W., & Kim, Y. (1992). *Communicating with strangers: An approach to intercultural communication* (2nd ed.). New York: McGraw-Hill.

Janus, M., Hertzman, C., Guhn, M., Brinkman, S., & Goldfeld, S. (2009). Reply to Li, D'Angiulli and Kendall: The Early Development Index and children from culturally and linguistically diverse backgrounds. *Early Years, 29*(1), 83–87.

Kagan, S. L., & Neuman, M. J. (2003). Integrating early care and education. *Educational Leadership, 60*(7), 58–63.

Kagan, S. L., Britto, P. R., & Engle, P. (2005). Early learning standards: What can America learn? What can America teach? *Phi Delta Kappan, 87*(3), 205–208.

LeVine, R. A. (2002). Populations, communication, and child development. *Human Development, 45*, 291–293.

Lloyd, B., & Howe, N. (2003). Solitary play and convergent and divergent thinking skills in preschool children. *Early Childhood Research Quarterly, 18*(1), 22–41.

Lonigan, C. J., Schatschneider, C., & Westberg, L. (2007). Identification of children's skills and abilities linked to later outcomes in reading writing, and spelling. In National Institute for Literacy (Ed.), *Report of the National Literacy Panel*. Washington, DC: National Institute for Literacy.

Mallory, B. L. (1994). Inclusive policy, practice, and theory for young children with developmental differences. In B. L. Mallory & R. S. New (Eds.), *Diversity and developmentally appropriate practices: Challenges for early childhood education* (pp. 44–61). New York, NY: Teachers College Press.

Marsella, A. J. (2009). Diversity in a global era: The context and consequences of differences. *Counselling Psychology Quarterly, 22*(1), 119–135.

Mashburn, A. J. (2008). Quality of social and physical environments in preschools and children's development of academic, language, and literacy skills. *Applied Developmental Science, 3*(12), 113–127.

Mashburn, A. J., Justice, L. M., Downer, J. T., & Pianta, R. C. (2009). Peer effects on children's language achievement during pre-kindergarten. *Child Development, 80*(3), 686–702.

Miller, E., & Almon, J. (2009). *Crisis in the kindergarten: Why children need to play in school*. College Park, MD: Alliance for Childhood.

National Center for Health Statistics (2007, 2008). Prevalence of overweight, infants and children less than 2 years of age: United States, 2003–2004. http://www.cdc.gov/nchs/products/pubs/pubd/hestats/overweight/overwght_child_under02.htm. Accessed 18 July 2008.

National Institutes of Child Health and Human Development (2000). Health disparities: Bridging the gap. http://www.nichd.nih.gov/publications/pubs/upload/health_disparities.pdf. Accessed 15 Aug 2009.

Nonoyama-Tarumi, Y., & Bredenberg, K. (2009). Impact of school readiness program interventions on children's learning in Cambodia. *International Journal of Educational Development, 29*(1), 39–45.

Ogden, C. L., Carroll, M. D., & Flegal, K. M. (2008). High Body Mass Index for age among US children and adolescents, 2003–2006. *Journal of American Medical Association, 299*(20), 2401–2405.

Patrick, H., Nicklas, T. A., Hughes, S. O., & Morales, M. (2005). The benefits of authoritative feeding style: Caregiver feeding styles and children's food consumption patterns. *Appetite, 44*, 243–249.

Pianta, R. C., Cox, M. J., & Snow, K. L. (Eds.). (2007). *School readiness and the transition to kindergarten in the era of accountability*. Baltimore, MD: Paul Brookes.

Polednak, A. P. (2008). Estimating the number of US incident cancers attributable to obesity and the impact on temporal trends in incidence rates for obesity-related cancers. *Cancer Detection and Prevention, 32*(3), 190–199.

Rhee, K. E., Lumeng, J. C., Appugliese, D. P., Kaciroti, N., & Bradley, R. H. (2006). Parenting styles and overweight status in first grade. *Pediatrics, 117*(6), 2047–2054.

Ruddick, S. (2003). The politics of aging: Globalization and the restructuring of youth and childhood. *Antipode, 35*(2), 334–362.

Stearns, P. N. (2005). Conclusion: Change, globalization and childhood. *Journal of Social History, 38*(4), 1041–1046.

Taras, H., & Potts-Datema, W. (2005a). Chronic health conditions and student performance at school. *Journal of School Health, 75*(7), 255–266.

Taras, H., & Potts-Datema, W. (2005b). Obesity and student performance at school. *Journal of School Health, 75*(8), 291–295.

Trochim, W. M., Cabrera, D. A., Milstein, B., Gallagher, R. S., & Leischow, S. J. (2006). Practical challenges of systems thinking and modeling in public health. *American Journal of Public Health, 96*(3), 538–546.

US Department of Health and Human Services (2003). HHS, Education launch research to promote school readiness effort. http://www.hhs.gov/news. Accessed 7 Jan 2011.

Wang, G., & Dietz, W. H. (2002). Economic burden of obesity in youth aged 6 to 17 years: 1979–1999. *Pediatrics, 109,* E81.

Warren, E., Young, J., & de Vries, E. (2008). The impact of early numeracy engagement on four-year-old indigenous students. *Australian Journal of Early Childhood, 33*(4), 2–8.

Webster-Stratton, C., & Reid, M. J. (2004). Strengthening social and emotional competence in young children: The foundation for early school readiness and success. *Infants & Young Children, 17*(2), 96–113.

Weigel, D. J., & Martin, S. S. (2006). Identifying key early literacy and school readiness issues: Exploring a strategy for assessing community needs. *Early Childhood Research and Practice, 8*(2). http://ecrp.uiuc.edu/v8n2/weigel.html

Winter, S. M. (2007). *Inclusive early childhood education: A collaborative approach.* Upper Saddle River, NJ: Merrill Prentice Hall.

World Health Organization (2004). *Obesity: Preventing and managing the global epidemic. Report of a WHO consultation on obesity 1999.* Geneva: Author.

Young, M. E. (Ed.). (2002). *From early child development to human development: Investing in our children's future.* Herndon, VA: World Bank Publications.

Part III
International Perspectives

Chapter 12
Reconsidering Readiness

Should the Spotlight Be on Children or on Schools?

Nancy K. Freeman and Beth Powers-Costello

Ready Schools Efforts in the United States and Northern Italy

Promoting school readiness has become a critical issue worldwide. Many efforts have focused on how to help children become ready for formal schooling. Yet, little attention has been given to how ready kindergartens or primary school settings are to receive and support their newest students and their families. While preschools and preprimary programs may be "reaching up", few kindergartens or primary schools are reaching down or reaching out to children who are entering a formal setting for the first time.

This chapter provides a rationale for focusing on helping schools get ready for children rather than making children ready for school. Additionally, it describes the efforts of some schools in the United States and Northern Italy to smooth children's transitions to formal educational settings. Finally, it recommends ready school strategies, and considers the implications of investing in ready schools.

Ready Schools Address Factors that Put Children at Risk for School Failure

There are several factors known to put children at risk for school failure. Some, such as low birth-weight and parents' limited educational attainment, cannot be addressed by schools. Programs for young children can, however, address other risk-producing circumstances that are known to put children's chances for school

N. K. Freeman (✉)
Department of Instruction and Teacher Education, Early Childhood,
University of South Carolina, 225 Child Development Research Center,
1530 Wheat Street, Columbia, SC 20201, USA
e-mail: nfreeman@sc.edu

D. M. Laverick, M. R. Jalongo (eds.), *Transitions to Early Care and Education,*
Educating the Young Child 4, DOI 10.1007/978-94-007-0573-9_12,
© Springer Science+Business Media B.V. 2011

success in jeopardy. The ready schools initiative is inspired by this commitment to address factors that increase children's chances for school success. Ready schools take an ecological approach that works to strengthen the interconnections between the child, his or her family, and their community and school (Scott-Little 2009). Moreover, they recognize that there are specific issues that need to be addressed to help make a school ready for children.

Cultural Incongruity Between Home and School

Some of the biggest challenges young children and their families face as they enter the formal educational system are those created by a mismatch between their home culture and that of their school. These differences are reflected in families' goals for children (Doucet and Tudge 2007). They influence families' interactional styles (Heath 1983), for example their use of personal space; the meaning of eye contact, particularly between children and adults; and their conception of being "on time" (Gonzalez-Mena 2001; Miller 1989).

Effective strategies to overcome barriers created by cultural differences include home visits and orientation sessions designed for children and all interested family members. These activities help children and families learn about their school and have the added potential to inform school personnel about the cultures and values of the families and children they serve. They help schools become ready for children (Doucet and Tudge 2007).

The school's curriculum and pedagogy also present opportunities to strengthen its link to children and families, or to magnify differences, creating barriers that can last throughout children's educational careers. Schools that build on children's prior knowledge and the strengths of their families and communities make learning relevant and increase children's chances for school success.

Continuity Between Early Care and Education and Local Schools

Another factor that influences children's adjustment to their new school's environment is the continuity that exists between children's preschool experiences and the formal educational system they are preparing to enter (National Association for the Education of Young Children 2009). Child-centered preschools are often very different from the formal academic settings that house kindergartens and primary classrooms. Children experience these differences in teachers' and schools' expectations, routines, and interactional styles (Shore 1998).

Some preschools address this issue by attempting to prepare children with the skills they will need in a more formal setting. These efforts often involve "skill/drill" approaches to instruction which are designed to prime children to perform well on formal assessments. Another way to look at this issue, however, is to shift the focus from one that pressures children to complete inappropriately academic tasks, to one that puts the spotlight on those who shape children's early educational experiences (Katz and Chard 2000). This approach places the responsibility for creating learning environments that meet children's developmental needs at the feet of schools and teachers of young children, rather than expecting children to succeed and prosper in environments that do not reflect their cultural and developmental characteristics (Freeman and Brown 2008).

Programs that are committed to smoothing children's transitions from one setting to the next provide opportunities for preprimary and primary teachers to form partnerships and to share their philosophies, expectations, and curricula. Primary teachers working to smooth their future students' transitions to school may make home visits or telephone parents before school begins, or might partner with community preprimary teachers to plan for individual students' transitions. These efforts have been shown not only to improve children's chances for school success, but also to increase the likelihood that their families will be involved in their children's early education (Scott-Little 2009).

Expecting Every Child to Be Successful

Ready schools respond to each child's developmental and educational needs. They plan for varying levels of readiness and are prepared to individualize instruction rather than take a "one size fits all" approach to curriculum and pedagogy (Shore 1998). When schools take this individualized approach, they are much less likely to require struggling learners to repeat one of the early grades. This reluctance to retain young children is an important shift in policy, for research has consistently demonstrated retention is a detrimental policy that is strongly associated with increased incidence of high school dropout (Hong and Yu 2007; Jimerson 2001). In sum, individualized instruction benefits children in both the long and short term.

Efforts in the United States to Make Schools Ready for Children

All 50 states' governors adopted eight National Education Goals in 1990. They created a framework to guide America's efforts to increase every child's opportunities for success. The first goal directly addressed the challenges faced by young children who enter school lagging behind their peers. It created the expectation that "By the year 2000, all children in America will start school ready to learn" (National Education Goals Panel 2002). But, just as policy makers recognized the importance of providing all children access to high quality preschool programs, to supporting parents' efforts to be their children's first teachers, and to ensuring that children's nutritional and health care needs are met, they also recognized that schools have a responsibility to be ready for kindergartners beginning their formal education.

This realization led to the creation of the Goal 1 Ready Schools Resource Group. Relying on the work of respected scholars, reports of highly regarded task forces, and strategies of successful programs they identified ten specific policies that have been shown to increase the likelihood that young children could grow in competence and meet high expectations for performance as they entered school (Shore 1998). In short, this group asked "How can we make sure all schools are ready for the children and families they serve?"

The nation's governors demonstrated their continuing commitment to the National Education Goals they adopted in 1990 and to the work of the Ready Schools Resource Group by recommending that states enact policies focused on one or more of these three ready schools initiatives:

1. Support children's transitions into kindergarten.
2. Align learning standards from preschool through the early years so that all stakeholders have appropriate expectations about what young children should know and be able to do as they prepare for and enter the formal education system.
3. Provide support and make schools accountable for creating learning environments that support all children's success (National Governors Association Center for Best Practices 2005b).

As they focused ready school efforts in these three areas, governors have called on all stakeholders to "encourage innovative and promising practices at the local level" (National Governors Association Center for Best Practices 2005a, p. 11). Their challenge puts the responsibility for creating schools ready for all children in the hands of state and local advocates and policy makers.

While it is true that not all communities in every state have enacted the policies recommended by the ready schools initiative, successful efforts have been launched. Researchers have not yet identified "best practices" for school transitions, but innovative communities have embarked on a number of promising practices that may inspire others. Examples come from programs created by federal mandates, local initiatives, and the investments of a private foundation.

Head Start's Transition Mandate

Head Start mandates have led the way toward improving preschool quality. Head Start's most recent reauthorization requires programs to develop formal agreements with local public schools to smooth children's transitions from one setting to the next (Improving Head Start for School Readiness Act of 2007). Effective transition strategies used by Head Start include school meetings, home visits, parent education efforts aimed to help parents navigate the public school system to effectively access the services they and their children are eligible to receive, help with the registration process, and activities for children (SERVE n.d.).

Countdown to Kindergarten

Countdown to Kindergarten is an example of a community-based effort to ease children's transitions into the formal educational system. Boston launched its year-long Countdown to Kindergarten program in 2001. One of the initiative's goals is to establish robust home–school lines of communication before children begin kindergarten. One successful strategy has been registering children in January so they can begin developing a relationship with their teacher well before school starts in the fall. As opening day approaches, parents are encouraged to help children adjust to bedtime and wake-up routines and to develop independence by, for example, practicing opening juice boxes and riding the bus to and from school (Countdown to Kindergarten Boston n.d.).

Countdown to Kindergarten has been adapted by locales as diverse as North Dakota, Maryland, North Carolina, and South Carolina. In some instances the program replicates the Boston model, in others it has been significantly adapted. In South Carolina, for example, Countdown to Kindergarten's primary activity is a 10-week home visitation program conducted in the summer (Bohan-Baker and Little 2004). Maryland's Countdown to Kindergarten takes a different tack, providing materials to help parents prepare their children for school; producing public service announcements broadcast on local radio stations; and engaging libraries, museums, and other community partners to host local Countdown to Kindergarten events (Countdown to Kindergarten Maryland n.d.).

Foundation-Supported Efforts

The Supporting Partnerships to Assure Ready Kids (SPARK) project represents the investment of the W.K. Kellogg Foundation to guide policy development and support community efforts focused on preparing children for school success. This initiative has funded programs in seven states and the District of Columbia to serve as "incubators for what works" (Education Commission of the States 2009, p. 3). The project is guided by these four principles:

1. Strong partnerships link families, preschools, community organizations, and schools to ensure children's school success.
2. Investments in quality teachers and in teachers' professional development increase the likelihood that expectations about what children know and are able to do will be aligned.
3. Parents and families need continuous support, beginning in the preschool years and continuing through their children's transition into the formal educational system.
4. Administrators and teachers are essential partners in efforts designed to smooth transitions and create continuity across systems.

A three-pronged approach to policy development has grown out of SPARK's recommendations:

1. Effective teaching connects children's experiences as they move from home, to preschool, and into formal educational settings.
2. Programmatic policies take into account existing links between children's homes, schools, and their communities.
3. Policies address the early childhood infrastructure (Education Commission of the States 2009).

Participating states have taken idiosyncratic approaches to creating ready schools. All share, however, efforts aimed at easing transitions from community preschools into the formal educational system, involving parents in their children's learning, and aligning curriculum from preschool through grade twelve.

Efforts in Northern Italy to Make Schools Ready for Children

Italy is grappling with many of the same issues facing schools in the United States, including creating ready school environments for young children. It has been heralded as an exemplar due, in large measure, to laws and policies supporting young children and their families.

In 1968, compulsory government sponsored preprimary education was established and the *Orientamenti* policy established guidelines for high quality preschool. In 1971, government sponsored preprimary programs were established (Edwards et al. 1998).

In 1990, *Law 148* mandated continuity between preprimary and primary schools. This law not only stresses the importance of schools communicating with families, who are appreciated as knowledgeable authorities on children, but also specifically requires curriculum coordination between *scuolas materna* (preprimary programs) and local primary schools. The *Circolare Ministeriale n. 339* (Ministerial Circular number 339), passed in 1992 built on *Law 148,* focused particularly on meeting the needs of diverse families including those whose children have identified special needs. Additionally, this policy encouraged collaboration among social service agencies, health departments, schools, and families (Organization for Economic Cooperation & Development 2001).

These laws resonated particularly in the Emilia Romagna Provence in Northern Italy, where they aligned with the philosophy and practices fundamental to the Malaguzzi approach founded in the city of Reggio Emilia. This approach is based on an ever evolving but coherent set of theoretical perspectives including constructivist education as informed by Piaget and Vygotsky, European and American progressive education, and post World War II "left-reform" politics. At the heart of this philosophy is the idea that successful education is about "reciprocity, dialogue, and exchange" (Edwards et al. 1998, p. 10).

Although Malaguzzi's ideas influence pedagogy from birth through higher education, the biggest influence on curriculum has been on education and care for children ages 3–6 years of age, who typically remain in multi-age groupings throughout their preschool years. In recent years efforts have focused on developing curriculum for primary school settings.

Reggio Emilia Pedagogy: Environment as Third Teacher

An important component of Reggio Emilia's pedagogy is the view that the school environment is the child's third teacher (Edwards et al. 1998). This emphasis on the classroom setting is based on the belief that children can best make sense of their world in environments that enable them to explore "complex, varied, sustained, and changing relationships between people, the world of experience, ideas and the many ways of expressing ideas" (Caldwell 1997, p. 93).

Building on the cultural value of collective responsibility for children, teachers view families as equal members of the educational team. Family members are expected to actively participate in the school's administration and activities offered by the school such as informational lectures, work sessions to create educational materials and help with school maintenance, and special events and celebrations.

Reggio Emilia Pedagogy: Priming Events

Reggio educators strive to create an atmosphere that is conducive to communication, interaction, organization, aesthetic inspiration, and collaboration. A promising approach that some Reggio schools have employed to achieve these goals is the intentional implementation of priming events, which are repeated, predictable, routine activities, such as morning meeting, ongoing projects, special events, and field trips. These strategies continue to varying degrees in primary schools in the Reggio Provence which helps to create "ready school" environments (Corsaro and Molinari 2000).

Morning Meeting

During daily morning meetings, children discuss activities in which they participated outside of school, ongoing school-based projects, and other topics of interest. The main goal for these meetings is to provide all children with the opportunity "to have something to contribute to the group" (Corsaro and Molinari 2000, p. 19). *Discussione* (discussion and debate) is an integral part of Italian preschool culture which reflects the norms and expectations of their Northern Italian roots (Corsaro and Rizzo 1988). As the school year progresses, discussions center on older chil-

dren's transitioning to a new school. This practice reinforces all children's sense
of belonging to a group and gives the oldest children a beginning understanding of
their approaching role as primary school students.

Storia Personale

A second priming event that occurs in preschools is the ongoing creation of each
child's *storia personale* (personal story). This personal story documents three years
of the child's growth through photographs, descriptions of significant events, and
other artifacts of their growth and development. This personal story helps children
to see their growth over time and to celebrate both their own growth and learning,
and, for transitioning children their passage from one stage of childhood to another.
At the end of the final preschool year, teachers and parents work with children to
create daily entries on the coming transition to demonstrate that the past is giving
way to the future (Corsaro and Molinari 2000).

Group Literacy Projects

Children engage in literature-based group projects that can last for several months.
In one example of a literacy project, the children read the *Wizard of Oz* with their
teachers and classmates, discussed it in daily morning meetings, and each child
drew a picture of a particular scene in the story. The pictures were displayed on the
classroom walls until the final week of school. During this last week, the children
took their drawings off of the wall, placed them in the center of the room on the
floor, and working together, put each scene in order. The children then engaged in
a discussion about the events of the story. On the final day of school, children took
home their original artwork and a book that included copies of all of the drawings
(Corsaro and Molinari 2000). This project offered children developmentally appropriate activities while at the same time mirrored the structure and duration of many
primary school assignments.

Field Trips

Field trips to local primary schools are an example of a priming event that involves
just the children preparing for their transition into the formal educational setting.
Fifth grade students and their teachers lead preschoolers on a tour of the school,
children meet its principal, and spend some time in a primary classroom. Because
teachers typically stay with the same group of children through their elementary
years, the fifth graders' teachers are preparing to work with this group of children
when they enter in the fall. On the days following the visit to their new school,
children are encouraged to discuss their observations and pose questions about their
new school in classroom discussions.

Similarities in United States and Northern Italian Approaches to Making Schools Ready for Children

There are several commonalities between successful "ready schools" efforts in the United States and Northern Italy. They cluster around three issues addressed above: cultural incongruity between home and school, continuity between preschool and local schools, and the expectation that every child can succeed. The following is an overview of successful efforts in both countries.

Cultural Incongruity

Strategies that have been employed in both countries to overcome cultural incongruity between home and school include home visits, orientations, and other outreach events for families, as well as curriculum and pedagogy that strengthen schools' links between the school, children, and families.

In the United States, successful efforts have been made in a variety of arenas. Nationally, Head Start policies encourage home visits, parent education, and provide help for parents who are learning how to navigate formal educational settings. In some communities, Countdown to Kindergarten has effectively opened lines of communication between parents and schools while, at the same time, helping parents prepare children with some of the routines and skills they will need as they enter school. In other locales, programs that are part of the SPARK initiative have worked to build strong partnerships between primary schools, preschools, and their community organizations to ensure children's success.

In Italy, national policies emphasize the crucial importance of home–school relationships and the need for schools to communicate effectively with families, particularly those who come from diverse backgrounds and those who have children with special needs. The Reggio philosophy encourages positive relations among schools, children, and families. For example, parents play important roles in schools' governance, and are typically invited to participate in school-sponsored events. Moreover, cultural values prevalent in the Emilia Romagna Provence encourage communication and collaboration between schools and families. These efforts help to create ready school environments for children.

Continuity Between Preschools and Local Schools

Child-focused preschools are often very different from primary schools that expect children to be "ready for school." Efforts in both the United States and Italy have been made not only to make children ready for school, but also to make primary schools ready for children.

In the United States, the National Governors Association put the responsibility for continuity of care in the hands of state and local advocates as well as policy makers. For example, expect schools to be accountable for creating learning environments that support all children's success. The SPARK project encouraged school administrators and teachers to create continuity between school settings.

In Italy, *Law 148* specifically addresses continuity between preschools and primary schools. It specifically requires curriculum coordination between the two settings. The implementation of priming events in preschools and the prevalence of similar activities in primary schools contributes to consistency across settings.

Expecting Every Child to Succeed

Ready schools respond to each child's developmental and educational needs. In other words, instruction needs to be differentiated to meet the needs of individual learners. Additionally, extensive understanding of child development, developmentally appropriate practice, and culturally relevant pedagogy is required to ensure that realistic requirements are balanced with high expectations. Efforts have been made in both the United States and Italy to create learning conditions that are conducive to achieve this effectively.

In the United States, Kellogg Foundation-supported locally developed SPARK initiatives have served as incubators of innovation in support of policies and practices that support children and families as they prepare for the important transition into formal educational settings.

In Italy, the Reggio Emilia approach is rooted in the beliefs that all children have rights, are active co-constructers of knowledge, and that multiple forms of knowing are valuable and necessary to create meaning (Hewett 2004). In other words, their practices are rooted in the belief that all children can learn and develop. They also deserve to be seen and met not only as worthy individuals but also as valuable members of the collective community. Such values reinforce the belief that all children can and will succeed and works against one size fits all curriculum and practices.

Implications and Recommendations

Just as every child deserves access to a high quality preschool program all children also deserve the opportunity to enter primary schools that are ready for them to be successful. In other words, children do not need to be "made ready for school", but rather schools need to be made ready for children. Several strategies described in this chapter have the potential to facilitate the establishment of ready schools.

First, cultural congruence between home and school can significantly impact children's school success. Although there are risk factors that schools cannot remediate (e.g., low birth rate, poverty, and parents' low educational attainment), there are several factors that schools can address by focusing on a ready school environment. For example, cultural incongruity between school and home can be addressed by engaging in such activities as home visits, orientation sessions for children and families, and curriculum planning that centers on children and families.

Second, continuity between preschool and primary school is essential to ensuring that children experience a smooth transition as they move from one setting to the next. Smooth transitions are more likely when teachers and schools create partnerships so that expectations, routines, philosophies, and interactional styles are aligned.

Third, all ready schools expect that all children can be successful. Instead of schools trying to make children fit to their standards, schools need to be responsive to children's developmental and educational needs.

Fourth, cross-fertilization of efforts between the United States and Italy has the potential to increase the likelihood that schools will be ready for the young children as they begin their formal education. For example, schools in the United States would benefit from exploring how priming events might be employed to smooth children's transitions. Likewise, Italian schools might benefit from community efforts such as Countdown for Kindergarten's tactic of providing activities for children and families in venues such as libraries and other community centers.

Ready schools are committed to supporting all children, particularly those whose life circumstances may disadvantage them during the early years, as they transition into the formal educational system. Promising practices that help to ensure all children's school success include strategies that successfully link preschools with the formal education system, align standards so that there is a shared understanding about what children should know and be able to do at kindergarten entry, and engage families in their young children's school experiences have been implemented in communities across the United States and Northern Italy. These success stories have the potential to inspire other communities to invest in the ready schools initiative and hold promise for reducing some of the barriers all children face during this important transition into school.

References

Bohan-Baker, M., & Little, P. M. D. (2004). *A review of current research and promising practices to involve families.* Cambridge, MA: Harvard Family Research Project. http://www.indianat-ransition.org/13-C%20Transitioning%20into%20Kindergarten/Harvard-Transition%20to%20 Kindergarten.pdf. Accessed 2 Jan 1010.

Caldwell, L. (1997). *Bringing Reggio Emilia home: An innovative approach to early childhood education.* New York, NY: Teachers College Press.

Corsaro, W. A., & Molinari, L. (2000). Priming events and Italian children's transition from pre-school to elementary school: Representations and action. *Social Psychology Quarterly, 63*(1), 16–33.

Corsaro, W. A., & Rizzo, T. (1988). Discussion and friendship: Socialization processes in peer culture of Italian nursery school children. *American Sociological Review, 53,* 879–894.

Countdown to Kindergarten Boston (n.d.). http://countdowntokindergarten.com. Accessed 2 Jan 2010.

Countdown to Kindergarten Maryland (n.d.). http://www.countdownmd.org/countdown_home. html. Accessed 2 Jan 2010.

Doucet, F., & Tudge, J. (2007). Co-constructing the transition to school: Reframing the novice versus expert roles of children, parents, and teachers from a cultural perspective. In R. C. Pianta, M. J. Cox, & K. L. Snow (Eds.), *School readiness and the transition to kindergarten in an era of accountability* (pp. 307–328). Baltimore, MD: Brookes.

Education Commission of the States (2009). *Linking ready kids to ready schools: A report on policy insights from the Governors' Forum Series.* http://www.ecs.org/docs/4208_COMC_report_forweb.pdf. Accessed 4 Jan 2010.

Edwards, C., Gandini, L., & Forman, G. (Eds.). (1998). *The hundred languages of children: The Reggio Emilia approach advanced reflections* (2nd ed.). Norwood, NJ: Ablex.

Freeman, N. K., & Brown, M. (2008). An authentic approach to assessing pre-kindergarten programs: Redefining readiness. *Childhood Education, 84*(5), 267–273.

Gonzalez-Mena, J. (2001). *Multicultural issues in childcare* (3rd ed.). Mountain View, CA: Mayfield.

Heath, S. B. (1983). *Ways with words: Language, life, and work in communities and classrooms.* New York: Cambridge University Press.

Hewett, V. M. (2004). Examining the Reggio Emilia approach to early childhood education. *Early Childhood Education Journal, 29*(2), 95–100.

Hong, G., & Yu, B. (2007). Early-grade retention and children's reading and math learning in elementary years. *Educational Evaluation and Policy, 29*(4), 239–261.

Improving Head Start for School Readiness Act of 2007, Public Law 134. 110th Cong. (2007). http://eclkc.ohs.acf.hhs.gov/hslc/Program%20Design%20and%20Management/Head%20Start%20Requirements/Head%20Start%20Act. Accessed 2 Jan 2010.

Jimerson, S. R. (2001). Meta-analysis of grade retention research: Implications for practice in the 21st century. *School Psychology Review, 30*(3), 420–437.

Katz, L. G., & Chard, S. C. (2000). *Engaging children's minds: The project approach.* Norwood, NJ: Ablex.

Miller, D. F. (1989). *First steps toward cultural difference: Socialization in infant/toddler day care.* Washington, DC: Child Welfare League of America.

National Association for the Education of Young Children (2009). *NAEYC Position Statement: Developmentally appropriate practice in early childhood programs serving children from birth though age 8.* Washington, DC: National Association for the Education of Young Children. http://www.naeyc.org/files/naeyc/file/positions/PSDAP.pdf. Accessed 2 Jan 2010.

National Education Goals Panel (2002). http://govinfo.library.unt.edu/negp/index-1.htm. Accessed 2 Jan 2010.

National Governors Association Center for Best Practices (2005a). *A governor's guide to school readiness: Building the foundation for bright futures.* Washington, DC: National Governors Association Center for Best Practices. http://www.nga.org/Files/pdf/0501GOVGUIDEREADINESS. pdf. Accessed 5 Jan 2010.

National Governors Association Center for Best Practices (2005b). *Building the foundation for bright futures: Final report of the NGA task force on school readiness.* Washington, DC: National Governors Association Center for Best Practices. http://www.nga.org/Files/pdf/0501TaskForceReadiness.pdf. Accessed 5 Jan 2010.

Organization for Economic Cooperation & Development (2001). *Early childhood education and care policy in Italy.* http://www.oecd.org/dataoecd/15/17/33915831.pdf. Accessed 8 Jan 2010.

Scott-Little, C. (2009). Children's readiness for success in school. In S. Feeney, A. Galper, & C. Seefeldt (Eds.), *Continuing issues in early childhood education* (3rd ed., pp. 100–128). Upper Saddle River, NJ: Pearson.

SERVE (n.d.). The *transition from Head Start to school: A team approach.* http://www.serve.org/TT/hs_tco.html. Accessed 2 Jan 2010.

Shore, R. (1998). *Ready schools: A report of the Goal 1 Ready Schools Resource Group.* Washington, DC: National Education Goals Panel (ED 416 582).

Chapter 13
Preparing Young Children for Schools in China

Critical Transitions for Chinese Children

Yaoying Xu

Overview

This chapter provides an introduction to the early educational system in China and discusses several major transitions for Chinese young children. The public school system in China consists of a 12-year formal education: 6-year elementary school, 3-year middle school (junior high), and 3-year high school. China provides a 9-year compulsory education. Before they enter the grade schools, young children may go through three types of early education programs: childcare or nursery programs for infants and toddlers (birth to 3), kindergarten programs for children 3 to 6 years of age, and a 1-year pre-primary program for children in rural areas prior to primary school. To avoid confusion for early childhood professionals from Western cultures, the term "pre-primary" was used throughout this chapter instead of the term "preschool," which typically refers to programs for 3- to 5-year-olds in the Western world. The term "kindergarten" in this chapter refers to programs serving 3- to 6-year-olds.

Although education has been valued and emphasized throughout the long history of China, early childhood education as a field is a relatively new discipline. The contemporary public school system in Mainland China has been established since 1949 when the Chinese Communist Party took over the government. This chapter begins with a review of the foundations of the Chinese early childhood education, followed by an exploration of the curriculum evolution. Then the transitions in three major stages in early childhood are discussed. Finally, the social and cultural influences in preparing young children for schools are examined.

Y. Xu (✉)
Virginia Commonwealth University, 1015 W Main St., P.O. Box 842020,
Richmond, VA 23284, USA
e-mail: yxu2@vcu.edu

D. M. Laverick, M. R. Jalongo (eds.), *Transitions to Early Care and Education,*
Educating the Young Child 4, DOI 10.1007/978-94-007-0573-9_13,
© Springer Science+Business Media B.V. 2011

Foundations of Early Childhood Education in China

Early childhood education today in China has been influenced by historical factors and recent developmental theories from Western cultures. The Chinese traditional culture has always played a significant role in the pedagogical and philosophical foundations in early childhood education. Since the educational reform in the early 1980s, Western theories and philosophies have been accepted and practiced by more and more Chinese educators and researchers.

Historical Background

Education has been valued throughout the history of China. The term "education" in the Chinese language consists of two words: *jiao* (teach) and *yu* (nurture). To teach and to nurture are two major concepts involved in education. While this literal interpretation may carry some true meaning of the educational philosophy in China, the significance of early childhood education for an individual's development was formally recognized in the early twentieth century (Vong 2008). Historically, the Chinese formal educational system consisted of only the elementary education (for children 7–15 years old) and higher education (for students over 15 years old). Instead of receiving public education, children younger than school age received private instruction from private tutors or home teachers (Bai 2000).

Confucianism has played a significant role in the Chinese educational ideology except during the Cultural Revolution period (1966–1976) when the formal educational system was abandoned and Confucianism was criticized. Social order and collectivism have been valued and reflected through the educational policies as well as conceptual framework. Interpersonal relationships among individuals in the same society were emphasized (Triandis 1990). This is especially important for the contemporary early childhood educators and researchers in China because the "One Child One Family" policy since 1979 has put more responsibility upon early childhood professionals to provide social interaction opportunities for young children to interact with their peers, who otherwise would interact primarily with their siblings in home settings.

Theoretical Foundations

Compared to the long history of education since the time of Confucius, kindergarten or preschool education in China was a more recent concept that evolved from Western educational ideas. Western educational theories such as those of Dewey, Montessori, Bronfenbrenner, Bruner, Piaget, and Vygosky were introduced to the field of early childhood education curricula, especially after China's economic reform and Open-Door policy beginning in the 1980s (Vong 2008; Zhu and Zhang 2008). These Western theories have influenced the Chinese early childhood educators in reforming the early childhood programs. Between 1949 and 1979, early childhood education in China was dominated by a teacher-directed, skill-oriented approach, an influence from the former Soviet Union theories as well as the Chinese culture's values of collectivity and discipline. In this approach, play was not emphasized and was often replaced by structured group lessons. Children's individual characteristics had to give in to group goals.

Since the early 1980s, developmental theories of Vygotsky and Piaget have received special attention among Chinese early childhood educators. Different from traditional teacher-led instruction, hands-on manipulation of objects and interactions with peers within a meaningful context are encouraged. Child-centered curricula that value children's intrinsic learning through free play activities have been developed. Vygotsky's socio-cultural theory, characterized by the zone of proximal development concept, is used in explaining the pedagogy observed in early childhood classrooms (Vong 2008). While these Western theories have influenced the Chinese early childhood educators in developing and reforming the early childhood programs, they also challenge the early childhood education system that had existed for more than 30 years since 1949.

The Evolution of the Early Childhood Education Curricula

Top-Down Model of the Kindergarten Reform

The reform in early childhood education in China came along with its widely known economic reform since the early 1980s (Liu and Feng 2005). Kindergarten educational reform began as a small scale, experimental format that emerged spontaneously in different parts of the country in the early 1980s, and gradually expanded to a large scale reform. Eventually it developed into a top-down model, led by the central government based on the *Regulations on Kindergarten Education Practice* issued by the National Education Committee of the People's Republic of China in 1989. Since then, the early childhood programs have been increasing every year. By 2008, the number of kindergartens nationwide was 133,700, an increase of 4,600 from the previous year, serving 24,749,600 children 3–6 years old, an increase of 1,261,300 (Ministry of Education 2009).

One primary goal of the early childhood education reform was to incorporate new educational theories and learner-centered approaches to early education, with the purposes of improving the quality of kindergarten education and strengthening the instructional skills of kindergarten teachers. As a top-down model, this reform was carried out through administrative policies to all levels of administrative organizations and kindergartens. Compared with the traditional model that was teacher-directed and skill-oriented, the reformed model emphasized child-initiated activities, individual differences, play-based performance, integrated curricula, and the process of learning (Zhu and Zhang 2008). As a result, a variety of curriculum approaches have been adopted including the Project Approach, Reggio Emilia, High/Scope, and Montessori (Li and Li 2003). Developmentally appropriate practice (DAP) was introduced as the framework for curriculum development.

Under this new model, play has been identified as a major way of young children's learning instead of structured group lessons. Early childhood educators started to observe children's play behaviors during activities as part of the evaluation process. Identifying individual differences of young children was another major component of the reform, which has also been the most challenging part of the reform because it caused conflicts with the traditional value of collectivism. Respecting children as individual persons is a new concept for many Chinese educators and parents. For example, it has always been valued and emphasized in the Chinese education curriculum that the interests of the collective group supersede the interests of oneself. It was viewed as being selfish if an individual put his or her own interests above those of the group.

Despite these challenges, educators have been carrying out the reform based on the modern theories and practices that respect young children as a group with similar developmental patterns while, at the same time, recognizing them as individuals with their own characteristics. As a learner-centered approach, the current Chinese kindergarten programs have been revitalized with new ideas of interacting with young children. Educators and parents have begun to appreciate that young children are not just being protected by the adult society, they should be respected as individuals with independent personality and dignity, and respected as persons with their own rights to learn and develop (Liu et al. 2005).

Goals and Standards

The goals and standards in early childhood education in China have been changed since 1979. According to the *Education Law of the People's Republic of China* (National People's Congress 1999), early childhood education has been regarded as the foundation of overall education. To ensure the quality of early education, national guidelines of policies for early childhood education were established by the central government as a general framework; the local governments and communities have established their own developmental plans (Wong and Pang 2002). The national *Kindergarten Work Regulation* recommends that kindergarten programs provide care and education for young children 3–6 years old by focusing on the development of the child as a whole and emphasizing play-based, integrated curricula; this was a gradual movement from a teacher-directed to a child-centered approach (Li 2006; Wong and Pang 2002). Five developmental and learning domains were addressed including health, social/emotional, science, language, and art, upon which the following goals were developed:

1. To prepare a healthy environment
2. To promote cognitive and language development
3. To foster children's moral and social development
4. To develop children's appreciation for the arts

One essential change in the new approach to kindergarten curricula is the emphasis on young children's active learning through exploration with the environment and interaction with peers in hands-on activities. Constructivism and social/cultural interactive learning has played a major role in the development of this new approach. Instead of learning through structured instruction as a collective group, young children now are encouraged to "construct," to build their own knowledge through active process of learning. While this change has inspired many Chinese early childhood educators to be creative and reflective, it also has caused challenges because it affects the fundamental ideology in the Chinese education system. In the traditional Chinese culture, learning was more extrinsic than intrinsic. This has much to do with a fundamental value rooted in the Chinese culture: namely that you learn with the main purpose of benefiting the collective group other than simply for the purpose of enjoying yourself. When these two purposes do not align, conflicts may arise.

Types of Early Childhood Programs

There are three main types of early childhood programs serving children three to six years of age. Most of these programs are regulated or licensed nationally and provincially with specific standards of health, safety, nutrition, and teacher training. The class/group size and staff-child ratios are also specified for each age group. Annual inspections are implemented to maintain the standards.

Full-Day Kindergarten Programs

The most popular early childhood programs serving children 3–6 years of age are full-day programs that operate about 8 hours a day from 8 a.m. to 4 p.m. Different classes are grouped by age: junior class for 3- to 4-year-olds; middle class for 4- to 5-year-olds, and senior class for 5- to 6-year-olds. According to the *Kindergarten Work Regulation*, the maximum class size is 25 for junior class and 30 for middle and senior classes. Full-day kindergartens are especially popular in large cities where both parents are employed.

Part-Day or Seasonal Programs

Part-day or seasonal programs may have temporary schedules that allow for adjustment and change to accommodate working parents' schedules. This type of program is common in state-run industries and large corporations where employees have to work by different shifts. The quality of these programs varies tremendously, from basic care with minimal resources to high-quality care and education with a variety of resources and supports.

Boarding Programs

Boarding programs operate 24 hours a day, five days a week throughout the year. Despite the criticism from Western early childhood professionals, boarding programs in early childhood are common and more prevalent in large cities. Children typically go home on Friday night and come back on Sunday night. Boarding programs typically have smaller group/class sizes. To ensure qualities of boarding programs, the government has established strict rules for regulating and monitoring all aspects of the program in care and education.

In addition to the three types of programs mentioned above, another type of early childhood provision is a 1-year early childhood program, which has been developed and implemented since the late 1980s, particularly in rural areas. The purpose of this type of program is to prepare young children for primary school, especially for children in rural areas who may not have the opportunities for receiving 2 or 3 years of early education.

Pre-Primary Programs

In China, over 50% of the population lives in rural areas (Zhao and Hu 2008). However, young children from rural or underdeveloped areas had not been guaranteed early education for several decades since 1949. The agricultural communities have unique needs and challenges in terms of young children's care and education due to the lack of resources and limits of funding, among many other factors. Lower enrollment in elementary schools and higher school dropout rates had been major issues in many rural areas. Since the economic reform and the Open Door Policy, the government established national guidelines that specifically focused on early childhood education in serving children in rural areas. In 1983, the central government released *Concern about Early Childhood Education in Rural Areas* specifying the critical role of early childhood education with policy guidelines.

The new guidelines encourage small towns and villages to take more active roles in developing and implementing early care and education programs to serve the local communities. As a minimum requirement, children 5–6 years old are offered a 1-year pre-primary program before they enter the primary school. As the lowest administrative organization, the village committees generally sponsored the pre-primary program. Most of these classes are hosted and administered through the village elementary schools. Many local governments and communities have started providing services for children 3–5 years old, with the eventual goal to provide a 3-year early education program for all young children 3–6 years old.

In addition to the shortage of financial resources, one big challenge for this type of program is the shortage of teaching staff. Most of the pre-primary classes are taught by elementary school teachers who may not receive formal training in early childhood education. Even for those who are licensed in early childhood education, many teachers in rural areas have not adopted the child-centered approach as recommended by kindergarten guidelines and supported by researchers (Zhang and Zhou 2005). These teachers tend to teach young children as they would older children. Age appropriate hands-on activities are very limited and children's individual needs and social/emotional development are often overlooked. Play is not encouraged, if it is allowed at all. Often times the curriculum and content are a version of the first grade program with discrete skills and intellectual abilities as the focus.

Despite these challenges, the number of kindergartens in China has been increasing in general and the pre-primary program has been implemented in most rural areas as the initial provision for young children prior to first grade. According to the *Chinese Children Development Outline: 2001–2010*, the focus of early care and education is on children's rights to health and education under the principles of Children First (Zhao and Hu 2008). While children from economically developed areas often receive three years of early education prior to primary school, it is the government's goal that the majority of children in rural areas will receive at least 1 year of pre-primary education.

Infants and Toddlers Programs

There is an increasing trend that young children in China enter kindergarten at a younger age. One reason for this trend is the demand from working parents in urban areas. Recent research also contributes to this growing trend (Zhu and Wang 2005). Consequently, many kindergarten programs expand their programs to infants and toddlers and many traditional nurseries start offering both care and education by improving the quality of the child care personnel. It is not uncommon that many infants and toddlers spend their whole day in nurseries or kindergartens for three to five days a week. Besides meeting the needs of working parents, some early childhood professionals and parents believe that quality early childcare and education programs may actually benefit these young children in terms of social interactions with their age appropriate peers, which has been limited at home settings in a one-child family (Li and Wang 2008).

Private Early Childhood Programs

Another characteristic in early childhood education is the rapidly growing trend of private early care and education programs as a result of the economic impact and change of governmental policies. In terms of funding sources, kindergartens in China used to have four categories: kindergartens sponsored directly by the government for its personnel at all levels; kindergartens sponsored by state-owned enterprises and large corporations as a support for their employees; kindergartens co-sponsored between parents and local communities in urban areas; and kindergartens sponsored by local rural governments in the countryside (Zeng 2008). All these kindergarten programs were considered public early childhood programs with full or partial support from the different levels of government and agencies. Private early childhood programs came into existence as a new concept along with the economic reform.

The central government in China started to shift its responsibilities for funding and managing early childhood education to nongovernmental agencies or private sectors since the 1990s (Li and Wang 2008). As a result, some public early childhood programs were forced to transform into self-funded enterprises when the budget was cut from the local governments. This change of policy has caused controversy among parents and educators. For example, Li and Wang's study (2008) suggested that many people were concerned about the quality and standards of self-funded programs when the transformation to private sectors changed the nature of teaching profession, whereas others expressed their support because the transformation might elicit fair market competition and might lead to a more reasonable distribution of educational resources.

Early Childhood Transitions

Young children in China may experience three major transitions during their early childhood period: (1) transition from home to nursery; (2) transition from nursery to kindergarten; and (3) transition from kindergarten to primary school. For children in rural areas, they may experience at least two transitions: from home to pre-primary and from pre-primary to primary school.

From Home to Nursery

Since 1949 Chinese women have been encouraged to join the workforce from all aspects of the society and this trend has only been strengthened in the last several decades. Accordingly, most parents of young children in urban settings are both employed. More and more parents start to enroll their infants and toddlers in childcare programs or nurseries as early as age one. Even though some grandparents may provide childcare for their grandchild, many parents still choose to enroll the child in an early care program for the benefit of the child. The transition of the infant or toddler from home to nursery typically is gradual for two main reasons. First, most working mothers are provided three to four months maternal leave so that they are able to stay at home for the first few months. Second, many retired grandparents offer childcare at least for the first year. Even after the first year, grandparents may enroll the child in a childcare program for certain hours a day, for example, two hours a day to play with other children in the center.

Traditionally the primary goal of the nurseries was to provide childcare. However, recent research has influenced the curriculum of childcare programs by looking at the impact of early education on the development of young children. Therefore, many childcare centers have adopted a child-centered curriculum and started to pay attention to young children's social/emotional development. Social interaction and play are essential for these programs through developmentally appropriate environment and materials.

From Nursery to Kindergarten

For many young children this is their first major transition in early childhood. Typically, most children in urban settings around the age of three would experience this transition, either from a childcare center, or from a home setting where childcare was provided by grandparents or other caregivers. For the next three years prior to primary school, children would experience three levels of early care and education through three kindergarten classes: junior, middle, and senior. The transition between the classes is gradual, although the focus of each year changes. With the introduction of Western approaches such as the Project Approach, the Reggio Emilia approach, High/Scope curriculum, and Montessori method, individual children's needs and characteristics have received more attention and respect, especially during the transition period. For example, children are allowed to follow their own pace in completing a project and parents or other primary caregivers are invited to spend some time with the child in the center.

In recent years, there has been an increasing effort to integrate nurseries and kindergarten programs to form continuous care and education for children from birth to age 6. Historically, nurseries were separated from kindergarten programs and were overseen by the Ministry of Health, whereas kindergartens were administered under the Ministry of Education. Nurseries used to focus on health and care, and their personnel were trained as "nurses" rather than educators. In recent years, the educational reform and early childhood research have promoted the concept of "edu-care" by integrating care and education for infant and toddler programs (Zhu 2002). Many kindergartens have begun to enroll children as young as 2 or 3 years old and many others have collaborated with nurseries in providing educational services to young children and their families.

Kindergarten to Primary

The new approach to kindergarten curriculum is child-centered and play-based with developmentally appropriate environments that allow for children's free exploration and interaction. The setting of primary schools is more structured and teacher-directed. Free play is limited and school readiness skills such as early language and literacy skills, early math and science concepts, and social interaction skills are expected for first graders. Therefore, the senior class of a kindergarten program has more skill-oriented objectives to teach children in specific academic areas, such as counting, writing basic words, and introducing the pronunciation system (*pin yin*). Additionally, common knowledge, such as school rules, is taught.

To ensure attainment of the learning objectives, informal assessment such as direct observation and sometimes formal testing (e.g., one-on-one oral testing) is administered as part of the evaluation. Some kindergarten programs even start to assign homework every day to prepare children for primary schools. Although classroom rules are taught through play or planned activities, instructional sessions become longer.

Pre-primary to Primary

As mentioned in previous sections, early childhood education in rural or underdeveloped areas has not been offered as the same scope as these programs in urban settings due to the limited resources. The main goal of the government is to provide a 1-year pre-primary program for young children prior to primary schools. More than 70% of these pre-primary classes are provided through the local elementary schools. The rationale is that the existing resources such as teaching personnel, classrooms, and materials from the local elementary schools can be shared while these young children are prepared for primary schools. Pre-primary programs are offered either as full-day or half-day programs for children 5–6 years old.

This approach has been effective in meeting the immediate needs of preparing young children for basic academic skills required by primary schools in rural and underdeveloped areas. Compared with the early childhood programs in urban and more developed communities, however, the pre-primary program has several limitations. First, the curriculum focuses on academic skills similar to elementary education. While it may prepare young children with basic skills such as language, literacy, and early math, developmentally appropriate activities are replaced with formal class sessions. Second, the approach to instruction is mostly teacher-directed with drills and worksheets that would be more appropriate for older children. As a result, whether these programs have long-term benefits for young children's development remains unknown.

Social and Cultural Influence in Preparing Young Children for Schools

The appropriateness of education is always defined within the relevant social and cultural contexts. The contemporary early childhood education in China reflects the influence from social, cultural, and political changes. From its current pedagogy and curricula, interactions among traditional Chinese values, Western standards, and the communist principles are evident. China's early childhood curricula reflect a hybrid of these three cultures (Wang and Spodek 2000; Zhu and Wang 2005).

Traditional Values

Traditionally, Chinese culture is viewed as more oriented to the group, while Western culture is more oriented toward the individual (Tobin et al. 1989; Liu 2003). Because group interests are placed above the individual ones, extrinsic motivation is encouraged, such as working hard to make other people proud or to make the community look good. In this traditional value, intrinsic motivation is not emphasized. For example, young children would not be encouraged to do something simply because it makes them *feel* good. Children as young as 3 years old are taught to do the *right* things, to love their hometowns, to be respectful of the elders, and to be patriotic to their motherland. These values always have been embedded into the educational system in China since the time of Confucius. It would be culturally inappropriate if the early childhood curricula totally abandoned these traditional values because they are rooted in Chinese people's everyday life as well as the country's ideological system.

Discipline is another value that can be easily traced back to the tradition. Accurate recitation, rote memorization, and disciplined behavior were some of the criteria required for young children from their private teachers or tutors at old times. Historically, corporal punishment was part of the routine as well. Young students could be punished because of an error in their recitation of a poem or a question being asked during the teacher's instructional time. After receiving the corporal punishment, students were supposed to express their appreciation to the teacher for the care and attention they received from the teacher.

Western Standards

It is well known that the Western culture values individualism, independence, and self-determination. Early childhood curricula based on Western values establish their standards by creativity, free expression of speech, and problem solving skills. While it is a natural component in an American early childhood curriculum, these are new concepts for the Chinese ideology. Thus there could be a discrepancy between what was understood and what was accepted. In other words, even when teachers say they understand and accept the new curriculum, they may not implement it if the new approach conflicts with their fundamental educational beliefs and philosophy. For example, Chinese teachers emphasize the accuracy in diction or strokes when children learn a new word whereas American educators tend to teach a new word within a context that helps the child make connections through creative processes. While Chinese children are taught to follow the rules and learn the consequence of bad behavior, American children are encouraged to ask questions about the rules. An American teacher may tell a child to "take your turn because it is *fair*," whereas her Chinese counterpart may tell the child to "take your turn because it is *right*."

Western standards may or may not fit the traditional values. For the curriculum reform to be successful, it is critical that educators view the Western standards within the Chinese culture.

Political Priority

The principles of the Chinese Communist Party have significantly influenced the development of curriculum goals of early childhood education in China. During the Mao period (1949–1976), political priority dominated all levels of the educational system. The Communist Party encouraged schools to prepare students in three main domains: political education, cognitive education, and physical education. This priority has changed in the post-Mao era (1976–Present) with an emphasis on cognitive education. However, although Western values such as individualism and independence have been accepted by Chinese early childhood educators, the communist culture still influences today's early childhood curriculum in areas such as organization, discipline, and manual labor.

The influence from different cultures on education is ever-changing across time. Education is contextual, dynamic, as well as interactive (Li 2006; Zhu and Zhang 2008). The Western approach only makes sense to children and teachers when it is embedded within the Chinese country's traditions and political principles. While the influence of the communist culture is strong in practical aspects, the traditional culture has had a profound influence on the ideological foundation for the early childhood education in Mainland China.

References

Bai, L. (2000). The Chinese kindergarten movement. In R. Wollons (Ed.), *Kindergarten and culture: The global diffusion of an idea* (pp. 137–165). New Haven, CT: Yale University Press.

Li, H., & Li, P. (2003). Lessons from implanting Reggio Emilia and Montessori curriculum in China. [In Chinese.] *Preschool Education, 9*, 4–5.

Li, H., & Wang, C. (2008). Transformation of public kindergartens in Shenzhen: Internet study of public views. *Chinese Education and Society, 41*(2), 41–70.

Li, S. (2006). Development of kindergarten care and education in the People's Republic of China since the 1990s. In E. Melhuish & K. Petrogiannis (Eds.), *Early childhood care and education: International perspectives* (pp. 151–166). London: Taylor & Francis.

Liu, Q. (2003). Understanding different culture patterns or orientations between East and West. *Investigationes Linguisticae, 9*, 21–30.

Liu, Y., & Feng, X. (2005). Kindergarten educational reform during the past two decades in Mainland China: Achievements and problems. *International Journal of Early Years Education, 13*(2), 93–99.

Liu, Y., Pan, Y., & Sun, H. (2005). Comparative research on young children's perceptions of play: An approach to observing the effects of kindergarten educational reform. *International Journal of Early Years Education, 13*(2), 101–112.

Ministry of Education (2009). Statistical communiqué on national educational development in 2008. http://www.moe.gov.cn/edoas/en/. Accessed 30 Jan 2010.

National Education Committee of the People's Republic of China. (1989). Kindergarten work regulations and procedures. http://www.moe.gov.cn/. Accessed 29 Jan 2010.

National People's Congress (1999). Teachers' law of the People's Republic of China (1993). In Chinese Preschool Education Research Society (Ed.), *A collection of major documents on early childhood education in the People's Republic of China* (pp. 13–20). Beijing: Beijing Normal University.

Tobin, J., Wu, D., & Davidson, D. (1989). *Preschool in three cultures: Japan, China, and the United States*. New Haven, CT: Yale University Press.

Triandis, H. C. (1990). Cross-cultural studies of individualism and collectivism. In J. J. Berman (Ed.), *Cross-cultural perspective: Current theory and research in motivation* (pp. 41–133). Lincoln, NE: University of Nebraska Press.

Vong, K. (2008). *Evolving creativity: New pedagogies for young children in China*. Oakhill, VA: Trentham.

Wang, X. C., & Spodek, B. (2000). *Early childhood education in China: A hybrid of the traditional, communist, and Western culture*. Paper presented at the Annual Conference of the National Association for the Education of Young Children, Atlanta, GA.

Wong, N. C. M., & Pang, L. J. (2002). Early childhood education in China: Issues and development. In L. K. S. Chan & E. J. Mellor (Eds.), *International developments in early childhood services* (pp. 53–69). New York, NY: Lang.

Zeng, X. (2008). A design of an appropriate early childhood education funding system in China. *Chinese Education and Society, 41*(2), 8–19.

Zhang, Y. T., & Zhou, Q. Q. (2005). Countermeasures and present condition of the preschool education in the countryside. [In Chinese.] *Journal of Sichuan College of Education, 9*, 41–42.

Zhao, L., & Hu, X. (2008). The development of early childhood education in rural areas in China. *Early Years, 28*(2), 197–209.

Zhu, J. (2002). *Early childhood care and education in P.R. China*. Paper presented at 2002 KEDI-UNESCO Bangkok Joint Seminar and Study Tour on Early Childhood Care and Education, Seoul, Korea.

Zhu, J., & Wang, C. (2005). Contemporary early childhood education research in China. In B. Spodek & O. N. Saracho (Eds.), *International perspectives on research in early childhood education* (pp. 55–77). Charlotte, NC: Information Age.

Zhu, J., & Zhang, J. (2008). Contemporary trends and developments in early childhood education in China. *Early Years, 28*(2), 173–182.

Chapter 14
The Socio-Cultural Contexts of Early Education in Caribbean Societies

A Focus on Transition to Primary School

Jaipaul L. Roopnarine and James E. Johnson

Following global trends, there has been a steady increase in preschool/primary enrollments in the Caribbean and Latin American region (about 43% growth in Caribbean region between 1999 and 2004; UNESCO 2006). As in many other societies across the world (see Dakar Framework for Action, UNESCO 2000), Caribbean countries have placed a good deal of stock on early childhood development and education as a way of improving the life chances of children later on (Logie 2009; Samms-Vaughan 2004; Spijk et al. 2008). Accordingly, a number of Caribbean countries have embraced the promise of educational, social, and economic returns from long-term, large- and small-scale early intervention and early childhood programs (Grantham-McGregor et al. 2007; Spijk et al. 2008; Weikart and Schweinhart 2009; Zigler and Styfco 2004). Indeed, there is credible evidence on the salubrious effects of parent-child programs in Turkey, Colombia, Bangladesh, Jamaica, and Bolivia, and from integrated models of service delivery that provide nutritional supplements, parental support, and direct involvement with children in India (Integrated Child Development Services) and Bolivia (Proyecto Integral de Desarollo Infantil); see Engle et al. (2007).

With increasing emphasis on quality early childhood education in Caribbean countries, a growing concern among Ministries of Education, educational policy-makers, educators, and parents is how young children make the successful transition from early childhood education settings to primary school. Although identified some time ago (Rodrigues 1994), it has been a difficult issue to address because of the strong emphasis on academic training early in children's lives and pressures due to sparse resources and family structural organization within different developmental niches in Caribbean countries. That is, the exigencies of poverty and other transitions in children's and families' lives (e.g., mate-shifting and child-shifting, parental migration) may also influence children's entrance into formal schooling in profound ways (see Samms-Vaughan 2004). In this chapter, we take a closer look at the cultural meaning of transition to primary school in English-speaking Caribbean

J. L. Roopnarine (✉)
Department of Child and Family Studies, Syracuse University, Syracuse, NY 13244, USA
e-mail: jroopnar@syr.edu

D. M. Laverick, M. R. Jalongo (eds.), *Transitions to Early Care and Education,*
Educating the Young Child 4, DOI 10.1007/978-94-007-0573-9_14,
© Springer Science+Business Media B.V. 2011

countries. After providing a cultural context for family socialization practices and early education, we discuss the findings of recent studies on academic and social skills as indicators of the readiness to make the transition to primary school. Despite the fact that English-speaking countries share a history of colonization and commonalities are evident in childrearing and educational beliefs and practices among families (see Roopnarine et al. in press; Williams et al. 2006), the early childhood systems in different countries encompass an array of educational practices with children of different ages (e.g., Basic School begins at 3 in Jamaica; preschool begins at 3 years 9 months in Guyana and ends at 5 years 9 months, then children move on to preparatory school; for more detailed descriptions see Austin 2005; Leo-Rhynie et al. 2009; Samms-Vaughan 2004). Because of this and the lack of data on children's first experiences with out-of-home care/education, the focus is limited to children's transition from preschool to primary school.

Framing the Meaning of Transition in Caribbean Countries

Until fairly recently, researchers have viewed childhood transitions primarily in terms of developmental processes that are common to children worldwide. Cultural and cross-cultural theorists and researchers emphasize the multiple developmental pathways to the acquisition of cognitive and social skills in young children (Greenfield et al. 2003; Super and Harkness 1997), and to cultural variations in the manner in which parents prioritize childrearing goals in caring for young children and in devising investment strategies for early learning and education (LeVine 1974, 2004). Some (e.g., Gaskins 2006) have argued rather persuasively that a general goal of developmental models is to explain early socialization in humans as a species and as such do not adequately account for developmental trajectories within specific cultural groups. Thus, while childhood transitions may be universally present, they may hold different meanings across cultural communities and the potential exists that they may be expressed and achieved differently.

In Caribbean societies, transition to early schooling is approached with less fanfare and angst than in the technologically developed world because families must devote greater attention to other concurrent and challenging events in their lives that are crucial to the survival and well-being of the family. This being so, Caribbean children's entrance into early childhood and primary education programs is neither linear nor unidimensional. As in several other cultural communities, it involves factors within the home (e.g., parental belief systems, socioeconomic resources), schools/early childhood settings (e.g., teacher visits to children's homes, parent-teacher contacts, and the readiness of schools), and the larger community (Rimm-Kaufman and Pianta 2000; Samms-Vaughan 2004; Vogler et al. 2008). However, the transition to school in the Caribbean has other added dimensions that may make the process more complicated. For instance, due to economic circumstances and family life-course practices young Caribbean children are often forced to negotiate multiple transitions (prolonged parental separations due to mate-shifting, child-shifting, external migration that may separate parent and child for up to 5 years) simultaneously, relatively unaided. The widespread depressive impact of consistent harsh social and economic conditions (e.g., crowding, household possessions, parental occupation, and violence) on family functioning, physical health, and school outcomes are well-documented (Samms-Vaughan 2004), and so too are the negative effects of paternal instability due to mate-shifting (see Roopnarine et al. in press; Roopnarine in press) and parental absence, as a function of external migration, on childhood achievement and social adjustment in Jamaican children (Pottinger 2005).

But there appear to be other important cultural differences pertaining to which factors weigh more systematically and heavily during the transition process in the English-speaking Caribbean countries compared to the technologically developed world. First, the much touted home–school interface is not as prominent in the Caribbean as it is in the technologically developed societies. There is an entrenched sociocultural system whereby Caribbean families explicitly rely on schools as the primary authority in educating children and often defer to these institutions on matters relating to schooling. As a result, they may not perceive the need to assist their children in psychologically negotiating the early schooling process. Second, and equally important, the transition to school is enveloped in preparation for the rigors of academic training in the primary school years, in narrowing gender disparities in academic performance associated with boys being "at greater risk" for underachievement and school dropout later on (see Goolsarran 2009), and in continuity in the curriculum from preschool to primary school (see Leo-Rhynie et al. 2009). For example, Guyana's national preschool program is deeply entrenched in academic preparation for pre-primary and primary education (see Sukhdeo 2008) and for that matter, so are the preparatory and private preschools in Jamaica (Samms-Vaughan 2004) and Trinidad and Tobago (Logie 2009). Put differently, the early childhood "curriculum" in several Caribbean countries is geared toward learning basic skills and manners at the expense of not attending to social-psychological processes related to childhood transitions. As will become obvious later, this focus meshes well with teachers' and parents' cultural expectations of what children should learn in preschools.

Why might English-speaking Caribbean parents accord such overwhelming emphasis on academic preparedness for transition to primary school? A possible answer resides in the ecological niche where there are pressures for academic socialization for immediate educational returns in order to ensure a positive long-term developmental trajectory for children (see Kaplan and Bock 2001, for a discussion of embodied capital theory). In other words, in harsh ecological niches, parents and teachers may bank heavily on educational investment early in the child's life to set the pace for long-term gains to break out of the cycle of poverty. Parents explicitly state that the preschool years are crucial for the development of basic academic skills and find play-based education unappealing (Leo-Rhynie et al. 2009; Roopnarine et al. 2004). Furthermore, educational success achieved in the early school years is likely to affect investment strategies in children's education in subsequent years—whether there is continued educational support or allocation of adequate resources. These cost-benefit decisions are not independent of family organization patterns, socialization practices, or beliefs about early development and education.

It is to a consideration of these issues and their implications for transition to primary school that we turn to next.

Childrearing Practices and Transition

In the multi-ethnic communities (e.g., African Caribbean, Indo Caribbean, Amerindians, Mixed-ethnic, European Caribbean) of the English-speaking Caribbean, it is often difficult to speak in a uniform voice about childrearing practices. Nonetheless, there are a few prevailing childrearing practices in the region that may shed light on processes within the family that could aid or abet the transition to early schooling. The interpersonal strength and positive parenting attributes of English-speaking Caribbean families have been described in several reviews (Williams et al. 2006; Roopnarine et al. in press). Among them are collectivistic childrearing practices where there are multiple caregivers and nurturers of children (Roopnarine et al. 1997), religiosity (Anderson 2007), maternal commitment to childrearing in the face of extreme economic hardship, and social network support or functional extendedness (Roopnarine et al. in press). No doubt these attributes would more likely contribute in positive ways to the transition to primary school. But, a resilient, strengths-based model on transition to schools in Caribbean countries is yet to be proffered, much less tested. Having said that, there are partner relationships/practices and parenting tendencies among Caribbean families that may undermine children's successful adjustment to early schooling.

The studies on family organization patterns and childrearing practices have been conducted on two primary ethnic groups: African Caribbean families, a dominant group across most Caribbean countries, and Indo Caribbean families residing predominantly in Trinidad and Tobago and Guyana. These two groups have different mating/marital strategies: marriage is more common among Indo Caribbean families, whereas it occurs less frequently and much later in African Caribbean families, after progressive mating in visiting and common-law relationships (Anderson 2007; Brown and Barker 2003; Roopnarine et al. in press). Different mating/marital strategies have been shown to influence resource allocation, the nature and quality of parenting investment in young children, and child-shifting. For instance, Trinidadian men interacted less and directed more negative interactions to non-biological than biological offspring (Flinn 1992), and in a Jamaican sample there was a significant relationship between multiple father figures and withdrawn behavior in preschoolers (Samms-Vaughan 2004). Further, children who are shifted to other residences due to mate-shifting, external migration, or economic hardship may have to cope with the loss of attachment figures while establishing new social ties with alternative caregivers (Roopnarine and Krishnakumar 2006). Instability in residential patterns has been shown to contribute to conduct problems in children (Crawford-Brown 1997). Thus, even though mate-shifting and child-shifting (estimates range between 15% and 33%; Russell-Brown et al. 1997) are normative practices in Caribbean countries, both could have spillover and/or carryover effects on the transition to school.

There are other insidious factors embedded within the family system that may influence children's schooling experiences: parenting styles and harsh discipline. It has been repeatedly asserted that Caribbean families use a mixture of authoritarian and indulgent parenting practices—warmth mixed with punitiveness (Leo-Rhynie 1997). In two recent cluster analyses of parenting in Indo-Guyanese (N = 139 mothers) and a group of multi-ethnic Trinidadian families (N = 180 mother–father pairs), this admixture of parenting practices received support (Roopnarine and Krishnakumar 2010). In both samples, parents were high in warmth and behavioral control, but the analyses revealed two clusters of parents. Interestingly, the two groups were similar in warmth and control but differed in degree of hostility, neglect, and undifferentiated rejection. These findings indicate that within the confines of warmth, parents use harsher means of controlling and managing children's behaviors. In this vein, they use shame, social threats (e.g., "the strange woman down the street will come and get you" in Guyana), negative comments/denigration (e.g., "you are a hardened child" in Trinidad and Tobago), forceful commands and insults, and criticisms—behaviors that indicate some aspects of psychological control. Along with physical punishment, which is quite prevalent in the Caribbean, these behaviors are used to curb undesirable behaviors (see reviews by Roopnarine et al. in press; Williams et al. 2006). Praise or rewards are sporadic and public displays of affection are rare in Caribbean families. In one survey, about 23.6% of children received praise for doing something that pleased the parent (Leo-Rhynie 1997).

In the absence of outcome data in Caribbean countries, it is difficult to determine what these parenting practices mean for childhood adjustment in harsh ecological niches. Data from within Caribbean countries indicate that rigidity in family functioning had positive associations with behavioral difficulties in Jamaican preschoolers (Samms-Vaughan 2004), and that the frequency and severity of physical punishment predicted aggressive behaviors in Trinidadian preschoolers (Roopnarine and Krishnakumar 2010). Research from other societies clearly indicates that physical punishment is associated with aggression (see meta-analysis by Gershoff 2002) and that psychological control has a deleterious effect on children's social adjustment through the transition from kindergarten to primary school (Aunola and Nurmi 2005). It is worth noting that, depending on the severity of conditions within the developmental niche, the parenting practices among Caribbean parents could be inhibitory or facilitative in meeting day to day childrearing goals.

Parental Beliefs and Expectations of Young Children

Eco-cultural theorists (e.g., Super and Harkness 1997; Weisner 1998) propose that parental beliefs or internal working models about childrearing (e.g., discipline, early education, when young children acquire cognitive and social skills) are instrumental in guiding and structuring everyday cognitive and social activities for children, which, in turn, could have direct and indirect effects on different aspects of childhood development (see Sigel and McGillicuddy-DeLisi 2002). Parents' beliefs or ethnotheories about childcare, childhood development, and early education vary a good deal across cultural communities (see Rogoff 2003; Roopnarine and Metindogan 2006; Super and Harkness 1997), and some have questioned the symmetry in meaning of parenting beliefs and practices for child development outcomes across cultures (see Chao 1994; LeVine 2004; Roopnarine et al. 2004; Super and Harkness 1997). In some cultural groups, parents have earlier developmental expectations of children (Goodnow et al. 1984) and engage in the practice of "concerted cultivation" (Lareau 2003), whereas in others, parents believe that children acquire social and cognitive skills "naturally" or through observation (Gaskins 2006; Roopnarine and Metindogan 2006) and that playful activities are peripheral to childhood development (Roopnarine in press).

African Caribbean and Indo Caribbean parents believe that children should be obedient and compliant, and show unilateral respect to adults and proper conduct in their presence (Durbrow 1999; Wilson et al. 2003). An overwhelming majority of parents in Antigua, St. Kitts, St. Lucia, St. Vincent, Barbados, and Jamaica thought that children should obey their parents (Grant et al. 1983). Other studies show that Guyanese adults chose obedience as the most desirable socialization orientation (Wilson et al. 2003), and Dominican parents described childhood competence in terms of respect for and obedience to adults, academic skills, proficiency in chores, getting along with peers, and engaging in activities in the larger community and school (Durbrow 1999). Dominicans almost never see their children as *bwen lave* (well brought up), and regularly describe children's behaviors in negative terms (*A-betant* or troublesome, *Ka Raisonne* or rude, miserable, lazy/idle). Before three years of age, *A-betant* carries less of a negative stigma; it is viewed positively (Durbrow 1999).

Developmental expectations of Caribbean children can be unrealistic, especially among low-income families. Together, Indo Caribbean and African Caribbean parents have a poor understanding of developmental milestones as parental expectations often do not match children's behavioral skills or competencies. When parents in Guyana, Jamaica, and St. Vincent and the Grenadines were asked what preschoolers should be able to do, their responses were almost identical across the three countries. Guyanese parents believed that their children should be able to write, dress self, read, verbally express self, identify numbers and count, and take care of self; Jamaican parents believed that their children should be able to write, read, dress self, and verbally express self; and parents in St. Vincent and the Grenadines believed that their children should be able to write their names, letters, and numbers, take care of self, dress self, and count/identify numbers. In the social skills area, parents in all three countries thought that children should be courteous (i.e., display manners) above all other behaviors (Leo-Rhynie et al. 2009).

School Readiness as an Emerging Transition Issue in Caribbean Countries

As there are virtually no data on children's adjustment to day care or preschool in Caribbean countries, a basic strategy in research on transition from preschool to pre-primary and primary schools has been to document different levels of academic performance and behavioral skills of young children toward the end of the pre-school years in order to determine whether they are "prepared" for formal schooling. A widespread assumption is that children who perform at high levels of academic competence will find the transition to primary school more congenial. In this segment of the chapter, we discuss the findings of three such studies (Leo-Rhynie et al. 2009; Roopnarine and Krishnakumar 2010; Samms-Vaughan 2004) that provide some insights into the school readiness phenomenon. Again, the early childhood systems across Caribbean countries vary considerably in terms of length of time spent in preschools, teacher training across sites, quality of the home and early childhood environments, age of entry into preschools, and educational approaches/curricula. Consequently, school readiness comparisons across countries should be interpreted cautiously.

In an attempt to better understand the ability of children to make the transition to primary school, Leo-Rhynie et al. (2009) assessed a range of academic and social skills among 99 preschool-aged children in Guyana (three urban and three rural nursery schools), 89 children in Jamaica (five pre-primary programs—two basic schools, two infant schools and one preparatory school), and 94 children in St. Vincent and the Grenadines (three urban and three rural preschools). Assessments were conducted during the children's final year of preschool and involved the use of classroom observations, focus groups, teacher interviews, standard instruments (the Early Years Evaluation (EYE) Test and the Student Worksheet), and parent and teacher questionnaires. The EYE instrument provides indices of school preparedness and emergent literacy of 4-6 year-olds in the following domains: awareness of self and environment, social skills, behavior, and approaches to learning, cognitive skills, language and communication, and physical development. The Student Worksheet was designed along the lines of the Jamaican Ministry of Education Grade One Inventory and assesses children's academic readiness skills that are deemed important for success in grade school (visual motor coordination, visual perception discrimination, auditory perception, and letter and number knowledge). Of obvious interest to the present discussion are the cognitive and social data on children and those on teachers' and parents' perceptions of school readiness as children prepare for entry into primary school.

On the different components of the Student Worksheet most children were at or near mastery levels. For instance, on visual and motor coordination 66% of children in St. Vincent and the Grenadines, 98% in Guyana, and 98% in Jamaica achieved mastery; on visual perception discrimination 69% of children in St. Vincent and the Grenadines, 46% in Guyana, and 97% in Jamaica achieved mastery; and on auditory perception 64% of children in St. Vincent and the Grenadines, 71% in Guyana, and 94% in Jamaica achieved mastery at the end of preschool. Overall, Jamaican children appeared better prepared for first grade than Guyanese children or children from St. Vincent and the Grenadines. The disparities were greatest in the mastery of letter and number knowledge area between children in St. Vincent and the Grenadines (60%) and Guyana (67%) and Jamaica (94%). A similar pattern emerged when children's performance on the EYE is considered. More than 90% of Jamaican children were judged to be in the high competence area on language and communication, awareness of self and environment, social skills and behavior, and physical development, and 88% were in the high competence area on cognitive skills. By comparison, only 35% of children in St. Vincent and the Grenadines and 50% in Guyana were in the high competence categories. Correspondingly, 13% of children in the Guyanese sample and 23% of children in the St. Vincent and Grenadines sample were in the low competence category (Leo-Rhynie et al. 2009). These discrepancies may mean that a greater number of children in St. Vincent and the Grenadines and Guyana are "at risk" for educational difficulties. In a group of Jamaican preschoolers who were followed through third grade, the achievement trajectory for low-achieving children got progressively worse over time (Samms-Vaughan 2004).

Teachers' perceptions of school readiness for primary education were remarkably similar across the three countries. They mentioned that the mastery of academic skills placed children on good footing for the transition to primary school. More specifically, Guyanese teachers mentioned identifying letters and their sounds, writing, counting, following instructions, and communication skills as major criteria for school readiness. Their counterparts in the other two countries agreed with these beliefs, but Jamaican teachers thought teaching/learning materials, the classroom environment, teaching strategies, community involvement, and social skills were also important, and teachers in St. Vincent and the Grenadines thought that educational tours, children's knowledge of themselves, and social skills contributed to the transition process as well. The anticipated academic readiness skills for primary school were also firmly planted in parents' aspirations for their children (e.g., number recognition, writing, reading and spelling) (Leo-Rhynie et al. 2009).

Although not primarily designed to assess transition to primary school, a study (Roopnarine and Krishnakumar 2010), conducted over a 2-year period in Guyana and focused on parenting practices (e.g., parental warmth, hostility, undifferentiated rejection, behavioral control, and indifference and neglect) and academic and social outcomes in 139 preschool-aged children, provides some additional insights into the academic and social readiness of rural Guyanese children for formal schooling. Using an instrument developed by the Ministry of Education in Guyana, data were gathered on the psychomotor (e.g., gross-motor, fine-motor, body balance, eye-hand coordination), intellectual (e.g., use of oral language, symbolic play and imitation, displaying memory and attention, logico-mathematical thought), and socio-emotional (e.g., respect for others, conformity to rules, cooperative activities, friendships) development of children at the end of three marking periods per year for two years. Only data from the final term of children's second year in preschool (prior to entry into primary school) are discussed here.

Teachers' assessments of children revealed a pattern of findings that is congruent with those of the study just discussed. On key intellectual skill areas, only about a third of rural Guyanese children were judged to be in the high performing range: use of oral language (30%), logico-mathematical thought (38%), interpersonal communication (32%), written expression (37%), artistic expression (30%), imagination (31%), expression of ideas and thoughts (32%), perceptive abilities (32%), and displaying memory and attention (30%). On most of these measures, however, about two-thirds of the 139 children performed above average. Children fared a little better on assessments of social skills, but less than 50% received a superior rating in most categories: sense of self (49%), independence (54%), respect for others (33%), consideration for others (34%), conformity to rules (35%), interaction with others (43%), and cooperative skills (48%). Needless to say, these findings confirm the overwhelming emphasis on academic skills in the early training of young children in Caribbean countries and match parental expectations of what children should acquire from enrollment in preschool. It appears that there is far less attention paid, by parents or teachers, to social adjustment or general psychological difficulties (e.g., school phobia, enuresis, teeth grinding) that children may encounter as they move to primary school. It is not the case that Caribbean parents and children are immune to the adjustment difficulties witnessed during major transitions in families' and children's lives in other cultural communities or that they are unaware of school readiness issues for primary education. Their concerns seem to surround academic training. There is a lackluster attitude toward children's psychological difficulties during the early childhood years that may stem from a demanding academic regimen (Leo-Rhynie et al. 2009). On this count, teachers are also generally ill-prepared to deal with psycho-social issues emanating from the home or school environment. To the detriment of children, many teachers assume that good academic preparation=successful adjustment to primary school.

It is noteworthy that in both studies, there were very few gender differences in academic or social skills between boys and girls during the preschool years. This was also the case for the achievement and cognitive scores obtained for preschoolers in the Jamaican Profiles study discussed next. The better academic achievement of girls over boys in Caribbean countries (Goolsarran 2009; Samms-Vaughan 2004) seems to emerge much later after children have made the transition to primary school. Among Jamaican first-graders there were no gender differences in the Wide Range Achievement Test (WRAT). The underlying cause for the divergence in academic performance in boys and girls as children progress through their school careers is not readily apparent to us and not a major focus of the issues considered herein.

To more adequately address transition to primary school, we draw upon longitudinal data from the "Profiles" project in Jamaica (Samms-Vaughan 2004). Two-hundred and forty-five children (5–6 years of age) were followed through Grade 3. About 180 of the children attended community preschools (Basic Schools). A range of assessments were conducted on family functioning and general mental health (e.g., FACES II, BSI, PSI), physical health, the home environment (e.g., HOME), children's school achievement and cognitive functioning using standardized tests (e.g., PPVT; Raven's Progressive Matrices, McCarthy Scales of Children's Abilities) and on children's behaviors (e.g., Jamaica Youth Checklist). The children were from diverse family unions (7.1% visiting; 30% common-law; 24% married, and 38% in no relationship) with 42% of families having both biological parents present in the home. Although most families were connected, 37% were considered separated or disengaged with respect to family functioning as measured by FACES II. Not surprisingly, children whose families were classified as rigid and disengaged had greater behavioral difficulties (Samms-Vaughan 2004).

The preschool assessments indicated that children from lower socioeconomic backgrounds had home environments that were less stimulating and that they had significantly lower achievement and cognitive scores than children who were more privileged. Children who attended private preschools had better cognitive and achievement outcomes than children attending basic community-based schools. Whereas children who attended all types of preschools made gains in cognitive functioning during the transition to first grade (based on N = 130 of original sample), the differences attributed to type of school attended earlier persisted and became magnified over time. Only half the children were reading at the Grade 1 level. Assessments of the learning environments of the children in different schools provided a rather bleak picture. The classroom environments were deemed inappropriate for learning at the early childhood level; math and number activities were most available, but books and language rich materials were not. Opportunities for dramatic and other types of play were rare. Not surprisingly, the presence of books in classrooms and encouragement to engage in verbal communication were associated with higher reading scores in children (Samms-Vaughan 2004).

The findings of this ambitious study begin to capture the complexity of Caribbean children's transition to primary school. The transition event itself may play a secondary role in how children negotiate their way to first grade amid poor economic conditions, community violence, inadequate school resources, and changing family configurations. Unfortunately, the behavioral difficulties of children, if any, were not determined once the children entered first grade, and further analysis was not computed on the predictive power of the family process variables on childhood outcomes in grade school. That aside, there may be a message in these findings; family functioning and socioeconomic status have an enduring effect on children's academic performance as they embark on their educational journeys. In the technologically developing nations, it makes little sense to ignore economic conditions and family process variables within the immediate ecological niches because they are likely to have primary effects on children's transition to school. There is a basic need to develop more culturally-sensitive models on transitions to school that may guide research on within-culture developmental trajectories.

Recommendations and Conclusion

Within a child's rights perspective, several august bodies (e.g., UNESCO, UNICEF, Ministries of Education) and private foundations (e.g., Bernard van Leer) have proposed global approaches on how to successfully aid the transition from early childhood settings to formal schooling. Among them are stronger partnerships between the home and school environments, making school more ready for children of different developmental abilities, assuring linguistic continuity, attending to poverty, building curriculum continuity, redefining pedagogy (e.g., by merging the concepts of caring, nurturing, and early education), and improving early childhood teacher training (Woodhead and Moss 2007). These are laudable goals and would add immensely to improving the transition to formal schooling. In the resource starved countries of the English-speaking Caribbean, these lofty goals are often discussed but rarely implemented. Even in the oil-rich nation of Trinidad and Tobago, sweeping reforms of the early childhood education system (e.g., improved teacher training, introducing developmentally-appropriate curriculum) is proving to be daunting.

Regional bodies have begun to identify more culture-specific approaches to transition to school by focusing on the child, family, and the educational agent (OAS Caribbean Countries: Proposals for Concrete Actions in Transition, 2009–2011). The intent is to familiarize children and parents with the transition process through greater guidance and involvement from Ministries of Education and early childhood agents. These partnerships would acknowledge early childhood development curricula based on Caribbean learning goals and outcomes and Caribbean Community (CARICOM) guidelines. This stance implicitly and explicitly takes into account diverse factors within local ecological niches in the Caribbean that are so crucial to advancing educational change and eventually nation building. This is an essential first step, if we are to encourage parents and teachers to move beyond their beliefs about rigorous academic training toward a more holistic approach to nurturing the intellectual and social lives of Caribbean children.

References

Anderson, P. (2007). *The changing roles of fathers in the context of Jamaican family life*. Kingston: Planning Institute of Jamaica and the University of the West Indies.

Aunola, K., & Nurmi, J. E. (2005). The role of parenting styles in children's problem behavior. *Child Development, 76*, 1144–1159.

Austin, C. (2005). *The role of school administrators in and some strategies that can facilitate the transition process from nursery to primary school. Early Childhood Education and Development in Guyana* (pp. 27–38). Georgetown: University of Guyana.

Brown, J., & Barker, G. (2003). *Global diversity and trends in patterns of fatherhood. In supporting fathers: Contributions from the International Fatherhood Summit 2003*. The Hague: Bernard van Leer Foundation.

Chao, R. (1994). Beyond parental control and authoritarian parenting style: Understanding Chinese parenting through the cultural notion of training. *Child Development, 65*, 1111–1119.

Crawford-Brown, C. (1997). The impact of parent–child socialization on the development of conduct disorder in Jamaican male adolescents. In J. L. Roopnarine & J. Brown (Eds.), *Caribbean families: Diversity among ethnic groups* (pp. 205–222). Norwood, NJ: Ablex.

Durbrow, E. H. (1999). Cultural processes in child competence: How rural Caribbean parents evaluate their children. In A. S. Masten (Ed.), *Cultural processes in child development: The Minnesota symposia on child psychology* (Vol. 29, pp. 97–121). Mahwah, NJ: Erlbaum.

Engle, P., Black, M. M., Behrman, J. R., Cabral de Mello, M., Gertler, P. J., Kapirri, L., et al. (2007). Strategies to avoid loss of developmental potential in more than 200 million children in the developing world. *Lancet, 369*, 229–242.

Flinn, M. (1992). Paternal care in a Caribbean village. In B. Hewlett (Ed.), *Father–child relations: Cultural and biosocial contexts* (pp. 57–84). New York: de Gruyter.

Gaskins, S. (2006). Cultural perspectives on infant-caregiver interaction. In J. Enfeld & S. C. Levinson (Eds.), *Roots of human sociality: Culture, cognition, and interaction* (pp. 279–298). Oxford: Berg.

Gershoff, E. T. (2002). Corporal punishment by parents and associated child behaviors and experiences: A meta-analytic and theoretical review. *Psychological Bulletin, 128,* 539–579.

Goodnow, J. J., Cashmore, J. A., Cotton, S., & Knight, R. (1984). Mothers' developmental timetables in two cultural groups. *International Journal of Psychology, 19,* 193–205.

Goolsarran, M. (2009). *National Summary Report: 2009.* Georgetown: National Centre for Educational Resource Development.

Grant, D. B. R., Leo-Rhynie, E., & Alexander, G. (1983). *Life style study: Children of the lesser world in the English speaking Caribbean. Vol. 5: Household structures and settings.* Kingston: Bernard Van Leer Foundation—Center for Early Childhood Education.

Grantham-McGregor, S., Cheung, Y. B., Cueto, S., Glewwe, P., Richter, L., & Strupp, B. (2007). Developmental potential in the first 5 years for children in the developing countries. *Lancet, 269,* 60–70.

Greenfield, P. M., Keller, H., Fuligni, A., & Maynard, A. (2003). Cultural pathways through universal development. *Annual Review of Psychology, 54,* 461–490.

Inter American Symposium on Policies and Strategies for the Child's Successful Transition to Socialization and School (2009). Organization of American States (OAS) and the National Association of Preschools in Chile in collaboration with regional offices of UNICEF and UNESCO, Valparaiso, Chile, May 27–29.

Kaplan, H., & Bock, J. (2001). Fertility theory: The embodied capital theory of human life history evolution. In N. J. Smelser & P. B. Bakes (Eds.), *The international encyclopedia of the social and behavioral sciences* (pp. 5561–5568). Oxford: Elsevier.

Lareau, A. (2003). *Unequal childhoods: Class, race, and family life.* Berkeley, CA: University of California Press.

Leo-Rhynie, E. (1997). Class, race, and gender issues in child rearing in the Caribbean. In J. L. Roopnarine & J. Brown (Eds.), *Caribbean families: Diversity among ethnic groups* (pp. 25–55). Norwood, NJ: Ablex.

Leo-Rhynie, E., Minott, C., Gift, S., McBean, M., Scott, A. K., & Wilson, K. (2009). *Competency of children in Guyana, rural Jamaica, and St. Vincent and the Grenadines making the transition from pre-primary school with special emphasis on gender differences.* Kingston: Dudley Grant Memorial Trust.

LeVine, R. (1974). Parental goals: A cross-cultural view. *Teachers College Record, 76,* 226–239.

LeVine, R. (2004). Challenging expert knowledge: Findings from an African study of infant care and development. In U. P. Gielen & J. Roopnarine (Eds.), *Childhood and adolescence: Cross-cultural perspectives and applications* (pp. 149–165). Westport, CT: Praeger.

Logie, C. (2009). *White paper on early child care and early education.* White Paper, Ministry of Education, Trinidad and Tobago.

Pottinger, A. M. (2005). Children's experience of loss by parental migration in inner-city Jamaica. *American Journal of Orthopsychiatry, 75,* 485–496.

Rimm-Kaufmann, S. E., & Pianta, R. C. (2000). An ecological perspective on the transition to kindergarten: A theoretical framework to guide empirical research. *Journal of Applied Developmental Psychology, 21*(5), 491–511.

Rodrigues, M. (1994). *Moving from nursery to primary: Experiences of nine schools in Regions 4 and 10 Guyana.* Working Paper No. 1, University of Guyana, Georgetown.

Rogoff, B. (2003). *The cultural nature of human development.* New York: Oxford University Press.

Roopnarine, J. L. (in press). Cultural variations in beliefs about play, parent–child play, and children's play: Meaning for childhood development. In A. Pelligrini (Ed.), *Oxford encyclopedia on play.* Oxford: Oxford University Press.

Roopnarine, J. L., & Krishnakumar, A. (2006). Conceptual and research considerations in the determinants of child outcomes among English-speaking Caribbean immigrants in the United States: A cultural-ecological approach. In R. Mahalingam (Ed.), *Cultural psychology of immigrants.* Mahwah, NJ: Erlbaum.

Roopnarine, J. L., & Krishnakumar, A. (2010). *Parenting styles and childhood outcomes in Trinidadian and Guyanese families.* Unpublished manuscript, Syracuse University.

Roopnarine, J. L., & Metindogan, A. (2006). Cross-national early childhood education research. In B. Spodek & O. Saracho (Eds.), *Handbook of research on the education of young children*. Mahwah, NJ: Erlbaum.

Roopnarine, J., Snell-White, P., Riegraf, N., Wolfsenberger, J., Hossain, Z., & Mathur, S. (1997). Family socialization in an east Indian village in Guyana: A focus on fathers. In J. L. Roopnarine & J. Brown (Eds.), *Caribbean families: Diversity among ethnic groups* (pp. 57–83). Norwood, NJ: Ablex.

Roopnarine, J. L., Bynoe, P. F., & Singh, R. (2004). Factors tied to the schooling of children of English-speaking Caribbean immigrants in the United States. In U. P. Gielen & J. Roopnarine (Eds.), *Childhood and adolescence: Cross-cultural perspectives and applications* (pp. 319–349). Westport, CT: Praeger.

Roopnarine, J. L., Evans, M., & Pant, P. (in press). Parenting and socialization practices among Caribbean families: A focus on fathers. In D. Chadee & J. Young (Eds.), *Current themes in social psychology*. Mona: University of the West Indies Press.

Russell-Brown, P., Norville, B., & Griffith, C. (1997). Child shifting: A survival strategy for teenage mothers. In J. L. Roopnarine & J. Brown (Eds.), *Caribbean families: Diversity among ethnic groups* (pp. 223–242). Norwood, NJ: Ablex.

Samms-Vaughan, M. (2004). *The Jamaican pre-school child: The status of early childhood development in Jamaica*. Kingston: Planning Institute of Jamaica.

Sigel, I., & McGillicuddy-DeLisi, A. (2002). Parental beliefs are cognitions: The dynamic belief systems model. In M. H. Bornstein (Ed.), *Handbook on parenting* (2nd ed., Vol. 3.). Mahwah, NJ: Erlbaum.

Spijk, J. V., Rosemberg, C., & Janssens, W. (2008). *RCP impact evaluation in St. Lucia*. Amsterdam: Amsterdam Institute for International Development.

Sukhdeo, F. (2008). *Basic access and management support program*. Georgetown: Ministry of Education.

Super, C., & Harkness, S. (1997). The cultural structuring of child development. In J. Berry, P. Dasen, & T. Saraswathi (Eds.), *Handbook of cross-cultural psychology. Vol. 2: Basic processes and human development* (pp. 1–39). Needham, MA: Allyn & Bacon.

UNESCO (2000). *Dakar framework for action: Education for all—meeting our collective commitments*. Adopted by the World Education Forum, Dakar, Senegal, pp. 26–28.

UNESCO (2006). *Strong foundations: Early childhood care and education*. 2007 Education for All Global Monitoring Report. Paris: UNESCO.

Vogler, P., Crivello, G., & Woodhead, M. (2008). *Early childhood transition research: A review of concepts, theory and practice*. Working Paper No. 48. The Hague: Bernard van Leer Foundation.

Weikart, D., & Schweinhart, L. J. (2009). The HighScope Curriculum for early child care and education. J. L. Roopnarine & J. E. Johnson (Eds.), *Approaches to early childhood education* (5th ed.). Columbus, OH: Merrill/Prentice Hall.

Weisner, T. (1998). Human development, child well-being, and the cultural project of development. In D. Sharma & K. Fischer (Eds.), *Socioemotional development across cultures. New directions in child development* (pp. 69–85). San Francisco, CA: Jossey-Bass.

Williams, S., Brown, J., & Roopnarine, J. L. (2006). *Childrearing in the Caribbean*. Technical report, Caribbean Child Support Initiative, Barbados.

Wilson, L. C., Wilson, C. M., & Berkeley-Caines, L. (2003). Age, gender, and socioeconomic differences in parental socialization preferences in Guyana. *Journal of Comparative Family Studies, 34*, 213–227.

Woodhead, M., & Moss, P. (Eds.). (2007). *Early childhood and primary education*. Walton Hall: Open University Press.

Zigler, E., & Styfco, S. J. (2004). *The Head Start debates*. Baltimore, MD: Brookes.

Chapter 15
Transition to School

Child, Family, and Community-Level Determinants

Magdalena Janus

Transition to school is a complex process for any child and his or her family. Balancing the expectations with excitement, known with unknown, the process of adjusting to school starts well before children actually cross the threshold of the school building. It is not the first, and certainly not the last of the many transitions that humans have to experience through their lives, but it is one of the most important. Successful adjustment to the school environment increases the child's enjoyment of school-based life, including play, education, and social relations with other children and adults.

Children's school readiness used to be synonymous with the basic cognitive skills required to enter formal education, and utilized as a testable characteristic determining the child's right to school entry (Meisels 1999; La Paro and Pianta 2000). Modern thinking and understanding of child development has moved significantly from this narrow concept (e.g. Kagan 1992; Meisels 1999), by encompassing children's developmental health at school entry under the term of "school readiness" (Janus and Offord 2007), and acknowledging the complexity of neurological and social processes that contribute to it (Snow 2006).

Ecological models of child development have long postulated that any individual unit is embedded within larger units that exert reciprocal influences over each other (Bronfenbrenner 1979). In this chapter, I will first briefly review the biological basis of early development as it impacts outcomes at school entry; second, describe how child and family level characteristics influence children's outcomes in kindergarten in two countries (Canada and Mexico); and finally, use results from Canada to illustrate how parent-driven engagement of the child and family into the community and school can have a profound impact on broad developmental domains. Throughout, I hope to illustrate the mutual influences of factors at many levels and highlight the ones that first, have strong impact on children's outcomes in kindergarten; and second, can be targeted at the community level to improve children's experience in transition to school.

M. Janus (✉)
Offord Centre for Child Studies, McMaster University, Hamilton, ON L8N 3Z5, Canada
e-mail: janusm@mcmaster.ca

D. M. Laverick, M. R. Jalongo (eds.), *Transitions to Early Care and Education,*
Educating the Young Child 4, DOI 10.1007/978-94-007-0573-9_15,

Biological Basis of Early Development

Neuroscientists characterize early brain development as rapid, plastic, complex, and flexible (Shore 1997). Speed of the early development exceeds any other period in life. It proceeds in waves: different areas of the brain become active at different times and at varying intensity. Babies and children reach milestones sometimes suddenly, sometimes after a prolonged practice. Plasticity allows the brain to recover from a trauma, and in some cases to develop a compensatory mechanism to deal with a deficit. On the other hand, if a child is not exposed to the experience she needs, the particular connection may not develop early enough—or even not at all. This could be simply physiological: a child who was born deaf will not be able to develop speech in the same way a typical child would. However, this also means that there are times when exposure to negative stimuli—or even lack of appropriate stimulation—may have long-term consequences. In some cases, these windows in development are very specific in relation to the skill. This is true, for example, for things like vision and hearing (Kuhl 2001). It is more difficult to establish whether similar windows occur for more broadly based skills, like emotion regulation for example. In many skills, the plasticity aspect helps if a skill has not developed, but often it could be harder to master the skills outside of the critical period. Studies following up early intervention programs have clearly shown that preschool-level intervention has higher chance to improve children's outcomes than a later-age intervention (Schweinhart et al. 1993). Another type of evidence is provided by studies of children adopted from orphanages at different ages. Children who spent more than the first eight months of life in an orphanage exhibited more deviant behaviours and less attachment security than those who were adopted after a shorter amount of time (Chisholm 1998). Clearly, therefore, a child's brain reacts to both positive and negative stimuli, and both of those can have long-lasting consequences.

There are striking disparities in what children know and can do at each stage of their development, and these often are clear before they reach kindergarten. The broad range of individual differences among young children often makes it difficult to distinguish normal variations and maturational delays from transient disorders and persistent impairments. These differences are strongly associated with physical, social, and economic circumstances and are usually highly predictive of future school success.

School Readiness

The concept that is measurable and focused on the issues reviewed thus far could be described as "school readiness", or even "readiness for school". This zooms in on the qualities necessary for the child to have an enjoyable, successful, and fulfilling experience in school. The "school readiness" concept needs to be culturally inclusive, regardless of context. This is especially important in large countries with a dominant language and culture, where there are many other languages and cultures,

which may not be perceived as equal—such as Australia, Canada, United States—
but also in countries that have culture and customs that differ from these mostly
English-speaking countries. While children's development progresses through the
same milestones regardless of their place of birth and ethnicity, there are socially
and culturally-influenced variations in encouragement, acceptability, and manifes-
tations of development.

The shift in the age between 5 and 7 years has been termed as "the age of reason
and responsibility", the transition between the preschool and the school-age child
(Sameroff and Haith 1996). Children's ways of thinking and behaviour changes
dramatically in this period, acquiring the precursors of later maturity. Rogoff et al.
(1975) investigated the roles and expectations of children in 50 communities across
the world. They found that these change dramatically in the period between 5 and
7, when children are given increased responsibility for various culture-appropriate
tasks (e.g. tending animals, caring for younger children, helping in household chores,
etc.), which required trust and independence. Moreover, it was in this age-range that
children were expected to become "teachable". Indeed, it is not a simple coincidence
that in many countries the age range between 5 and 7 is the time when children start
school. Therefore, "school readiness" is a convenient shortcut to children's developmental health at the cusp of early years and school-age development. A measurement taken at school entry is a convenient marker for the 5- to 7-year-old age range.

During the first few years, development occurs in many domains all at once.
When a parent cuddles a toddler while reading a story, this event provides social,
emotional, linguistic, cognitive, and possibly even moral or regulatory experiences.
Divisions into domains are approximate at the early stages: some issues can clearly
be labelled as one or the other, but they contribute to the child's development in their
totality. By the time one can talk about being ready for school, the developmental domains crystallize to a certain extent, and it is possible to distinguish several domains
that are highly relevant to child's success at school (Doherty 1997; Kagan 1992).
These are: physical health and well-being, social and emotional competence, approaches to learning, cognitive and language competence, and communication skills.

In many ways, the term "school readiness" is a shortcut to—or a snapshot of—
the outcome of the transition process. Children face many transitions in their lives,
but this one—from home, or even preschool—to school, where they assume the
full role of the student is probably the most dramatic and potentially traumatic one
for many children, especially in the face of serious systems discontinuities between
the preschool and school environments (Kagan and Neville 1996). In most western
countries, children start kindergarten at age 5—thus, Grade 1 at 6—and there are
many places that offer an earlier version of kindergarten, the junior kindergarten
at age 4. The transition to school does not all happen on the first day; there could
be some consequences of the events of that day (Pianta and McCoy 1997), but the
process of adjustment to the new environment, learning about learning and about
the teacher, and about the school, takes time. The starting point before Grade 1 is
a combination of what the child brings to school as an outcome of his or her first
five years in his family, in the neighbourhood, in an idiosyncratic combination with
the child's age and gender, and the school practices towards easing the transition
process (Meisels 1999). Since these tend to be similar across the school divisions,

it is fairly safe to assume that children bring with them a much larger proportion of variance than could be accounted for by schools. So what has to be captured by the concept of school readiness is really that "whole child" view of their adjustment for formal education as it is offered by the school system. It cannot be an assessment of one skill, ability, or social competence. It has to be a combination of many, set in a developmental perspective, sensitive to differences between and within children as they pertain to different skills (Love et al. 1994; Meisels 1999), and in a context of early experiences. For example, if adults do not talk to a pre-verbal child, she will not develop adequate language skills, even though she has the propensity to do so, as development is an interactive process, and not simply a maturational one.

While much of the detailed research on transition to school has been carried out in the developed world, there is a consistent, international theme that flows through our understanding of which children, through no fault of their own, have difficulties in making the transition in adjustment to school. Inadequate nutrition, absence of a caring early environment, and health issues are common factors for school difficulties in any latitude. These children are the ones who need schools and educational systems to be there for them—simply because no one else will. Schooling is the most universal service that children have access to—albeit some of them briefly—and it behooves us to ensure that it is delivered in a way that would increase a child's success for a happy transition and a fulfilled life.

School readiness, measured in kindergarten, allows for considering an outcome for which children have to live in a neighbourhood for several years, thus adding the validity for measuring the actual contribution of neighbourhood. In addition, the kindergarten age is a fascinating one to study: these children are at an important developmental junction in transition to grade school and their developmental outcomes can still be attributed to the history of their first five years.

The Offord Centre at McMaster University in Hamilton, Canada, houses an extensive national database on the developmental status of Canadian kindergarten children. This database is used to investigate the research questions. In many communities in Canada standardized data on children's readiness to learn at school are collected with the Early Development Instrument (EDI). A number of other countries have also adapted the EDI (Janus et al. 2007, 2010). The EDI is completed by teachers and provides kindergarten outcome measures in the domains of Physical Health and Well-being, Social Competence, Emotional Maturity, Language and Cognitive Development, and Communication and General Knowledge (Janus and Offord 2007). Four of those are further divided into subdomains. Table 15.1 outlines domains, subdomains, and examples of items.

Concurrent Determinants of Kindergarten Outcomes in Canada and Mexico

Kindergarten teachers in Canada and Mexico assessed children's kindergarten outcomes in the five developmental domains measured by the EDI, and parents provided additional information on children and families. Janus and Duku (2007) explored

Table 15.1 Domains, subdomains, and sample questions on the EDI

EDI domains	Subdomains	Example items
Physical health and well-being	Physical readiness for school day	Arrives to school hungry
	Physical independence	Has well-coordinated movements
	Gross and fine motor skills	Is able to manipulate objects
Social competence	Overall social competence	Able to get along with other children
	Responsibility and respect	Accepts responsibility for actions
	Approaches to learning	Works independently
	Readiness to explore new things	Eager to explore new items
Emotional maturity	Prosocial and helping behaviour	Helps other children in distress
	Anxious and fearful behaviour	Appears unhappy or sad
	Aggressive behaviour	Gets into physical fights
	Hyperactivity and inattention	Is restless
Language and cognitive development	Basic literacy	Able to write own name
	Interest in literacy/numeracy and memory	Interested in games involving numbers
	Advanced literacy	Able to read sentences
	Basic numeracy	Able to count to 20
Communication skills and general knowledge	(No subdomains)	Able to clearly communicate one's own needs and understand others' needs
		Shows interest in general knowledge about the world

variables in five risk areas: socio-economic status (SES), family status, child health, parent health, and parent involvement for their contribution to children's kindergarten outcomes. In a series of logistic regression analyses, the strongest indicator from each of the five areas was retained and entered into final regression. The same methodology was used for both the Canadian and Mexican sample, except for the parent health and parent involvement as the indicators used in the Mexican parent survey contained too much missing data (Gaskin et al. 2009). However, participation in a government-funded early child care program, which requires parental involvement, called Centro del Desarrollo Infantil (CENDI), was added to the regression model in the Mexican sample. In total, 2196 Canadian 5-year-olds contributed to the data from Canada, and 1672 Mexican 5-year-olds contributed to the data from Mexico.

In Canada, the strongest SES indicator was income; in Mexico it was maternal education. Each strongly contributed to children's outcomes: in Canada, a child from a low-income family was 2.016 times more likely to score below the 10th percentile in more than one of the five developmental domains measured by the EDI; in Mexico, a child of mother with low education was 1.759 times more likely to have low scores. The odds ratio values were similar, around 1.8, for family characteristics: in Canada, it was the lack of "intact" status of the family (*not* the same original two-parent family since child's birth), in Mexico, lack of mother's married status had the negative impact. Child's gender also had similar effect on outcomes: boys in both samples were more likely to score low, although in Canada the odds ratio was higher than in Mexico (2.324 as compared to 1.410). In Canada, child's health status and age (above mean) also had impact on the kindergarten outcomes, but not in Mexico. Finally, child's enrolment in the CENDI child care program was also associated with positive outcomes: children attending other programs were 1.440 times more likely to have low scores.

Family status, socio-economic circumstances and child's gender proved to have a meaningful association with children's kindergarten outcomes in both Canada and Mexico. In the next section of this chapter, the parent engagement with a child is briefly reviewed, then examined in several communities in Canada.

Does Parent Engagement Make a Difference for School Readiness?

Throughout the preschool years, families create a unique environment fostering their children's development of learning and exploratory skills, with parents as the main agents. Parental engagement in this process could be represented by direct involvement, as exemplified by the qualities of the parent-child relationship, or playing, reading, singing with the child, or an indirect influence, for example promoting child's participation in community-based activities, or even attending child care or school events.

Empirical research on parent involvement, largely carried out with older children, suggests that parental involvement—especially in the child's school-work—is associated with more positive outcomes (e.g. Domina 2005; Hango 2007). However, at a kindergarten level the impact of parent-child activities and children's outcomes is more challenging to study, which is reflected in a relatively small number of studies. A cross-sectional study of association between parental behaviours, expectations and school involvement with pre-reading and pre-math scores of senior kindergarten children (Hill 2001) indicated that maternal acceptance and expectations for grades were positively associated with both school readiness measures. Parental home involvement and the teachers' perceptions of involvement were positively associated with academic achievement among children studied from grade 1 to grade 6 in the Netherlands (Bakker et al. 2007). Children of parents considered highly involved in home-based activities with their child had higher achievement in reading and mathematics than those of less-involved parents (McWayne et al. 2004), and they also were reported to have higher social skills, more cooperation, self-control, and pro-social engagement in home and school. School-based transition to kindergarten practices, meant to engage parents and ease the process for families also have been shown to be associated with higher academic scores at the end of kindergarten (Schulting et al. 2005). Although the pattern of association was similar for all children, the strength of the correlation was highest for children from families from low SES backgrounds.

When parents of preschool and kindergarten children attend many school activities and volunteer frequently children are more likely to score higher on tests of reading achievement and are less likely to be held back a grade (Miedel and Reynolds 2000). Parents who believe that being engaged in the child's education is important and that their involvement with the child and school will impact the child's learning are the ones most likely to demonstrate high levels of actual involvement (e.g. Wyrick and Rudasill 2009). Regardless of their motivation, parent involvement matters: not only in education, but also in making it possible for the child to participate in athletics and other organized activities. Children who consistently participated in extracurricular activities during kindergarten and grade one were found to have higher standardized test scores than children who did not, controlling for child and family factors (NICHD Early Child Care Research Network 2004).

While the central question about the child's environment in the process of transition is what can be changed or improved about the educational system to make it more welcoming to the ever-younger child, it is equally important to ask about the conditions prior to school entry that may influence the successful adjustment. Drawing on parent information linked to their children's outcomes in kindergarten, I am going to describe the types of parent-child activities that appear to be meaningful in this context.

Empirical Study of Parent Engagement and Children's Kindergarten Outcomes

Parents of kindergarten-age children in several communities in Southern Ontario in Canada completed a Kindergarten Parent Survey (KPS), (Gaskin et al. 2008). KPS includes questions on parent activities with children at home, children's participation in activities in the community (organized or casual), and parent involvement in school. Children's outcomes were measured using the Early Development Instrument (Janus and Offord 2007). In total, data were available for about 2,800 5-year-olds representing approximately 40% of all kindergarten children in these communities.

Parents were asked about frequency of seven types of home-based activities with their children over the last week: telling/reading a story; teaching letters, words, or numbers; teaching songs or music; working on arts and crafts; playing; taking child along while doing errands; and involving child in household chores. They were also asked about child's previous year's participation in the community-based activities, which fell into two categories, *casual*, available at the "drop-in" basis and not requiring commitment: play-based parent-child programs, family reading programs, recreational programs without an instructor or coach, and faith-related programs; and *sessional*, organized and likely to require a time commitment: organized team sports, participation in physical activity programs with a coach/instructor, dance, music, and arts programs. These activities were also classified in regard to developmental area into four types: *athletic* programs (organized and not organized sports, dance), *art* programs (music and art activities), *play/read* programs (play-based programs with parents, and reading programs), and *faith* programs (faith-based programs).

Home-Based Activities with Parents

Frequency of home-based activities was recoded into "minimal", "moderate", and "frequent", based on the summary score for all seven activities (Janus and Graham 2007). Over 70% of parents reported frequent engagement in activities with their children; 23.4% reported moderate engagement, and only 5% reported minimal engagement. This group of children scored significantly lowest in three developmental domains of the EDI: Social Competence, Language and Cognitive Development, and Communication Skills.

Casual and Sessional Community Activities

Each activity was given a score of either 1 or 0 for participation or no participation, respectively. Scores were summed to produce a total score for child participation in either casual or sessional activities.

For both categories, one-fifth of the population participated in no activities (19.6% for casual, and 16% for sessional), and a slightly larger proportion participated in more than three (19% for casual, and 27.3% for sessional). Participation in sessional, organized activities was higher among children who were on track in all five developmental domains on the EDI than among those who lagged behind on one or more (mean 1.8 vs. 1.2, effect size of the difference: 0.343). Regression analyses demonstrated that participation in sessional activities contributed a small proportion of variance to children's scores in all five domains, while the participation in the casual activities did not (Janus and Graham 2007).

Community Activities by Type

Mean attendance scores were created, and recoded into "no participation", "some participation" (mean less or equal 0.50), and "high participation" (mean greater than 0.50). Most children participated in athletic programs (only about 12% participated in none, and high participation was shown for 43%). In contrast, almost 74% of children did not participate in any art program, while participation in art programs was high for only 4.8%. Distribution of participation frequency in play/reading programs was fairly even: 41.3% in none, 30.7% in some, 28.4% with high participation. The strongest impact of the activities on kindergarten outcomes emerged for athletic activities: children who were doing well in kindergarten had significantly higher participation in such programs (effect size of the difference 0.409).

Athletic activities consistently contributed positively to outcomes in each of the five developmental domains, with the highest beta values in Communication Skills and General Knowledge areas (Sears and Janus 2009). Participation in faith-based programs also contributed significantly to children's scores in Language and Cognitive Development and Communication domains. Interestingly, participation in play/read activities had a negative association with both these domains, indicating perhaps that parents were more likely to engage the child in such programs if they perceived difficulty in language/communication areas.

Overall Parent Engagement Results

Taken all together, the strongest and most consistent impact on children's outcomes was due to their participation in sessional activities, in particular the athletically-oriented ones. Parent activities with child at home contributed to children's social competence, emotional maturity, and language/cognitive development (all analyses were controlled for education and income).

Since the measures used in our studies did not reflect intensity but rather the simple fact of having been involved in at least one of the activities listed on the questionnaire, these results by no means indicate that enrolling children in many organized activities is beneficial for them. Rather, this points out that impact on children's school readiness can happen through involvement in organized activities that are not necessarily focused on academic achievement. This finding emphasizes and confirms the health and holistic focus of the concept of school readiness used in our approach.

Conclusions

Facilitating transition to school requires a collaborative effort among the teachers, the school, the parents, and the whole community. The dialectical relationships that exist between children and families, and early care or educational institutions such as child care centres or kindergarten are part of the fabric of the transition and ultimately of the process of child's adjustment. Many years of evidence-based intervention strategies exemplified by the Head Start in the United States have not brought the panacea nor yielded all the benefits that were expected. While individual, intense, targeted interventions are documented to have high success (e.g. Schweinhart et al. 1993), they are not easy to generalize and implement at the population level.

Through the description of the research on determinants of children's outcomes as they experience transition to school, I attempted to demonstrate that first, the broad family and socio-economic factors that impact children's outcomes can be compared across countries; second, that parental agency in being engaged with the child in creating an activity-rich preschool social environment is among the finer factors that could be enhanced to improve the transition experience. Making schools ready for children means making communities ready to support children before they enter school and giving them and their families opportunities to be involved in their communities, and thus promote child development in all domains contributing to their successful transition to school and fulfillment throughout life.

References

Bakker, J., Denessen, E., & Brus-Laeven, M. (2007). Socio-economic background, parental involvement and teacher perceptions of these in relation to pupil achievement. *Educational Studies, 33*(2), 177–192.

Bronfenbrenner, U. (1979). *The ecology of human development: Experiments by nature and design.* Cambridge, MA: Harvard University Press.

Chisholm, K. (1998). A three year follow-up of attachment and indiscriminate friendliness in children adopted from Romanian orphanages. *Child Development, 69*(4), 1092–1106.

Doherty, G. (1997). *Zero to six: The basis for school readiness* (Research Paper R-97-8E). Ottawa: Human Resources Development Canada.

Domina, T. (2005). Leveling the home advantage: Assessing the effectiveness of parental involvement in elementary school. *Sociology of Education, 78*(3), 233–249.

Gaskin, A., Duku, E., & Janus, M. (2008). *The Kindergarten Parent Survey: Bridging the gap between early environment and school readiness outcomes.* Poster presented at the 20th Annual Research Day, Department of Psychiatry and Behavioural Neurosciences, McMaster University, Hamilton, Ontario, Canada.

Gaskin, A., Duku, E., & Janus, M. (2009). *Correlates and risk factors of the school entry gap in a group of pre-school children in Monterrey, Mexico.* Poster presented at the meeting of the Society for Research in Child Development, Denver, Colorado.

Hango, D. (2007). Parental investment in childhood and educational qualifications: Can greater parental involvement mediate the effects of socioeconomic disadvantage? *Social Science Research, 36,* 1371–1390.

Hill, N. E. (2001). Parenting and academic socialization as they relate to school readiness: The roles of ethnicity and family income. *Journal of Education Psychology, 93*(4), 686–697.

Janus, M., & Duku, E. (2007). The school entry gap: Socioeconomic, family, and health factors associated with children's school readiness to learn. *Early Education and Development, 18*(3), 375–403.

Janus, M., & Graham, S. (2007). *Parent engagement correlates of child school readiness.* Unpublished manuscript, Hamilton, ON, McMaster University.

Janus, M., & Offord, D. (2007). Development and psychometric properties of the Early Development Instrument (EDI): A measure of children's school readiness. *Canadian Journal of Behavioral Science, 39*(1), 1–22.

Janus, M., Brinkman, S., Duku, E., Hertzman, C., Santos, R., Sayers, M., et al. (2007). *The Early Development Instrument: A population-based measure for communities. A handbook on development, properties, and use.* Hamilton, ON: Offord Centre for Child Studies.

Janus, M., Brinkman, S., & Duku, E. (2010). Validity and psychometric properties of Early Development Instrument in Canada, Australia, United States, and Jamaica. *Social Indicators Research* (in press).

Kagan, S. L. (1992). Readiness past, present, and future: Shaping the agenda. *Young Children, 11,* 48–53.

Kagan, S. L., & Neville, P. R. (1996). Combining endogenous and exogenous factors in the shift years: The transition to school. In A. J. Sameroff & M. M. Haith (Eds.), *The five to seven year shift: The age of reason and responsibility* (pp. 337–405). Chicago, IL: University of Chicago Press.

Kuhl, P. (2001). Language and the brain: A "critical period" for learning. In F. Lamb-Parker, J. Hagen, & R. Robinson (Eds.), *Developmental and contextual transitions of children and families: Implications for research, policy, and practice* (pp. 49–57). Washington, DC: The Head Start Bureau.

La Paro, K. M., & Pianta, R. C. (2000). Predicting children's competence in the early school years: A meta-analytic review. *Review of Educational Research, 70*, 443–484.

Love, J. M., Aber, J. L., & Brooks-Gunn, J. (1994). *Strategies for assessing community progress toward achieving the First National Educational Goal.* Princeton, NJ: Mathematica Policy Research.

McWayne, C., Hampton, V., Fantuzzo, J., Cohen, H. L., & Sekino, Y. (2004). A multivariate examination of parent involvement and the social and academic competencies of urban kindergarten children. *Psychology in the Schools, 41*(3), 363–377.

Meisels, S. J. (1999). Assessing readiness. In R. C. Pianta & M. J. Cox (Eds.), *The transition to kindergarten* (pp. 39–66). Baltimore, MD: Brookes.

Miedel, W., & Reynolds, A. (2000). Parent involvement in early intervention for disadvantaged children: Does it matter? *Journal of School Psychology, 37*(4), 379–402.

NICHD Early Child Care Research Network. (2004). Are child developmental outcomes related to before-, after-school care arrangements? Results form NICHD study on early child care. *Child Development, 75*(1), 280–295.

Pianta, R. C., & McCoy, S. J. (1997). The first day of school: The predictive validity of early school screening. *Journal of Applied Developmental Psychology, 18*, 1–22.

Rogoff, B., Sellers, M. J., Pirotta, S., Fox, N., & White, S. H. (1975). Age of assignment of roles and responsibilities to children: A cross-cultural survey. *Human Development, 18*, 353–369.

Sameroff, A. J., & Haith, M. M. (1996). Interpreting developmental transitions. In A. J. Sameroff & M. M. Haith (Eds.), *The five to seven year shift: The age of reason and responsibility* (pp. 3–30). Chicago, IL: University of Chicago Press.

Schulting, A. B., Malone, P. S., & Dodge, K. A. (2005). The effect of school-based kindergarten transition policies and practices on child academic outcomes. *Developmental Psychology, 41*(6), 860–871.

Schweinhart, L., Barnes, H., Weikart, D., Barnett, W. S., & Epstein, A. S. (1993). *Significant benefits: The High/Scope Perry Preschool study through age 27* (Monographs of the High/Scope Educational Research Foundation, Number 10). Ypsilanti, MI: The High/Scope Press.

Sears, J., & Janus, M. (2009). *Parental involvement with kindergarten children in rural and urban communities.* Poster presented at the Early Development Imperative: A Pan-Canadian Conference on Population Level Measurement of Children's Development, Winnipeg, Manitoba.

Shore, R. (1997). *Rethinking the brain: New insights into early development.* New York, NY: Families and Work Institute.

Snow, K. L. (2006). Measuring school readiness: Conceptual and practical considerations. *Early Education & Development, 17*, 7–41.

Wyrick, A. J., & Rudasill, K. M. (2009). Parent involvement as a predictor of teacher–child relationship quality in third grade. *Early Education & Development, 20*(5), 845–864.

Chapter 16
Schools as Integrated Hubs for Young Children and Families

A Canadian Experiment in Community Readiness: The Toronto First Duty Project

Tomoko N. Arimura, Carl Corter, Janette Pelletier, Zeenat Janmohamed, Sejal Patel, Palmina Ioannone and Saba Mir

Perspectives on "School Readiness"

School readiness has been most commonly defined in terms of children's school entry competencies that are important for later school success (e.g. Snow 2006; Rimm-Kaufman and Pianta 2000). Extensive research has established that many child characteristics predict children's adjustment as they transition into school. Although this perspective on school readiness has generated a wealth of knowledge about the influence of child characteristics, they account for less than one quarter of the variance in understanding school outcomes (La Paro and Pianta 2000). Moreover, this approach has been criticized as lacking explanatory power in accounting for factors and processes that explain *how* children acquire these competencies (Mashburn and Pianta 2006).

More recently, scholars have begun to take a contextualized approach to understanding the development of child competencies. The general premise of this approach is that children's adjustment is influenced by the various contexts (i.e. family, peers, school, and neighbourhood) that surround them (Dockett and Perry 2007). However, there is variation in how the relations between contextual variables and child competencies are conceptualized. For example, studies utilizing a direct model of influence have examined direct effects of contextual factors such as, the quality of the learning environment, class size, parent sensitivity and stimulation, peer relationships, and family or neighbourhood characteristics as correlates of readiness (e.g. Farkas and Hibel 2008). Others have utilized models that ac-

By "parent" we mean the adult(s) who deal with services such as the parent, stepparent, guardian, grandparent, etc. We generally use the term "family" as a more inclusive term, but occasionally use the term "parent" for clarity in reporting research results or common usage in the literature (e.g. "parent involvement").

T. N. Arimura (✉)
Ontario Institute for Studies in Education, University of Toronto, Toronto, ON, Canada
e-mail: t.arimura@utoronto.ca

D. M. Laverick, M. R. Jalongo (eds.), *Transitions to Early Care and Education,*
Educating the Young Child 4, DOI 10.1007/978-94-007-0573-9_16,
© Springer Science+Business Media B.V. 2011

knowledge both direct and indirect effects and the transactional process of influence between child and contextual factors (Sameroff 1975). This ecological/transactional perspective takes on a more process-oriented approach to defining readiness. For example, Pianta and colleagues (Mashburn and Pianta 2006; Rimm-Kaufman and Pianta 2000) proposed a transactional theory of readiness that defines it as a function of an organized system of interactions among people, settings, and institutions across time. Furthermore, they argue that the primary mechanism through which children acquire readiness-related competencies are social relationships that children form with peers, parents, and teachers.

Based on ecological/transactional conceptualizations of school readiness, interventions must address the contexts in which children develop and the interconnections between them in order to optimize their developmental outcomes. In particular, schools should be ready to support the unique developmental needs of children (e.g. Arnold et al. 2008; Dockett and Perry 2007; Rimm-Kaufman and Pianta 2000). While there is increasing recognition among policy-makers and educators of this, to date, school readiness strategies in many jurisdictions still reflect a limited "ready child" view (Snow 2006).

A Universal Community Strategy for Improving Readiness: Schools as Integrated Hubs

Local, provincial/state, and national policymakers seeking better transitions face the challenge of determining how school readiness might best be nurtured and enhanced. A major component of this dilemma includes the question of to whom and how the intervention should be offered. There is increasing evidence to suggest that the best early childhood development programs are those that are comprehensive, integrated, and universally available to all families regardless of their socioeconomic background (e.g. McCain et al. 2007). Thus, "ready schools" recognize that children can benefit from support outside the school, including non-academic supports relating to health care, nutrition, and social services (Shore 1998). In some cases, schools become hubs of early childhood services, making the school one of a family's major ties with the community (Corter et al. 2002; Desimone et al. 2000).

For school readiness/transition initiatives, universal approaches include all young children and their families and schools, while targeted approaches concentrate on families with one or more known risk factors for low rates of school readiness, such as income or family, or on communities with high levels of risk. A major challenge facing such programs is that targeted programs may fail to reach a significant percentage of the vulnerable children. For example, Willms' (2002) analyses of the Canadian National Longitudinal Survey of Children (NLSCY) suggest that 80% of young children manifesting serious cognitive, emotional, and behavioural problems do not come from "high-risk" families, but rather from two-parent families with adequate income and parental education. Thus, targeted problems for high-risk children or families, even if they are highly effective, may have little impact on the community rates for early childhood difficulties. Moreover, there is additional evidence to suggest that targeted programs reach only a very small proportion of the intended, targeted families (Barnett et al. 2004). Given these limitations of high-risk, targeted programs for early childhood development, there is an increased interest in universal programs for young children and their families (e.g. Schulman and Barnett 2005; Zigler et al. 2006).

This approach is consistent with the population health perspective that focuses on the social structures that shape health experiences at the population level (Hertzman and Wiens 1996). This perspective recognizes early childhood development to be an important determinant of health and well-being over the life course (Low et al. 2005); the early years of life are a period of considerable opportunity for growth and vulnerability to harm, consequences that can have a lifelong impact on health and well-being (Hertzman 1994). Rather than simply aiming interventions to promote change at the individual level, a population health approach targets change at the community or neighbourhood level, thereby promoting the health and well-being of all children and families within a specific setting at a specific time. Thus, equitable provision of early childhood services that support the daily lives of all young children and their families is seen as a key strategy for narrowing the "readiness gap" for children at the community level, a point of view that may be extended to the provincial/state or national level.

But why should services be integrated as well as universal? Advocates of integration have identified a range of practical and conceptual reasons for bringing together early childhood services: (a) supporting the holistic development of children (Zigler et al. 2006), (b) promoting equitable access to services (Colley 2006), (c) and enhancing continuity for children in early childhood service settings (Pelletier and Corter 2006). Continuity can take shape in a variety of different ways, but, generally, it implies that children experience greater consistency in their daily interactions across settings or over a span of time as a result of fewer transitions.

Integration strategies can reduce and even eliminate some transitions. For example, *horizontal transitions* that require children to move from one type of setting to another at one point in time can be reduced when school and child care professionals engage in collaborative practice to deliver seamless programs including kindergarten, child care and family supports. Sharing of space, use of a common pedagogical framework, and governance structures can all lead to a cohesive learning environment for children. Moreover, *vertical transitions* that require children to adjust to developmental transitions (e.g. entering kindergarten) can be minimized when schools make efforts to reach out to families and prior-to-school services in the community. This enables schools to be in a better position to plan for individual children, anticipate supports for families, and build relationships. Evidence suggests that continuity fostered through integration strategies can lead to higher quality of learning environments for children (Henrich et al. 2006) and levels of parent/family involvement (Pianta et al. 2001; Mashburn and Pianta 2006).

But why make schools the hub for universal, integrated services? Considering that schools are a public resource and already serve children and families in neighbourhoods, they have multiple advantages as the universal platform for delivering early childhood services (McCain et al. 2007; McCain and Mustard 1999; Pelletier and Corter 2006). The idea of using schools for various "non-academic" services is part of the community school movement that began several decades ago (Dryfoos et al. 2005). From an international policy perspective, many counties integrate early childhood programs under one ministry or department, usually education. In Europe, early childhood programs are often set up to deliver care and education to preschool children in one seamless program (OECD 2006).

There are of course some arguments for not using the school as the site for delivering programs to enhance children's development. Zigler and Finn-Stevenson (2007) note that, "lack of space, a poor track record in serving low-income and non-English speaking children, an overburdened educational system, and presumed parental dissatisfaction with schools" are some of the arguments voiced against placing early childhood programs in schools (p. 178). Another major concern is that since schools are traditionally associated with more direct academic instructional orientations, children in school-based early childhood programs will be subjected to formal didactic instruction in academic skills at younger ages (Finn-Stevenson and Zigler 1999). Nevertheless, the school hub model appears to be viable. Edward Zigler's School of the 21st Century (21C) is one of the most widely implemented models of school-based, integrated delivery of early childhood services (Finn-Stevenson and Zigler 2006; Zigler et al. 1995; Zigler and Finn-Stevenson 2006). Implemented across more than 1, 400 schools in more than 20 states, 21C delivers a comprehensive system of child care, early education, and family support for children birth to 12 years of age, all operating from the neighbourhood school. Findings reported in evaluation studies of the 21C suggest that integration and comprehensive delivery of programs were associated with higher quality of care, improved academic outcomes for children, lower kindergarten absenteeism rates, fewer grade retentions, and fewer special education referrals (Henrich et al. 2006; James-Burdumy et al. 2005).

In Canada, several provinces, including Ontario, are moving towards policies based on early childhood service integration. In Ontario, some of this movement came from the Toronto First Duty (TFD) project, which demonstrated how kindergarten, child care, and family support programs can be combined in a seamless, integrated early childhood program based in public schools. In the following section, we describe the core components of the TFD model and outline the readiness/transitions strategies embedded within the integrated delivery of services. We then briefly describe the evaluation framework, key findings and implications for practice and policy.

The Toronto First Duty (TFD) Project: A Universal Model for Delivering Integrated Early Childhood Services

The integrated early childhood service delivery model in TFD combines regulated, publicly-supported child care, kindergarten and family support services consolidated into a single, accessible program, located in primary schools and coordinated with early intervention and family health services. In this delivery model, a professional team of kindergarten teachers, early childhood educators, family support staff and teaching assistants plan and deliver the program. Space and resources are combined. There is a single intake procedure and flexible enrolment options. Children and families are linked to specialized resources as required.

The goal of TFD is to develop a universal, accessible service that promotes the healthy development of children from conception through primary school and that supports parents' work or study and offering support to their parenting role. Universal access, combined with outreach from the neighbourhood school hub, is designed to reduce social inequities in service uptake and outcomes.

The project is designed to inform public policy by demonstrating the feasibility of a comprehensive approach to the transformation of the existing patchwork of programs into a single, integrated and comprehensive early childhood program embedded in communities and in the education system.

Policy Context: From Readiness to Population Health

Over the last two decades, early childhood programs in Canada and related conceptions of school readiness have increasingly moved from a "child-centred" perspective to "society-centred" (Pelletier & Corter, 2002). Strategies for supporting school readiness/transition in the TFD model are consistent with the society-centred population health approach to child development. This approach, outlined by Hertzman and colleagues (e.g. Hertzman and Keating 1999) has influenced government thinking from the provincial (e.g. Government of British Columbia, Ministry of Children and Family Development 2002) to the federal level (e.g. Human Resources and Social Development Canada 2004). There are a number of defining features associated with this approach: (a) starting early with prevention and promotion programs for healthy child development, including education; (b) equity and better outcomes for all children through universal programs; (c) supporting parents to support children; (d) delivering programs and supports at the community level; (e) addressing the social determinants of healthy development (e.g. minority status, poverty, neighbourhoods, educational opportunity); and (f) using indicators to track needs, determinants and outcomes. The Early Development Instrument (EDI), described by Janus in this volume, is an example of a community-level indicator of child development. The EDI has been used across Canada to mobilize community and government action for early childhood programs consistent with the population health perspective (e.g. Carpiano et al. 2009; Lloyd and Hertzman 2009; Oliver et al. 2007). It has also been employed in the TFD evaluation research as a measure of outcome and as an indicator used by sites to design programming (Corter et al. 2008).

Following the population health perspective, TFD aims to build healthy child development in all realms of child development, not just pre-academics, and it aims to build more cohesive social ecologies supporting children and parenting. Better integration of services, families and communities provides for more successful and seamless transitions, with greater continuity from home to care to school across developmental transitions (vertical continuity) and as the child and parent move across settings at one point in time (horizontal continuity) (Pelletier and Corter 2006). Improved quality, as well as continuity, in children's environments is also a key goal of the TFD approach. Service integration and family involvement are designed to foster higher quality care and education in early learning settings and to support improved family life and parenting.

One core element of the TFD strategy is an integrated staff team buying into the model and delivering an integrated curriculum during a seamless day for children, and connecting to other services such as parent-child drop-in literacy centres. Full day learning and care is provided for four- and five-year-olds. Briefer programs are available for younger children and for their parents, and at some school hubs; on-site childcare for younger children is also available. The staff team works across these programs to foster continuity and to improve quality. The team combines complementary expertise and professional backgrounds in teaching, early childhood education, and family support.

A second core element of the TFD strategy is support and engagement of parents. Parents are involved and welcomed into the services that traditionally focus on the child (i.e. child care and kindergarten). Parents themselves are supported by child care in their needs to work and study and through parenting support programs, which include parent education in areas such as family literacy and behaviour management.

The core TFD elements of improving continuity and quality through staff teams and engaged parents require strategic *leadership* at three levels: (1) the school principal, (2) a school-community steering committee, and (3) the organizations overseeing the schools and other services on site, in this case, the school district and municipality. Principal leadership at the school level is crucial in supporting the staff team and in welcoming community connections to other service agencies and organizations as well as parents. The local steering committee comprised of parent and organizational representatives from service agencies, as well as the principal and school representatives, provides shared leadership to help implement the model.

TFD Evaluation Framework

The overall approach for the TFD evaluation was a mixed-method, longitudinal case study analysis, which combines quantitative and qualitative data to understand the design, implementation, and possible effects of TFD (Pelletier and Corter 2006). The narrative information helped to explain the quantitative data. Each of the five implementation sites was treated as a separate case study to explore how a common approach would work in five different communities. Each case study combined information about changes in service access and delivery over time, evidence about the impact on children and families, and descriptions of the community context. In addition, the implementation and management of the project was treated as a case study of organizational development, placed in the context of the city, school board, and charitable foundation working together in a complex social and policy context. Quasi-experimental designs were also used to assess effects on parents (Arimura 2008; Patel 2004) and children (Corter et al. 2008). In these designs, the functioning of children and parents in TFD sites was compared to families in matched community sites without integrated services.

The research team used a variety of techniques to gather data, including document collection, meeting notes and observations, focus groups, interviews, direct observation, and surveys. Continuous monitoring of program utilization also took place. We used ECERS-R (Harms et al. 1998) to measure program quality. A new tool, *TFD Indicators of Change*,[1] was developed to monitor and measure integration benchmarks for each of the key elements of the TFD model (local governance, seamless access, early learning environment, early years staff team and parent participation). The EDI (Janus et al. 2008; Offord Centre for Child Studies 2008, 2009) was used to measure child outcomes across time (pre-post comparisons) and across settings (quasi-experimental analysis comparing TFD and matched community sites without TFD). A practitioner survey was developed to monitor how practitioners were handling the challenges and possibilities of the TFD model and a series of questionnaires, interviews and focus groups were employed to assess families' use of programs, parent involvement, parental self-efficacy, and daily hassles.

Key Findings and Implications for Practice and Policy

The TFD project utilized an integrated service model to improve the experiences and outcomes of children and parents from preschool into the traditional time of "transition" to school. By merging child care, kindergarten and other support services at school sites, the evidence suggests that disruptive transitions were reduced, both during the child's day and across developmental time. However, it is likely that the success of the model was not due simply to greater continuity in children's days or across time. Evidence from our research suggests that integration also improved the quality of the child's experience in both the school and home settings. And in parallel, the experiences of parents and professionals improved in communities where the integrated model was implemented. These findings parallel reports from qualitative analysis of the 21C model developed by Edward Zigler and his colleagues in the United States (Desimone et al. 2004).

Child Outcomes

In the design of TFD, learning and school success were not the only desired outcomes, but academic success remains the touchstone of concern with transition and

---

[1] The tool can be accessed online at: http://www.toronto.ca/firstduty/index.htm.

readiness. How did integrated school hubs perform in this respect? Although we have not followed students to look at later academic success, ratings of kindergarten children on the EDI point to benefits of the integrated experience. Kindergarten children in TFD communities were more advanced in social-emotional development in comparison to children in demographically matched schools (Corter et al. 2008). This difference in community level outcomes for children parallels the finding from the UK Sure Start evaluation (Melhuish 2008). In that large-scale study children in Sure Start communities with integrated preschool services were more advanced in measures of social-emotional development.

In the TFD project further evidence on value of integrated service experience for "child readiness" comes from tracking data on the number of hours children and families used services *within* TFD communities. Dose-response analyses suggested that more hours of experience led to better child outcomes in other areas such as physical health and well-being, language and cognitive development (Patel 2009). A very important point about these outcome findings is that the effects were not limited by demographic factors such as maternal education or minority language status. Both enrolment and intensity of participation reflected the makeup of the TFD communities and drew evenly across demographic lines (Patel et al. 2008). Another important point from these findings is that the integrated programming has benefits for the whole child, not for pre-academic areas of development.

Integrated Professional and Parental Pathways to Better Transitions

In the evaluation of TFD we wanted to go beyond a narrow analysis of child outcomes by studying the implementation process and collateral benefits. We developed a theory-of-change that viewed outcomes for children as a function of two "process" pathways between service integration efforts and improvements in children's development. One pathway was improvement in learning environments through staff teamwork and continuity. The other pathway was through parent engagement and improved family life.

Our process evaluation showed that the integrated model could be successfully implemented in different communities with demonstrated progress on pulling together child care, kindergarten and family supports, along with other types of community services (Corter et al. 2007, 2008, 2009). The Indicators of Change tool was developed to assist sites in monitoring integration progress along different dimensions of integrated early learning environments, staff teams, governance, program access, and parent/community engagement. Predictable challenges to local integration efforts were found ranging from professional turf and regulation differences to availability of suitable space at the school. At the same time factors facilitating higher levels of integration included strong leadership, opportunities for staff time to meet, bottom-up teamwork together with top-down supports and pressure to build the model, and school space for co-location of care with kindergarten and other services. Despite common challenges and varying levels of facilitating factors, all TFD sites made progress in implementing integration with concomitant increases in program quality as measured by ECERS-R. With the greater integration, parental confidence and engagement with services also increased and stresses in the home were reduced.

Implications for Integrated Practice

Major implications for integrated practice from TFD cluster around the analysis of the professional and parents "pathways". As integration of staff teams proceeded, all professional groups grew in the feeling that they were benefiting professionally as they worked to improve programming. Increasing professional satisfaction energizes collaborative work. Staff also utilized feedback from the ECERS-R, from the Indicators of Change, and from the EDI (Corter et al. 2008). Focusing on results and indicators allows staff teams to monitor progress and improve. The process evaluation showed some other important success factors in growing teamwork; common professional development and regular time to meet to discuss programming were keys as professional differences were overcome and staff focused on what is best for the child and family. Leadership from the principal and collaborating local agencies was crucial, as would be expected in any school reform effort.

The implementation of integrated TFD services in school sites was also associated with stronger parent involvement, in terms of connections to services and the school, as well as in terms of parents' confidence in fostering learning at home (Corter et al. 2007; Patel and Corter 2006). This is an important finding since research shows that high quality environments – both in the home and in early childhood programs – contribute to child outcomes, with the home having even greater impact (e.g. Sylva et al. 2007). The finding also suggests that the preschool period and school-based hubs can be a key for boosting parent and school capacity for mutual engagement. A menu of services at the school serves to bring in diverse groups that ordinarily are not well connected to schools or other services (Patel et al. 2008).

The research also explored how integrated services can reach into and support everyday family life. Findings showed that integrated school-as-hub services were associated with lower levels of daily parenting hassles, greater satisfaction with some forms of support, and greater levels of continuity in children's days (Arimura 2008). In TFD sites, parents named both kindergarten teachers and early childhood educators as part of their social support network. In comparison sites, only early childhood educators were named. Children in TFD sites spoke about their experiences in a seamless way. In contrast, children from the non-integrated sites noted differences between their experiences at school and at the child care centre. A system that promotes continuity and better relationships across home and program settings may promote better outcomes for children and better quality of experiences for adults as well.

Policy Implications for School-as-Hub

The results of the TFD demonstration study show that embedding early childhood services in a school-as-hub model can be successfully implemented with positive effects. These findings are consistent with arguments for merging child care and education in government policy (OECD 2006) and in community level integration of early childhood services in local schools (Zigler et al. 2006). TFD showed that school leadership and school district leadership were critical to the success of the project at the community level, along with supports for teacher buy-in to the integrated staff team. Beyond the individual school sites, the school district, the Toronto District School Board developed new supports for scaling up the integrated approach beyond the five TFD demonstration sites, but with 400 other elementary schools in the district, along with limited resources, a voluntary approach, and no supports or mandate from the provincial level, "it's a slow moving train" (Corter et al. 2009, p. 28). This observation supports Michael Fullan's (Fullan and Levin 2009) conclusion that successful large scale education reform requires top-down pressures and supports, coupled with bottom-up buy-in from school teams focusing on results for children. In the case of early childhood, service reform is even more complex because it requires linkages that extend beyond the school and the education system. While the school district worked to integrate care and community support, the provincial Ministry of Education was not "pushing down" supports and pressure on schools to operate in new ways (Corter et al. 2009). Furthermore, as in many other jurisdictions in the world, the Ontario provincial education ministry and other ministries have done little in the past to integrate their approaches to children and families. For example, universal half-day kindergarten for 4- and 5-year olds is overseen by the education ministry and a patchwork of child care services is overseen by another ministry. Scaling up models like TFD require supports from integrated work at higher levels of government. Some of that work is now underway in Ontario as the government undertakes the implementation of universal full-day, school-based programs for 4- and 5-year olds with staffing by kindergarten teachers and child care professionals, and with the Ministry of Education in the lead.

Policy Implications for Universal Models of Transition

The universal TFD model of integrating core services of child care, kindergarten and family support was implemented successfully in different communities. It reached out effectively and equitably to both marginalized and middle class families. Lower SES and immigrant families were more likely to utilize integrated programs in the school hubs than scattered programs. Parents became more engaged with school and learning and child "readiness" increased independently of demographic factors. Benefits were not limited to higher risk groups. In these respects, the TFD model fits the population health strategy of universal, community-level programs to foster healthy development. Reaching middle-class families is important for two reasons.

One is that in countries like Canada with large middle-class populations, the greatest number of vulnerable children actually come from the middle class rather than higher risk but smaller segments of the population (e.g. McCain and Mustard 1999; Willms 2002). A second reason is that a universal program such as TFD may build political buy-in since there are potential benefits for all children and families, ranging from improved "readiness" to meeting family needs for quality care and fewer hassles in negotiating early childhood services. Political buy-in is necessary if the equity aims of better transitions are to be achieved through system reform rather than solely through isolated child-by-child, school-by-school, or community-by-community efforts.

Of course no model is a panacea and universal integrated preschool hubs are no exception. Thus the TFD approach is a work in progress, not a pre-packaged program with all the solutions. As a prime example, the TFD project showed how the universal platform of care, kindergarten and family support could produce general benefits, but it did not resolve how early identification, clinical services, and targeted programs would connect to the platform. However, the disconnections among these efforts are unlikely to be resolved without a universal point of integration such as school hubs.

The TFD model and the analyses we have presented may apply to jurisdictions, such as those in North America where early childhood services are relatively fragmented and not typically connected to schools. In other countries there are more coherent systems where children are not faced with disruptive transitions around 5 years of age as they enter school and within a year or two faced with regimes of academic learning. In contrast in some countries, notably the Nordic states, care and education are combined in the same government ministry and in the same universal early childhood programs. Whole child development and learning co-exist and gradually transition into higher grade levels at school (OECD 2006). In the North American context, demonstration projects such as TFD may illustrate the first steps along the way to large scale system reform leading to a truly seamless system.

Acknowledgments The Social Sciences and Humanities Research Council of Canada and the Atkinson Charitable Foundation provided major funding support for Toronto First Duty research, along with the City of Toronto. The City of Toronto and the Toronto District School Board also provided assistance in data gathering. We thank all the participants and the other members of the TFD research team for their generous contributions.

The opinions and interpretations in this paper are those of the authors and do not necessarily reflect those of the sponsors.

References

Arimura, T. N. (2008). *Daily routines, parenting hassles, and social support: The role that early childhood services play in parents' and children's daily life.* Unpublished master's thesis, Ontario Institute for Studies in Education at the University of Toronto, Toronto, ON, Canada.

Arnold, C., Bartlett, K., Gowani, S., & Shallwani, S. (2008). Transition to school: Reflections on readiness. *Journal of Developmental Processes, 3*(2), 26–38.

Barnett, W. S., Brown, K., & Shore, R. (2004). *The universal vs. targeted debate: Should the United States have preschool for all? Preschool Policy Matters.* New Brunswick, NJ: National Institute for Early Education Research.

Carpiano, R. M., Lloyd, J. E. V., & Hertzman, C. (2009). Concentrated affluence, concentrated disadvantage, and children's readiness for school: A population-based, multi-level investigation. *Social Science & Medicine, 69,* 420–432.

Colley, S. (2006). *Policy papers: How can integration of services for kindergarten-aged children be achieved?* Toronto, ON: Integration Network Project.

Corter, C., Bertrand, J., Griffin, T., Endler, M., Pelletier, J., & McKay, D. (2002). *Toronto First Duty Starting Gate report: Implementing integrated foundations for early childhood.* Toronto, ON: Atkinson Charitable Foundation. http://www.toronto.ca/firstduty/sg_report.pdf

Corter, C., Bertrand, J., Pelletier, J., Griffin, T., McKay, D., Patel, S., et al. (2007). *Toronto First Duty phase 1 final report: Evidence-based understanding of integrated foundations for early childhood.*Toronto, ON: Atkinson Centre for Society and Child Development. http://www.toronto.ca/firstduty/tfd_phase1_finalreport.pdf

Corter, C., Patel, S., Pelletier, J., & Bertrand, J. (2008). The early development instrument as an evaluation and improvement tool for school-based, integrated services for young children and parents: The Toronto First Duty project. *Early Education and Development, 19*(5), 773–794.

Corter, C., Pelletier, J., Jamohamed, Z., Bertrand, J., Arimura, T., Patel, S., et al. (2009). *Toronto First Duty phase 2, 2006–2008: Final research report.* Toronto: Atkinson Centre for Society and Child Development. http://www.toronto.ca/firstduty/TFD_phase2_final.pdf

Desimone, L., Finn-Stevenson, M., & Henrich, C. (2000). Whole school reform in a low-income African American community: The effects of the CoZi Model on teachers, parents, and students. *Urban Education, 35*(3), 269–323.

Desimone, L., Payne, B., Fedoravicius, N., Henrich, C., & Finn-Stevenson, M. (2004). Comprehensive school reform: An implementation study of preschool programs in elementary schools. *The Elementary School Journal, 104*(5), 369–389.

Dockett, S., & Perry, B. (2007). The role of school and communities in children's school transition. In R. E. Tremblay, R. G. Barr, R. D. Peters, & M. Boivin (Eds.), *Encyclopedia on early childhood development* (pp. 1–8). Montreal: Centre of Excellence for Early Childhood Development.

Dryfoos, J. J., Quinn, J., & Barkin, C. (Eds.). (2005). *Community schools in action: Lessons from a decade of practice.* New York, NY: Oxford University Press.

Farkas, G., & Hibel, J. (2008). Being unready for school: Factors affecting risk and resilience. In A. Booth & A. C. Crouter (Eds.), *Disparities in school readiness: How families contribute to transitions into school* (pp. 3–30). New York, NY: Erlbaum.

Finn-Stevenson, M., & Zigler, E. (1999). *Schools of the 21st century: Linking child care and education.* Boulder, CO: Westview.

Finn-Stevenson, M., & Zigler, E. (2006). What the schools of the 21st century can teach us about universal preschool. In E. Zigler, W. Gilliam, & S. M. Jones (Eds.), *A vision for universal preschool education* (pp. 194–215). New York, NY: Cambridge University Press.

Finn-Stevenson, M., Desimone, L., & Chung, A. (1998). Linking child care and support services with the school: Pilot evaluation of the school of the 21st century. *Children and Youth Services Review, 20*(3), 177–205.

Fullan, M., & Levin, B. (2009). *The fundamentals of whole-system reform. Education Week, 28*(35), 30–31. http://www.michaelfullan.ca/Articles_09/WholeSystemReform.pdf

Government of British Columbia, Ministry of Children and Family Development. (2002). *BC early childhood development action plan: A work in progress.* Victoria, BC: Government of British Columbia, Ministry of Children and Family Development. http://www.mcf.gov.bc.ca/early_childhood/pdf/ecd_action_plan_revised_june02.pdf

Harms, T., Clifford, R. M., & Cryer, D. (1998). *Early childhood environmental rating scale—revised.* New York, NY: Teachers College Press.

Henrich, C., Ginicola, M., Finn-Stevenson, M., & Zigler, E. (2006). *The school of the 21st century is making a difference: Findings from two evaluations (issue brief).* New Haven, CT: Yale University, Zigler Center in Child Development and Social Policy.

Hertzman, C. (1994). The lifelong impact of childhood experiences: A population health perspective. *Daedalus, 123*(4), 167–180.

Hertzman, C., & Keating, D. P. (Eds.). (1999). *Developmental health and the wealth of nations: Social, biological, and educational dynamics.* New York, NY: Guilford.

Hertzman, C., & Wiens, M. (1996). Child development and long-term outcomes: A population health perspective and summary of successful interventions. *Social Science & Medicine, 43*(7), 1083–1095.

Human Resources and Social Development Canada. (2004). *A Canada fit for children: Canada's plan for action in response to the May 2002 United Nations special session on children.* Ottawa, ON: Her Majesty the Queen in Right of Canada. http://www.hrsdc.gc.ca/eng/cs/sp/sdc/socpol/publications/2002-002483/canadafite.pdf

James-Burdumy, S., Dynarski, M., Moore, M., Deke, J., Mansfield, W., Pistorino, C., et al. (2005). *When schools stay open late: The national evaluation of the 21st century community learning centers program—final report.* Washington, DC: US Department of Education.

Janus, M., Brinkman, S., Duku, E., Hertzman, C., Santos, R., Sayers, M., et al. (2008). *The early development instrument: A population-based measure for communities. A handbook on development, properties, and use.* Hamilton, ON: McMaster University Press.

Johnson, L. C., & Mathien, J. (1998). *Early childhood services for kindergarten-age children in four Canadian provinces: Scope, nature and models for the future.* Ottawa, ON: Caledon Institute of Social Policy.

La Paro, K. M., & Pianta, R. C. (2000). Predicting children's competence in the early school years: A meta-analytic review. *Review of Educational Research, 70*(4), 443–484.

Lloyd, J. E. V., & Hertzman, C. (2009). From kindergarten readiness to fourth-grade assessment: Longitudinal analysis with linked population data. *Social Science & Medicine, 68*, 111–123.

Low, M. D., Low, B. J., Baumler, E. R., & Huynh, P. T. (2005). Can education policy be health policy? Implications of research on the social determinants of health. *Journal of Health Politics, Policy and Law, 30*(6), 1131–1162.

Mashburn, A. J., & Pianta, R. C. (2006). Social relationships and school readiness. *Early Education & Development, 17*(1), 151–176.

McCain, M. N., & Mustard, J. F. (1999). *The early years study: Reversing the real brain drain.* Toronto, ON: Ontario Children's Secretariat.

McCain, M. N., Mustard, J. F., & Shanker, S. (2007). *Early years study 2: Putting science into action.* Toronto, ON: Council for Early Child Development.

Melhuish, E., Belsky, J., Leyland, A. H., & Barnes, J. (2008). Effects of fully-established Sure Start local programmes on 3-year-old children and their families living in England: A quasi-experimental observational study. *The Lancet, 372*(9650), 1641–1647.

Offord Centre for Child Studies. (2008). *Early Development Instrument: A population-based measure for communities 2007/2008.* Hamilton, ON: McMaster University Press. http://www.offordcentre.com/readiness/files/EDI_2008_General_CON.PDF

Offord Centre for Child Studies. (2009). *Early Development Instrument guide 2008/2009.* Hamilton, ON: McMaster University Press.

Oliver, L. N., Dunn, J. R., Kohen, D. E., & Hertzman, C. (2007). Do neighbourhoods influence the readiness to learn of kindergarten children in Vancouver? A multilevel analysis of neighbourhood effects. *Environment and Planning, 39*, 848–868.

Organisation for Economic Co-operation and Development (OECD). (2006). *Starting strong II: Early childhood education and care.* Paris: OECD.

Patel, S. (2004). *Parents, services integration, and engagement in early childhood.* Unpublished master's thesis, Ontario Institute for Studies in Education at the University of Toronto, Toronto, ON, Canada.

Patel, S. (2009). *Integrated early childhood program participation, parenting, and child development outcomes:* The Toronto First Duty project. Unpublished doctoral dissertation, University of Toronto, Toronto, ON, Canada.

Patel, S., & Corter, C. (2006). *Parent-school involvement, diversity, and school-based preschool services hubs.* Paper presented at the annual meeting of the American Educational Research Association, San Francisco, CA, USA.

Patel, S., Corter, C., & Pelletier, J. (2008). What do families want? Understanding their goals for early childhood services. In M. M. Cornish (Ed.), *Promising practices for partnering with families in the early years* (pp. 103–123). Charlotte, NC: Information Age.

Pelletier, J., & Corter, C. (2002). Competing "world views" on early childhood care, education and development in the Canadian context. In L. Chan & E. Mellor (Eds.), *International developments in early childhood services* (pp. 29–52). New York, NY: Lang.

Pelletier, J., & Corter, C. (2006). Integration, innovation, and evaluation in school-based early childhood services. In B. Spodek & O. N. Saracho (Eds.), *Handbook of research on the education of young children* (2nd ed., pp. 477–496). Mahwah, NJ: Erlbaum.

Pianta, R. C., Kraft-Sayre, M., Rimm-Kaufman, S., Gercke, N., & Higgins, T. (2001). Collaboration in building partnerships between families and schools: The National Center for Early Development and Learning's kindergarten transition intervention. *Early Childhood Research Quarterly, 16*(1), 117–132.

Rimm-Kaufman, S. E., & Pianta, R. C. (2000). An ecological perspective on the transition to kindergarten. *Journal of Applied Developmental Psychology, 21*(5), 491–511.

Sameroff, A. J. (1975). Early influences on development: Fact of fancy? *Merrill-Palmer Quarterly, 21*, 267–294.

Schulman, K., & Barnett, W. S. (2005). *The benefits of prekindergarten for middle-income children*. New Brunswick, NJ: National Institute for Early Education Research.

Shore, R. (1998). *Ready schools: A report of the Goal 1 Ready School Resource Group*. Washington, DC: National Education Goals Panel.

Snow, K. L. (2006). Measuring school readiness: Conceptual and practical considerations. *Early Education & Development, 17*(1), 7–41.

Sylva, K., Melhuish, E., Sammons, P., Siraj-Blatchford, I., & Taggart, B. (2007). Promoting equality in the early years. Report to the equalities review. http://archive.cabinetoffice.gov.uk/equalitiesreview/publications.html

TDSB. (2007). *Working together for children's success: An early years integration strategy*. Toronto, ON: TDSB. http://www.tdsb.on.ca/wwwdocuments/programs/early_years/docs/WorkingTogether.pdf

Toronto First Duty Research Team. (2005). *First duty indicators of change*. Toronto, ON: Atkinson Charitable Foundation. http://www.toronto.ca/firstduty/indicators_oct2005.pdf

Willms, J. D. (2002). Socioeconomic gradients for childhood vulnerability. In J. D. Willms (Ed.), *Vulnerable children* (pp. 71–102). Edmonton, AB: The University of Alberta Press.

Zigler, E., & Finn-Stevenson, M. (2006). The school of the 21st century. In M. A. Constas & R. J. Sternberg (Eds.), *Translating theory and research into educational practice: Developments in content domains, large-scale reform, and intellectual capacity* (pp. 173–195). Mahwah, NJ: Erlbaum.

Zigler, E., & Finn-Stevenson, M. (2007). From research to policy and practice: The school of the 21st century. *American Journal of Orthopsychiatry, 77*(2), 175–181.

Zigler, E., Finn-Stevenson, M., & Marsland, K. W. (1995). Child day care in the schools: The school of the 21st century. *Child Welfare, 74*(6), 1301–1326.

Zigler, E., Gilliam, W. S., & Jones, S. M. (2006). *A vision for universal preschool education*, New York, NY: Cambridge University Press.

Index

D. M. Laverick, M. R. Jalongo (eds.), *Transitions to Early Care and Education,*
Educating the Young Child 4, DOI 10.1007/978-94-007-0573-9,
© Springer Science+Business Media B.V. 2011

9 789400 705722